Aesthetics of Film

Texas Film Studies Series
Thomas Schatz, Editor

AESTHETICS
OF FILM

JACQUES AUMONT

ALAIN BERGALA

MICHEL MARIE

MARC VERNET

TRANSLATED
AND REVISED BY
RICHARD NEUPERT

UNIVERSITY OF TEXAS PRESS   AUSTIN

To the Memory of Christian Metz

Library of Congress Cataloging-in-Publication Data

Esthétique du film. English.
    Aesthetics of film / Jacques Aumont . . . [et al.] ; translated and
revised by Richard Neupert. — 1st ed.
        p.   cm. — (Texas film studies series)
    Translation of: L'Esthétique du film.
    Includes bibliographical references and index.
    ISBN 0-292-70428-3. — ISBN 0-292-70437-2 (pbk.)
    1. Motion pictures—Aesthetics.   2. Cinematography.
I. Aumont, J. (Jacques)   II. Title.   III. Series.
PN1995.E7613   1992
791.43′01—dc20   91-33706

CONTENTS

TRANSLATOR'S NOTE

This book, originally published as *Esthétique du film* (Paris: Nathan, 1983), is a collective product of four film scholars whose names are by now quite familiar to American film students. Jacques Aumont, Michel Marie, and Marc Vernet have all taught at the American Film Program in Paris and have thus had a very strong personal influence on a large number of American film students and professors; many of us owe a great deal to their teaching and writing. Currently, all three are on the faculty of the cinema department at the Université de Paris III. Alain Bergala has been no less influential as editor and critic at *Cahiers du Cinéma*.

The French version was indeed begun as a collective project; though individuals were responsible for specific sections, all four authors read and commented upon each other's work. Jacques Aumont wrote chapters 1 and 2, part of the first section of chapter 5, and the conclusion. Alain Bergala wrote most of chapter 5. Michel Marie wrote the introduction, chapter 4, and part of the first section of chapter 5. Marc Vernet wrote chapter 3.

As translator I have made some revisions, updating several citations, but also substituting or adding film titles in order to guarantee clarity when the original examples may be relatively unknown outside of France. I also added the discussion of feminist theory at the end of chapter 5. This translation strives to remain faithful to the original tone and style, and I have retained the indented sections, which help add emphasis and also bracket related discussions.

I would like to thank each of the four authors for having trusted me with their prose. The fact that three of them are former professors of mine made the task more challenging yet more pleasurable. Finally, Marc Vernet deserves much credit and praise for having taken a great deal of time in answering specific questions and in reading and editing every word of the translation. His sense of humor and insight were also helpful in dealing with the delays and misunderstandings between publishers. I would also like to thank my wife, Catherine Jones, for her advice and time.

R.N.

INTRODUCTION

TYPOLOGIES OF WRITTEN WORK ON THE CINEMA

There are hundreds of books published each year on the cinema in French and English, while our countries also produce scores of monthly and quarterly magazines and journals covering a wide variety of interests in film (from film theory and criticism to technical reviews to information on the lives of the stars). The serious collector does not know where to stack all these books and journals, while the beginner does not know how to choose among them.

In order to situate the parameters of our text with some degree of precision, we will begin with a brief typological sketch of the range of discourses on the cinema. They may be divided globally into three groups, whose size will prove unequal: first, there are the popular magazines and books; second, the writings for cinephiles or serious film buffs; and finally, the theoretical and aesthetic works. These categories are certainly far from watertight since a book for film buffs may reach a very large audience and still possess some undeniable theoretical value. This sort of text is rare and typically involves film history; the books of Georges Sadoul serve as a good example in France.

Quite logically, publications on the cinema correspond to these categories of the film audience. French publishing is characterized by the volume directed toward the second sector destined for the cinephile.

The term "cinephile" was coined by Ricciotto Canudo in the early 1920s to designate an aware amateur of the cinema. There have been several generations of cinephiles, each with their own magazines and favorite authors. This body of cinephiles expanded rapidly after 1945, particularly in France. They exercised their influence in the form of specialized journals, the boom in film clubs and art houses, film retrospectives in museums, and of course the rise of screenings at film archives. The true cinephile constituted a veritable social type, particularly in places like Paris, London, New York, and Los Angeles where the options for filmgoers were especially rich. Moreover, in Paris they became one distinctive part of the cultural life and could (and still can) easily be recognized by several mimetic traits of behavior: they gather in cliques, never sit in the rear of the theater, and always evoke a passionate discourse on their favorite films. In fact, it is appropriate for us to distinguish this narrow subset of the cinephile with its maniacal dimension from the strictly amateur film buff.

The Popular Press

These are obviously the most numerous and most widely distributed publications. It is almost a rare exception to find popular publications that are not devoted to film actors, since they constitute the printed facet of the star system. Typical examples include *Premiere* magazine in the United States and *Première* in France, while *Ciné-Monde* was the most famous French example before World War II. In France, there were also a large number of "retold films," which were put out of business when the television series came along. Today in France the more scholarly *Avant-Scène Cinéma* has replaced these popular *films racontés*.

In any given year there may be thirty books published as monographs devoted to actors, most typically Marilyn Monroe or John Wayne. Actors' memoirs also proliferate, as well as the recollections of certain famous filmmakers. Furthermore, among the big sellers are books on prize-winning films and other gift or coffee table books such as luxurious editions devoted to the major studios (*The MGM Story, The Films of 20th Century Fox: A Pictorial History, The Universal Story*, etc.) or to popular genres (film noir, musicals, westerns). In general these coffee table books grant a large place to iconography since the written text often simply complements the beautiful photos.

If we bear in mind that a critical or theoretical approach must employ a certain aesthetic distancing of the object of study, it becomes clear that the discourse employed in this sector of film writing is not theoretical. Rather, this is the realm in which deliberately blind enthusiasm, total and mystified devotion, and the discourse of adoration all triumph. To the extent that film's cultural status continues to rest on a certain illegitimacy, this popular discourse will always find occasion to flourish. We must consider it, however, since in terms of size popular discourse constitutes the bulk of books and magazines devoted to the cinema and thereby provokes an effect of normality. Since the object of study is seen to be frivolous, it becomes normal that the discourse upon it depends on such babble.

Publications Directed at Cinephiles

Within the category of the cinephile, it is no longer the actor who triumphs, but the filmmaker. It is here we can see the fruit of efforts by directors of film clubs and archives as well as specialized critics: in order to prove that the cinema was more than a simple medium of entertainment they had to provide and herald auteurs or creators of its works. Numerous monographs bear witness to the successful promotion of the auteur-director: in France, Seghers published eighty such titles, covering directors from Georges Méliès to Marcel Pagnol; many other similar series exist in both English and French.

The second approach of literature for cinephiles is the collection of interviews with one or more directors. The canonical example of a critic leading a lengthy interrogation is certainly François Truffaut's *Hitchcock*, but many others exist. Within this same category we may add the genre studies that are more in depth than the photo collections of the more popular press, as well as studies of national cinemas and many film histories. Examples include books such as John Halliday's *Sirk on Sirk*, Alain Silver and Elizabeth Ward's *Film Noir*, and Victor Navasky's *Naming Names*.

It is easy to notice that such film criticism applies approaches traditional to literature, with its study of great auteurs and genres in relation to the history of important works. However, analysis of films requires tools different from those for literary works, and studying films as résumés of their scripts proceeds via a simplification as dangerous as it is difficult to avoid once one confronts large groups of films. It is important to add that the cinephile's discourse is most prevalent in monthly magazines that dominate this editorial terrain while, by contrast, books only occupy a small addendum.

Theoretical and Aesthetic Writings

This third sector is obviously the narrowest. Nonetheless, it is hardly new and has known certain moments of remarkable expansion owing to the hazards of research on the cinema. We will limit ourselves to two fairly recent French periods for examples. First, there was the creation of the Institute of Filmology at the Sorbonne after the liberation. From the institute sprang an influential journal, *Revue Internationale de Filmologie*, and the publication of a number of important essays, particularly *L'Univers filmique* by Etienne Souriau and *Essai sur les principes d'une philosophie du cinéma* by Gilbert Cohen-Séat. Second, from 1965 to 1970, the semiology of the cinema made its breakthrough at the Ecole des Hautes Etudes (School of Advanced Studies), while the structural analysis of film at the CNRS (National Center for Scientific Research) combined to generate publication of works by Christian Metz, Raymond Bellour, and the entire movement that surrounded them.

This sector was often more developed in places other than France and the United States. The classics of film theory are Soviet (*Poetika Kino*, and the writings of Lev Kuleshov and Sergei Eisenstein in the 1920s), Hungarian (*The Spirit of Film* by Béla Balázs, 1930), and German (with books by Rudolf Arnheim and Siegfried Kracauer). Moreover, the most important history of film theory is by the Italian Guido Aristarco.

If this theoretical sector has seen a marked revival in the last twenty years, it has been simultaneously paralleled by a steep decline in the sorts of studies that dominated academic writings in the 1950s and 1960s: the textbooks that introduced students to film aesthetics and film language or syntax. Obviously, these two phenomena are related. Essentially, these introductory manuals postulated the existence of a film language (we will return to this concept in chapter 4), while they presented a small dictionary of professional filmmaking, teaching shot scales, framing, and editing strategies. However, the actual study of such cinematic figures was typically limited to a tentative definition followed by the recital of numerous examples culled from regular film viewings.

The development of specialized research throughout the last two decades certainly hindered the publication of these other manuals, since the former began discussing film's theoretical bases. It was no longer possible to pose the problem of film language or syntax while bypassing semio-linguistically inspired analysis. Nor was it now permissible to investigate identification in the cinema without making a necessary detour into the realm of psychoanalytic theory or to study the film narrative while ignoring all the narratological work devoted to literary texts.

Attempting a didactic accounting of these different approaches to film is not a simple enterprise, yet that is the goal of this project.

Before launching into the midst of the subject, however, we must first tackle several theoretical and methodological preliminaries.

THEORIES OF THE CINEMA AND AESTHETICS OF THE CINEMA

Film theory is often assimilated with the aesthetic approach. However, these terms do not denote the same domains, and it is useful to distinguish them. Since its origins, film theory is equally the object of a polemic concerning the pertinence of approaches that are nonspecific to the cinema and that arise from disciplines exterior to its field. For example, linguistics, psychoanalysis, political economy, ideological theories, iconology, and gender studies are all disciplines that have been the locus of significant theoretical debates during recent years.

The cinema's cultural illegitimacy provokes an increase in chauvinism at the heart of theoretical attitudes that postulates that film theory can only be derived from film itself; exterior theories can only illuminate secondary and thus nonessential aspects of the cinema. This particular valorization of a cinematic specificity continues to weigh down theoretical processes; specifically, it helps prolong the isolation of film studies and thereby hinders the discipline's progress.

By postulating that a theory of the cinema can only be intrinsic, one impedes the possibility of developing hypotheses whose productivity is to be tested by analysis. Furthermore, such a position ignores a point we will demonstrate in this book: film is the meeting place of the cinema and many other elements that are not specifically cinematic.

An Indigenous Theory

There exists an internal tradition of film theory that is sometimes labeled "indigenous" theory. It results from the accumulative theorization of the most pertinent observations of film criticism when practiced with a certain finesse: the best example of this specific mode of theory is still André Bazin's *What Is Cinema?*

Conversely, Jean Mitry's *Esthétique et psychologie du cinéma*, an undeniable classic of French film theory, proves via the multiplicity and diversity of its theoretical references, which are exterior to the limited field of the cinema, that such an aesthetics cannot be con-

[handwritten marginal note: controversial discussion or argument]

stituted without contributions from logic, the psychology of perception, theory of the arts, etc.

A Descriptive Theory

Theory is a process that recovers the elaboration of concepts capable of analyzing an object. The term, however, has normative resonances that should be dispelled. A theory of the cinema, in the sense it is given here, does not concern a set of rules one must follow when directing a film. Theory here is instead descriptive; it strives to account for observable phenomena in films and also, by creating formal models, to envision figures not yet realized in actual works.

Film Theory and Aesthetics

To the extent that the cinema is susceptible to diverse approaches, there cannot be *one* theory of the cinema, but rather there must be *theories* of the cinema corresponding to these various approaches. One of these approaches involves aesthetics. Aesthetics covers reflection upon the phenomena of signification considered as artistic phenomena. The aesthetics of cinema is therefore the study of the cinema as an art and the study of films as artistic messages. It implies a conception of "beauty" and thus of the taste and pleasure of the spectator as well as the theoretician. Film aesthetics thereby depends upon general aesthetics, a philosophical discipline concerned with all arts.

Aesthetics of the cinema presents two facets: first, there is the general aspect that contemplates the aesthetic effects proper to the cinema; second, there is the specific aspect, centered on the analysis of particular works. This is film analysis, or criticism in the normal sense of the term, as it is used in the plastic arts and musicology.

Theory of the Cinema and Technical Practice

As we mentioned, introductory textbooks on film syntax often borrowed a great number of terms from the lexicon of film technicians. The characteristic of a theoretical approach is to study systematically these notions defined within the field of technical practice. The corporation of directors and technicians has led them to forge, each time it seems necessary, a certain number of words that serve to describe their practice. Most of these terms lack a rigorous base and their meaning can vary considerably according to the era, the country, and the modes of production practice particular to a certain group of filmmakers. These terms have then been displaced from the production stage to that of the films' reception by journalists and critics without the consequences of such transfers being analyzed. As a result, some technical categories mask the reality of the function of the processes of signification. This is the case, for instance, with the labels "sound on"/"sound off," as we will see in chapter 1.

By systematically interrogating these terms, film theory strives to grant them status as analytical concepts. The goal of our book is to summarize from a synthetic and didactic perspective the diverse theoretical attempts at examining these empirical notions, including ideas like frame vs. shot, terms from production crews' vocabularies, the notion of identification produced by critical vocabulary, etc.

↳ intending to teach, instruct

Film Theories

One cannot proceed to a definition of a theory of the cinema beginning with the object itself. More precisely, the distinctive feature of a theoretical approach is to constitute its object and elaborate a set of concepts that do not mask the empirical existence of phenomena but rather struggle to clarify them. The term "cinema," in its traditional sense, masks a distinct series of phenomena, each of which arises from a specific theoretical approach. It refers to an institution, in the legal-ideological sense, an industry, a signifying and aesthetic production, and a group of consumer practices, to cite several key aspects.

These diverse acceptances of the term thus come from particular theoretical approaches, which maintain relations of unequal proximity in regard to what one might take as the specific core of cinema phenomena. This specificity always remains illusory and is built on promotional and elitist attitudes. Film as an economic unit within the entertainment industry is no less specific than film considered as an artwork; what varies between the diverse functions of the object is the degree of cinematic specificity. (We confront the distinction specific/nonspecific in chapter 4.)

Many of these approaches come out of disciplines largely constituted outside of indigenous film theory. Thus, the film industry, the mode of production financing, and the mode of film distribution arise from economic theory that obviously exists outside the cinematic. It is probable that film theory in the narrowest sense of the term only contributed a minuscule portion of specific concepts, with general economic theory furnishing the essential concepts, or at least the large conceptual base categories.

All this holds true for the sociology of the cinema: ~~such an ap-~~ ~~proach must evidently take into account a series of attainments by~~ ~~sociology in relation to kindred cultural objects such as photography~~ ~~and art markets~~. Pierre Sorlin's *The Sociology of the Cinema* demonstrates the fruitfulness of such a strategy by integrating the work of Pierre Bourdieu into its project.

Our first two chapters, "Film as Audiovisual Representation" and "Montage," reconsider, in light of recent revolutionary work in film theory, material traditionally analyzed by introductory texts on film aesthetics. Their topics include narrative space in the cinema, depth of field, the shot, the role of sound, and the aesthetic, technical, and ideological aspects of editing.

Chapter 3, "Cinema and Narration," surveys film's narrative aspects. It begins with the accomplishments of literary narratology (notably Gérard Genette and Claude Brémond), defines the narrative cinema, and analyzes its components in terms of the status of fiction in the cinema and its relation to narration and history. It also presents several key concepts from new perspectives, namely, the notion of character, the problems of "realism," plausibility, and verisimilitude, and the impression of reality in the cinema.

The fourth chapter, "Cinema and Language," is devoted to a historic examination of the idea of film language since its origins and across diverse usages. It provides a clear synthesis of the way film theory now envisions the concept since the work of Christian Metz. The notion of language is also confronted in relation to the textual analysis of film, described in both its theoretical and aporial dimension.

"Film and Its Spectator," the fifth chapter, begins by examining classical film theory's conceptions of the film spectator according to the psychological mechanisms of comprehension and imaginary projection. Next, it confronts the complex question of identification and the cinema; finally, the chapter clarifies film's mechanisms by summarizing psychoanalytic theory's notions of identification. This didactic synthesis of Freudian theories became indispensable in light of the intrinsic difficulties in defining the mechanisms of primary and secondary identification in the cinema. The necessary side trip into psychoanalytic theory also sets the stage for our concluding discussion of gender and film spectatorship.

1 FILM AS AUDIOVISUAL REPRESENTATION

FILM SPACE

As we know, a film is composed of a great number of still images, called frames, placed in sequence on transparent film stock or celluloid. This strip of film, passing through the projector at a designated speed, gives birth to a much larger moving image. As a result, there are tremendous differences between the individual film frame and the image on the screen—to begin with, only the projected image creates the impression of movement; yet each is a flat image, surrounded by a border or "frame."[1]

These two material characteristics of the film image—its two-dimensionality and limited borders—are among the fundamental traits that guide our apprehension of film representation. For the moment let us consider the presence of the image's border, whose function is analogous to a picture frame. The image's border will be defined as "the limits of the image."

The image's border, whose necessity is obvious (it is difficult to imagine an infinitely large piece of celluloid), has its dimensions and proportions prescribed by two technological factors: first, the size or gauge of the film stock; and second, the dimensions of the camera's film gate. Taken together, these two given elements define what is called the film format. Many different film formats have existed since the cinema's origins. Even though the shift has been toward larger images, the standard format, which is used less and less today, is defined by its use of 35 mm film stock and a width-to-height ratio of 4:3 (or 1.33:1) for the image. This 1.33 ratio applied to almost all films shot until the 1950s. Films shot in 16 mm and Super-8 mm (which are still in 1.33:1) are referred to as substandard.

The image's border plays an important though varied role in the composition of the image, especially when the image is immobile (as, for example, in a freeze-frame) or nearly immobile (in the case of what is called a fixed or static shot wherein the framing does not change). Certain films, particularly during the silent era, exhibit a careful concern for equilibrium and expressivity within the image's composition rivaling that of painting. This is the case, for instance, in Carl Theodor Dreyer's *The Passion of Joan of Arc* (1928). In a general sense, one could say that the rectangular surface that delineates the area of the image is one of the first materials with which a filmmaker works.

One of the most visible techniques for working on the frame's surface is what we call the split screen, which is the division of the surface into several sections, whether equal or not, each filled with a partial image. Yet a true découpage, or division of the frame, may be obtained through other, more subtle approaches, as in Jacques Tati's *Playtime* (1967), for instance, where several distinct actions are often juxtaposed and framed while they unfold within the same shot.

Of course, even minimal experience watching films should prove that we react to the flat image as if we were actually seeing a portion of three-dimensional space analogous to the real space in which we live. In spite of its limitations (the presence of a border, absence of the third dimension, the artificial nature or even absence of color, etc.), this analogy is perceived as strongly authentic and carries with it an impression of reality that is specific to the cinema. This impression is primarily made manifest by the illusion of movement (see chapter 3) and the illusion of depth.

The reason the impression of depth is sufficiently strong for us now is merely that we are quite used to both the cinema and television. The first film viewers were, undoubtedly, more sensitive to the partial illusion of depth and the actual flatness of the image. Thus, Rudolf Arnheim writes in an essay published in 1933, but devoted essentially to silent film, that the effect produced by film was situated "between" two- and three-dimensionality, and that we perceive a film in terms of its surface and depth "at the same time." If, for instance, we shoot an approaching train from above, the resulting image will be perceived as both an illusory movement toward us and a real movement toward the bottom of the screen.[2]

The important thing to note here is that we react to the film im-

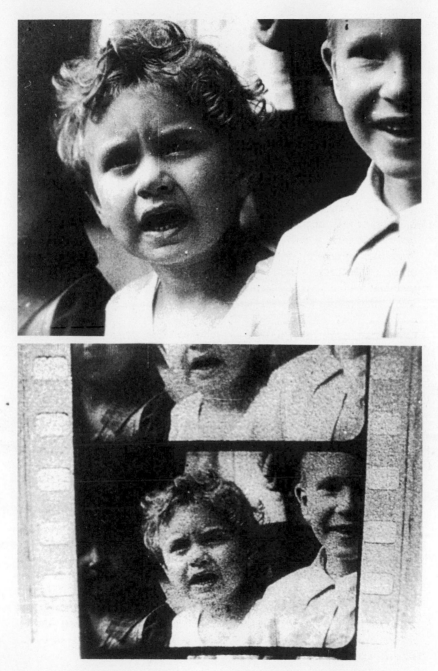

Top, a photo from *The Man with a Movie Camera* (Dziga Vertov, 1929); bottom, a photo showing the same image as a frame on the film stock.

Three carefully framed shots:
Top, *Nosferatu* (F. W. Murnau, 1922); middle, *Muriel* (Alain Resnais, 1963);
bottom, *Psycho* (Alfred Hitchcock, 1960).
Note how the *Psycho* shot's framing is echoed by the frames within the image.

age as a very realistic representation of an imaginary space that we
seem to perceive. More precisely, since the image is limited in size
by its border, we seem to perceive only a portion of the space. It is
this portion of the imaginary space that is contained inside the image's borders, which we will call "framing" or "onscreen space."

Like many terms in film vocabulary, the word "frame" is quite often
used without a carefully established meaning. On the shooting set, in
particular, the words "frame" and "shot" are often considered as equivalent, and they are often substituted for one another without any real problem. By contrast, for this book, which is less interested in the actual production of films than in the analysis of their viewing conditions, it will
be important to avoid any confusion of the terms "frame," "onscreen,"
and "shot."

The film image creates an analogy with real space; the resulting
impression is usually powerful enough to make us forget not only
the flatness of the image, but also, for example, the absence of color
if the film is black and white or the absence of sound in a silent film.
In addition, while we may not be led to forget the edges of the image,
which are always more or less consciously present in our perception,
we may be made to forget the fact that beyond those edges there is
no image. Moreover, the onscreen space is habitually perceived as
included within a more vast scenographic space. Even though the
onscreen space is the only visible part, this larger scenographic
space is nonetheless considered to exist around it. It is this notion
that allows André Bazin's famous formula translating the screen image as "mask" or a window onto the world,[3] a phrase borrowed from
Leon-Battista Alberti, the great Renaissance theoretician. Bazin's
point is that if the image works like a window to make a fragment
of the (imaginary) world visible, then there is no reason to suspect
that this world would stop at the image's edges.

There is much to criticize in this extreme embellishment of the
image as window. Nevertheless, this excessive stance (which is always partially valid when we are watching a film) does reveal that
an imagined space exists that is invisible yet extends the visible; we
call it "offscreen space." Offscreen space, therefore, is fundamentally bound to onscreen space because it only exists in relation to
onscreen space. The offscreen may be defined as the collection of
elements (characters, settings, etc.) that, while not being included
in the image itself, are nonetheless connected to that visible space
in imaginary fashion for the spectator.

The cinema learned very early on how to master a great number of the means of communication between the onscreen and offscreen space or, more precisely, how to construct the offscreen from within the onscreen. Without claiming to supply an exhaustive list, we can point out three principal kinds of spatial relations.

First, there is movement in and out of the onscreen space, most often occurring at the lateral sides of the image, but also possible at the top and bottom borders. It may even occur with the "front" and "back" of the onscreen space, demonstrating that the offscreen space is not limited to the edges of the onscreen, but may also be situated on its axis, in relative depth.

Second, there exist various direct interpellations of the offscreen by an onscreen element, typically a character. The most typical means used is the "glance offscreen," but we could also include here all the methods that an onscreen character may use to address an offscreen character, particularly speech and gesture.

Third, the offscreen may be exhibited by characters or other onscreen elements that are partially offscreen. A typical instance would be a tight close-up shot of a character, which almost automatically implies the presence of an offscreen space containing the person's unseen or "cut off" portion.

Thus, while there is a considerable difference between the two spaces (onscreen is visible, offscreen is not), in a way we can consider that they are both entitled to belong to the same perfectly homogeneous imaginary space that we will label the "film space" or "scenographic space." It may seem a bit strange to qualify onscreen and offscreen space as equally imaginary, in spite of the more concrete nature of the former, which is continuously present before our eyes. Certain critics, including Noël Burch (who has considered the issue in great detail),[4] reserve the term "imaginary" for the offscreen space, and then only for the offscreen space that has not yet been seen; they use the term "concrete" to designate space that is now offscreen but has already been presented. Our choice not to follow these critics is deliberate and aims to insist, first of all, upon the imaginary nature of the onscreen space (which is admittedly visible or concrete if you will, but hardly tangible); and second, upon the homogeneity and reversibility between onscreen and offscreen, which are both equally important for defining film space.

An additional cause for the equal importance of onscreen and offscreen lies in the fact that film space is defined by more than visual traits alone. First, sound plays a great role, partly because the ear cannot distinguish between a sound made "onscreen" or "offscreen." This homogeneity of sound is one of the major factors involved in the unification of film space as a whole.[5] Second, the temporal unfolding of the story, or narrative, necessitates taking into account the continual shift from onscreen to offscreen, thereby assuring their immediate communicativeness. We will return to these points later with regard to sound, editing, and the concept of diegesis.

It obviously remains necessary to clarify a point that has been left implicit up to now: all this reflection upon film space (and the adjoining definitions of onscreen and offscreen) only makes sense, after all, with regard to what we call the "narrative representational" cinema. That is, the discussion of film space pertains to films that, in one way or another, tell their story by situating it in some imaginary universe that they create in the resulting representation.

Actually, the borderlines of narrativity, like those of representation, are often difficult to sketch. Just as a cartoon or cubist painting may represent, or at least evoke, a three-dimensional space, there are films whose spatial representation, while schematic or abstract, is nonetheless present and effective. This is the case for many animated films or even some "abstract" films.

Ever since the beginning of the cinema, the so-called representational films have made up the vast majority of the world's production (including documentary production), even though, early on, this same type of cinema was sharply criticized. Among other things, critics have challenged the idea of a "window onto the world" and analogous formulae because such notions conveyed idealistic prejudices that encouraged accepting film's fictive universe for reality. Eventually we will return to the psychological aspects of this deception, which we may, in fact, consider to be more or less a component of the dominant contemporary conception of the cinema. We should note from the start that these criticisms have led to the proposal of another approach to the concept of the offscreen. Pascal Bonitzer, for example, proposes the idea of an "anticlassical" offscreen that is heterogeneous in relation to the onscreen and definable as the space of the production (in the largest sense of the word).[6]

Aside from its polemic and normative expression, such a perspective on the offscreen certainly holds some interest for us here. In particular, Bonitzer's approach has the virtue of putting strong emphasis on the deception that allows film representation systematically to cover over all traces of its own production. Nevertheless,

These ten frames, taken from ten successive shots in *La Chinoise* (Jean-Luc Godard, 1967), illustrate several methods of communication between on-screen and offscreen space: Shot no. 1 presents the Jean-Pierre Léaud character's entrance; all the other shots demonstrate various degrees of glances offscreen, culminating with the Léaud character pointing a finger toward the camera. In addition, the shot scales, which vary from close-up to medium long shot, provide a series of examples defining the offscreen by partially out-of-frame characters.

Additional examples of communication between onscreen and offscreen space. The top example from *Orpheus* (Jean Cocteau, 1950) shows the characters about to leave the shot by crossing through the mirror which coincides with the frame's bottom edge.

Beneath it is a shot from *Citizen Kane* (Orson Welles, 1941) seen through a mirror, in which Susan Alexander looks up at the other character, Kane, visible only because part of his back is in the mirror.

this deception—whose mechanism must be dismantled—is just as active in our perception of the onscreen space as three-dimensional as it is in the manifestation of an offscreen that is nonetheless invisible. It therefore seems preferable to retain the restricted meaning defined above for the term "offscreen." As for that space of the film production where the technical equipment, filmmaking activity, and, metaphorically, the work of *écriture* are all deployed and undertaken, it will be more useful to use the phrase "out of frame." This term may be inconvenient since it is rarely used, yet by way of compensation it offers the advantage of referring directly to the frame, that is, to an artifact of the film's production, and not to the screen space, which is already produced and taken in by the illusion.

The concept "out of frame" [*hors-cadre*] does not arrive without precedent in the history of film theory. In S. M. Eisenstein's writings in particular, we can find many references to questions of framing and the nature of the frame itself. In fact, Eisenstein advocated a cinema wherein the image's boundary would serve as a sort of caesura or division between two radically different worlds. While Eisenstein does not actually employ the phrase "out of frame" in the sense that we propose, his developments of the idea certainly support our own.

TECHNIQUES OF DEPTH

The impression of depth is certainly not unique to the cinema, and the cinema cannot pretend to have invented the illusion of depth. Nevertheless, the combination of processes used to produce this apparent depth in the cinema is quite singular and is, in and of itself, convincing testimony of the cinema's particular contribution to the history of methods of representation. Besides the reproduction of movement, which helps immensely in the perception of depth—and we will return to this notion in our discussion of the impression of reality—there are essentially two series of techniques that are used in the cinema: perspective and depth of field.

Perspective

The concept of perspective, as we know, made its appearance very early in relation to pictorial representation, yet it is interesting to note that the word itself did not appear with its current meaning until the Renaissance (the French having borrowed it from the Italian *prospettiva*, which was "invented" by the painter-theoreticians of the Quattrocento). Thus, the definition of perspective found in the dictionary is, in fact, inseparable from the history of thought on perspective. But it is also linked to the great theoretical upheaval by which this consideration of perspective left its mark on the European Renaissance.

We can briefly define perspective as "the art of representing objects on a flat surface in such a way that the representation resembles the visual perception that one may have of these same objects." This definition, as simple as its terms might be, is not without problems. It assumes, among other things, that we know how to define a representation that resembles direct perception. This notion of figurative analogy is, as we know, fairly elastic, while the limitations of the concept of resemblance are largely conventional. As E. H. Gombrich and Rudolf Arnheim, among others, have observed (from their diverse perspectives), representational arts depend upon a partial illusion that permits the difference between our vision of the real and its representation to be accepted.[7] (There is, for example, the fact that perspective does not take binocular vision into account.) We will consider this definition, therefore, to be intuitively acceptable, without, for the moment, seeking to be more precise. It is very important, however, to note that if the definition seems acceptable, and hence natural, it is because we are already extremely accustomed to a certain form of representational painting.

Indeed, the history of painting has known many systems of perspective and representation, several of which are quite removed from us in time and space and appear rather foreign to us now. In fact, the only system that we are accustomed to consider as normal, since it dominates the entire modern history of painting, is the one elaborated at the beginning of the fifteenth century under the name of *perspectiva artificialis* or monocular perspective.

This perspective system, so dominant today, is only one of those studied and proposed by the painters and theoreticians of the Renaissance. If monocular perspective was chosen in the end with fairly unanimous support, it was essentially due to two types of consideration:

—first, its "automatic" (*artificialis*) nature, allowing simple geometric construction to be developed from various devices (such as those proposed by Albrecht Dürer);

—second, thanks to its very construction it copies the vision of the human eye (hence the name "monocular") by trying to fix upon the canvas an image obtained by the same geometric laws as those for the retinal image (moreover, it does not take into account retinal curvature precisely because such distortion is strictly imperceptible to us);

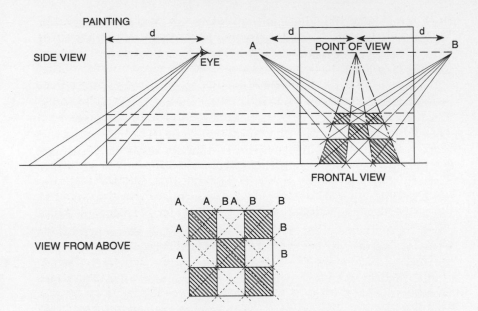

These diagrams demonstrate how, in *perspectiva artificialis*, one paints a checkerboard of three rows of three squares lying flat on the ground. Each group of parallel lines in the board is represented in the painting by a group of lines converging toward a ~~vanishing point~~. The vanishing point corresponding to the perpendicular lines within the painting is called the principal vanishing point or the *point of view*. As the diagram illustrates, the point of view's position varies with the height of the eye (it is at the same height), and the vanishing perspective is more pronounced the lower the eye becomes. Points A and B (vanishing points corresponding to lines 45° from the painting) are called ~~distance points~~; their distance to the point of view is equal to the distance from the eye to the painting.

—and, from this latter point, comes one of the system's essential characteristics, which is the establishment of a "~~point of view,~~" which is the technical term to designate the point where, by the process itself, the painting is supposed to correspond to the eye of the painter.

If we stress this process and the theoretical speculations that accompanied its origin, it is obviously because film perspective is none other than the exact replication of that representational tradition. The history of film perspective is actually intertwined with the successive invention of a wide variety of image-creating devices. We will not enter into a detailed discussion here of those inventions, but it is important to remember that the motion picture camera is, in fact, a relatively distant descendant of a very simple apparatus, the dark chamber (or camera obscura), which allowed the capturing of an image that obeyed the laws of monocular perspective without the aid of any optics. For our purposes at the moment, the photographic chamber, then the photo camera, and finally the modern motion picture camera are simply tiny versions of the camera obscura in which the opening that receives the light rays has been equipped with a more or less complex optical mechanism.

What is most important, moreover, is not so much to outline the relationship of cinema to painting as to evaluate the consequences of their common lineage. Thus, we should underline the fact that the apparatus for cinematic representation is historically linked to the emergence of humanism by its monocular perspective. More precisely, it is clear that both the long history of this perspectival form and the fact that centuries of painting have made us accustomed to it help account for the film image. But it is nonetheless important to admit that this perspective includes within the image, with its "point of view," a sign that the image is organized by and for an eye placed in front of it. Symbolically this allows us to say, among other things, that film representation assumes a subject who is watching, and whose eye is assigned a privileged viewing position.

Depth of Field

Let us now consider another parameter of representation that plays an equally important role in the illusion of depth: the sharpness of the image. In painting the matter is relatively simple: even if painters are more or less obliged to respect some perspectival law, they can play loosely with various degrees of the image's sharpness. For instance, a soft-focus or fuzzy effect has an expressive quality, especially in painting, that can be used to one's advantage. The situation is quite different in the cinema. The camera's construction imposes a certain correlation between various parameters (the amount of light entering the lens and focal length, among others) and the greater or lesser degree of sharpness in the image.[8]

In fact, these remarks must be doubly qualified:
—first, because the Renaissance painters tried to codify the ties between the sharpness of the image and the represented object's proximity. Compare this observation to Leonardo da Vinci's notion of "atmospheric perspective," which calls for treating distant objects as slightly hazy.
—second, because, inversely, many films toy with what are known as

"soft-focus art shots" that deliberately avoid sharp focus for part or all of the image in order to achieve expressive results.

Except for these special cases, the film image is sharp for an entire section of the field of vision, and the term used to distinguish the extent of this clearly focused zone is "depth of field." This depth is a technological factor of the image, which may be altered by varying the lens's focal length (depth of field is greatest when the focal length is shortest) or changing the f-stop (depth of field is greatest when the aperture is smallest). Thus, depth of field is defined as the depth measurement of the zone of sharply focused objects.

The concept of depth of field and its definition proceed from a factor that is determined by lens construction: for any given focus point—that is, for a given position on the lens's focus ring—one will obtain a very clear image of any object situated at a certain distance from the lens (the distance marked on the focus ring). For objects placed either a little farther from or closer to the camera, the image will be slightly out of focus; the further an object is moved toward "infinity" or toward the lens, the less clearly focused it will become. What we define as depth of field is the distance, measured along the axis of the lens, between the closest and farthest points that still provide a sharp image for a specific lens setting. Remember that this all assumes a conventional definition of sharp focus. For the 35 mm format, the image of an object point of extremely small dimensions is considered focused when the diameter of that image is less than 1/30 mm. Sharp focus is also defined by the technical determination of the "circle of confusion" projected onto the camera's film plane. Since a lens actually projects tiny circles onto the film instead of solid points, the smaller these so-called circles of confusion, the sharper the focus. This "circle of least confusion" becomes the standard for a given format's depth of field charts.

The importance of all this for us is obviously the aesthetic and expressive role played by the technical data. Actually the depth of field that we have just defined is not the depth of the field itself. This latter depth, which is the very phenomenon that we are trying to grasp in this chapter, is a result of various parameters of the film image, among them the use of depth of field. Depth of field is an important auxiliary method for the institution of the illusion of depth: if the depth of field is great, and the objects staged along the axis are all seen in focus, the perception of the perspective effect will be reinforced; if it is shallow, its very limitations will manifest a

"depth" of image, as, for instance, when a character comes into focus as s/he "approaches" the camera.

In addition to this basic function of accentuating the depth effect, depth
of field is often employed for its expressive virtues. In *Citizen Kane* (Orson Welles, 1941) the systematic use of short focal length and extreme
wide-angle lenses produces a very deep and hollowed-out space where
everything is presented in violently organized images. At the opposite
extreme, Sergio Leone's westerns use a great many very long focal length
lenses that flatten perspective and privilege a single object or character,
further emphasized by the soft focus of the surroundings.

If, therefore, depth of field is in itself a permanent factor of the
film image, its use has fluctuated quite a bit throughout the course
of film history. The primitive cinema, and the Lumière films in particular, benefited from a great depth of field that was a technical
consequence of the speed or relatively efficient light transmission of
the first lenses and the selection of very bright exterior subjects.
From an aesthetic point of view, this fairly uniform focus throughout the image, no matter what the object's distance from the lens, is
hardly immaterial since it allows these earliest films to approach
their pictorial ancestors. (It is worth recalling here Jean-Luc Godard's famous remark that Louis Lumière was actually a painter.)[9]
But the cinema's ultimate evolution would complicate matters.
During the entire period of the end of the silent era and the beginning of the sound cinema, depth of field virtually disappeared from
the cinema. The reasons, which are complex and multiple, involve
the upheaval surrounding the evolution of technical equipment,
which was in turn brought about by transformations in the conditions of credibility for film representations. This credibility, as
shown by Jean-Louis Comolli,[10] was transferred to the narrative
forms, the psychological verisimilitude, and the spatial-temporal
continuity of the classical stage.
Consequently, the massive and highly visible use of extreme
depth of field by certain films of the 1940s (begun in part by Jean
Renoir and then *Citizen Kane*) was taken as a real (re)discovery. This
reappearance, accompanied as it was by technical changes, is historically important as a sign of the cinema's reappropriation of a key
expressive technique that was all but forgotten. The revived depth
is also important because these films, and their by now very self-
conscious use of filming in depth, gave rise to André Bazin's elaboration of a theoretical discourse on the aesthetic of realism, a dis-

Examples of Depth of Field: top, *Citizen Kane* (Orson Welles, 1941); bottom, *The Lady from Shanghai* (Orson Welles, 1948).

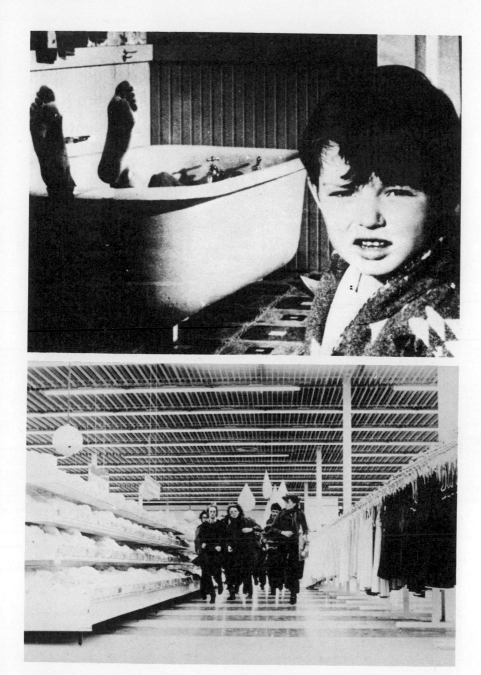

Top, *The Trouble with Harry* (Alfred Hitchcock, 1956); bottom, *Tout va bien*
(Jean-Luc Godard, 1972).

course that we have already mentioned and to which we will return throughout this study.

THE CONCEPT OF THE SHOT

Up to this point we have looked at the film image in terms of space (surface of the image, fictive depth of field, etc.) and have considered it a bit as we would a painting or photograph, or in any case as a unique fixed image, independent of time. However, the image is actually perceived much differently by the film spectator:

—first, it is not unique: any individual frame of the film is always taken from the middle of innumerable other frames;

—second, it is not independent of time: as it is perceived on the screen, the film image (which is itself always a series of successive, rapidly projected frames) is defined by a certain duration. This duration is dependent upon the speed with which the film moves through the projector and has been standardized for quite a long time now.[11]

—finally, the image is presented as moving: there is movement within the shot inducing the apprehension of movements in the field of action, such as character activity, for instance. There is also movement of the framing in relation to the framed material (or camera movements, if we are speaking in terms of the actual production).

Traditionally, we distinguish two large types of camera movement: tracking and panning/tilting. A tracking movement (or dolly) involves shifting the base of the camera, often along a line parallel to any movement by the filmed object (strictly defined as a track), or trucking in toward or out away from the object, as in a dolly movement. A special kind of camera movement is the crane shot, in which the camera actually leaves the ground, moving up or down, or, as in the case of Federico Fellini's famous "crab" crane, it may move in many different directions at once. (A more recent development, the steadicam, allows for even more elaborate and free-wheeling camera movement, which also makes camera movement more difficult to categorize). A panning movement, on the other hand, involves pivoting the camera horizontally while the camera pedestal remains fixed. A variation on the pan shot is the tilt, which pivots the camera vertically. Naturally, combinations of these kinds of movement exist as well; hence, one may speak of "track-pans," or the camera may be said to "dolly in and tilt up."

The introduction of the zoom lens, or variable focal length lens, brought options for simulated camera movement. For a given camera position, a short focal length lens provides a wide and deep field of vision, while the continuous shift to a longer focal length setting narrows the field, "enlarges" the objects in relation to the image's borders, and gives the impression that we are approaching the filmed objects. Hence, a "zoom shot" is also known as an "optical traveling" shot, but it is different from a camera movement in that the change to a longer focal length diminishes the depth of field.

This entire group of parameters—size, framing, point of view, as well as movement, duration, rhythm, and the image's relations with other images—makes up the very loose notion of a "shot." Once again we are using a word that belongs firmly to technical vocabulary and is very widely used during both actual film production and simple viewing practice.

During the shooting stage, "shot" is used as an approximate equivalent for "frame," "object field," and "take." Thus, it simultaneously designates a certain point of view on an event ("framing") and a certain duration.

During editing, the shot's definition is more precise, as it becomes the actual editing unit, meaning it is the minimal piece of film that, when assembled with the others, will make up the film.

In general, it is this second use that will govern the first. Most often, a shot is defined implicitly (and in a rather tautological manner) as "any piece of film contained between two shot changes or cuts." By extension, during filming the term "shot" is used to designate any piece of film that is running through the camera without interruption between the starting and stopping of the camera's motor.

The shot, as it figures in the edited film, is therefore a part of a shot exposed during the shooting. Actually, one of the most important operations during editing consists precisely of cutting down already filmed shots, taking out, on the one hand, technical sections (like the clapboard), and, on the other hand, all recorded elements that are considered unwanted or useless for the final cut version of the film.

If, then, "shot" is a frequently used and highly convenient word in actual film production, we must underline the fact that, for a theoretical approach to film, the term denotes a concept that remains difficult to handle, precisely because of its empirical origins. In the area of film aesthetics, the word "shot" is employed in at least three sorts of contexts.

1. *In terms of scale*: we traditionally define various shot "sizes" or proportions, and these are generally determined in relation to the

different framing options for shooting characters. The usual listing
includes the following scales: extreme long shot, long shot, medium
long shot, medium shot or *plan américain*, medium close-up, close-
up, and extreme close-up. The concept "shot scale" incorporates at
least two different issues:

—first, there is the question of framing, which is essentially no
different from other problems related to the boundaries of the image,
and which, on a larger plane, involves the establishment of a point
of view for the camera in relation to the represented event;

—second, a more general theoretical-ideological problem exists
precisely because the scale itself is determined in relation to the
human figure. We may perceive here, once again, echoes of Renaissance research on the proportions of the human body and the rules
for its representation. More concretely, this implicit reference of the
shot size to the human figure almost always functions to reduce all
representation to that of the character. This is especially clear in the
case of the close-up since it is nearly always used, at least in classical cinema, to show faces, that is, to erase what a "close-up point of
view" might possess that is atypical, excessive, or even troubling.

2. *In terms of mobility*: a paradigm would be proposed here between a "static shot," in which the camera remains immobile
throughout the shot, and various kinds of "mobile shots," including zooms. This problem is connected to the preceding one, and,
like shot scale, it also participates in the establishment of a point
of view.

We should note here the frequent interpretations given for camera
movements: the pan would be the equivalent of the eye's rotation,
or of someone turning his or her head; a tracking shot would be a
shift in someone's glance; and, as for the zoom, which is difficult to
interpret in terms of the simple position of the supposed subject of
the glance, it has often been read as the "focusing in" of a character's
attention. These interpretations, while occasionally accurate (especially in the case of what we call a "subjective point of view shot,"
that is, a shot seen through a character's eyes), have no general validity. At best they bear witness to the tendency in all reflection on
the cinema to equate the camera with the human eye. We will return to this point later during our discussion of identification in the
cinema.

3. *In terms of duration*: defining a shot as an "editing unit" implies in effect that very brief fragments (such as those less than one
second long) and very long segments (several minutes in duration)
both qualify as shots. Even though duration is the shot's essential
trait, given our empirical definition, it is here that the term's most

During this scene from *Rules of the Game* (Jean Renoir, 1939), the camera moves ever closer to the characters. We shift from an establishing shot of Geneviève and Robert to a medium long shot or *plan américain* of Geneviève alone, to a medium shot, then a medium close-up, and finally a close-up. Note how each shot includes significant mise-en-scène details.

The final sequence shot from *Muriel* (Alain Resnais, 1963): the camera follows the character while she explores the entire empty apartment.

complex problems surface. The most frequently studied aspect involves the appearance and use of the expression "shot-sequence," which designates a shot that is long enough to contain as many events as a sequence, that is, a string or succession of several distinct events.

Some critics, Jean Mitry and Christian Metz in particular, have clearly shown that a given shot is in fact equivalent to a sum of shorter fragments that are fairly easy to isolate. (In the next chapter we will return to this idea in relation to editing.) Thus, the shot sequence, if it is a *formal* shot (being set off, like all shots, by two splices), will nonetheless in most cases be considered interchangeable with a normal sequence. Naturally, everything here depends upon the approach that one brings to the film, whether one is simply trying to isolate and count the shots, isolate the unfolding of the narrative, or examine the editing pattern. In each case the shot sequence will be treated differently.

Due to all these reasons—the ambiguity in the word's meaning and the theoretical difficulties tied to any cutting of a film into smaller units—the word "shot" must be used cautiously or else avoided whenever possible. At the very least we should remain aware when using the term of what it *applies to* and what it *masks*.

THE CINEMA AS AUDIO REPRESENTATION

Sound reproduction is among the features that we expect from the current cinematic form, and synchronized sound is undoubtedly one of the most natural-appearing characteristics of the cinema. Yet for the very reason that sound *does* appear natural, it remains one of the least examined areas of film theory and aesthetics. Nonetheless, everyone realizes that sound is not a natural given of film representation and that the sound track's role and conception have varied in the past and still fluctuate widely from film to film. There are two necessary yet actively interfering determinants that control these audio variations.

The Economic-Technical Factors and Their History

As we know, the cinema first existed with an image track that was not accompanied by any recorded sound. The only sound accompanying a film's exhibition was usually music furnished by piano, organ, or violin soloists, or on occasion a small orchestra,[12] and of course the *benshi* or commentator in the Japanese cinema.[13]

The *cinématographe* emerged in 1895 as an apparatus devoid of synchronized sound, and the public would have to wait over thirty years for the first sound film (even though the technical problems were essentially solved by 1911 or 1912). This long silent period can be partially explained by prevailing market conditions. If the Lumière brothers commercialized their invention very quickly, it was undoubtedly due in part to their wanting to get a jump on Thomas Edison and his kinetoscope; after all, Edison did not want to market his invention without having solved the sound problem. In addition, after 1912, the commercial delay in the utilization of sound technology owes much to the well-known inertia of a system whose interests lie in using existing materials and techniques for as long as possible, without any new investments.

The appearance of the first sound films can also be explained in part, of course, by economic determinations. The telecommunications industry began branching out in a search for additional long-term applications for their sound reproduction equipment and investment bankers looked to Hollywood for potential clients. Furthermore, it was only after long-run profits seemed assured that the American studios moved wholeheartedly into the economically and stylistically costly process of sound films.[14]

The history of the advent of sound films is well known (it has even provided the subject matter for many films, including the famous *Singin' in the Rain* [Stanley Donen and Gene Kelly, 1952]); practically overnight, sound became an irreplaceable element of film representation. However, the evolution of sound technology did not end with this bursting of sound onto the film scene; in fact, we could say that since its beginnings sound technology has advanced considerably in two large areas. On the one hand, there has been a dramatic simplification of the actual sound recording process: the earliest set-ups required very cumbersome equipment, carried around in a "sound truck" designed specifically for exterior shooting. Accordingly, the invention of magnetic tape was a very important advance.

On the other hand, we find the appearance and perfection of the technology for postsynchronization and mixing, which is to say, quite generally, the ability to replace the live recorded sound from the actual shoot with another sound judged more appropriate and the addition of other sound sources such as supplementary sound effects and music. There currently exists a whole spectrum of audio techniques, from the most intricate—a postsynchronized sound track with accompanying sound effects, music, and special effects—to the simplest—synchronized sound recorded directly at the time of filming. This second technique saw a spectacular return to favor thanks to the invention of portable equipment and very quiet-running cameras during the late 1950s.

Aesthetic and Ideological Factors

The second large determination that is essential to our purposes is, in fact, inseparable from the technical-economic factors. By way of extreme simplification, we may state that there have always been two large tendencies in relation to film representation, which are then in turn incarnated by two large groups of filmmakers. In his article "The Evolution of the Language of Cinema," Bazin characterizes these two kinds of directors as "those who put their faith in the image" and "those who put their faith in reality."[15] In other words, there are filmmakers who make the act of representation itself their artistic and expressive goal, as opposed to directors who subordinate their representations to the most faithful restitution possible of a supposed truth or of some essence of reality.

There are numerous implications for these two different positions (we will return to all this later in the discussion of editing and the concept of transparency in the cinema). As for the reproduction of sound, this opposition was quickly translated into a form of opposing requirements for the sound track. Thus, one might easily argue that, during the 1920s anyway, there really existed two silent cinemas.

One cinema was authentically mute,[16] which is to say, literally deprived of speech. Thus, this cinema lacked speech and called out for the invention of a process of sound reproduction that would be faithful, truthful, and adequate to a visual representation that itself would be accepted as closely analogous to reality (in spite of its shortcomings, such as the continued lack of color).

But the other silent cinema, by contrast, assumed and sought out its own specificity in the language of images and the maximum expressivity of its visual means. This was the case, almost without exception, with all the great schools of the twenties—French surrealism and impressionism, Soviet montage and constructivism, and German expressionism, for instance. The important thing for these groups was that the cinema, to the greatest extent possible, try to develop toward this universal language of images. There was even a more utopian movement toward a "cinelanguage" that has left phantom traces in many articles of the period (see chapter 4).

It has often been pointed out that the mute cinema, whose expressive techniques are instilled with a certain coefficient of nonreality (no sound, no color), in some ways favored a considerable lack of realism in its narration and representation. Thus, the era of the silent film's zenith (the 1920s) was the period that saw the culmination of work on spatial construction, on the image's composition or frame (use of the iris and matte), and more generally on the nonfigurative materiality of the image (double exposures, unusual filming angles, tinting, etc.). Yet it was also an era that gave great attention to film themes involving dreams, the fantastic, the imaginary, as well as the "cosmic" dimension (to use an expression from Barthélémy Amengual) of people and their fate.[17]

Thus, it is not surprising that the arrival of the "talkie" encountered two radically different responses from these two opposing camps. For the first group, the sound film was hailed as the achievement of film language's "true vocation"—a vocation that had until now been delayed because of technical matters. At the most extreme, some people began to consider that, with the addition of sound, the cinema was only now really beginning and that henceforth the cinema would aim as much as possible at abolishing every barrier that separated film from being a perfect reflection of the real world. This position was, therefore, the product of critics and theorists; the most notable of these (because the most coherent, even in their excess) were André Bazin and his followers in the 1950s.

The second group, however, often perceived sound as a true instrument of degradation of the cinema. It was simply a device for making the cinema into a copy or double of reality, at the expense of work on the image and gesture. This position was adopted (often in an excessively negative form) by a number of directors, several of whom would require a very long time before accepting the presence of sound in films.

The late 1920s, therefore, saw a flurry of manifestos devoted to the sound cinema. For instance, in 1928, Grigori Alexandrov, Sergei Eisenstein, and Vsevolod Pudovkin co-signed a manifesto proposing that non-coincidence or counterpoint between sound and image was the minimal requirement for a sound cinema that would not submit to the theater.

For his part, Charlie Chaplin vehemently refused to accept talking films. In a *Motion Picture* interview in 1929, Chaplin attacked those favoring sound: "They are spoiling the oldest art in the world—the art of pantomime. They are ruining the great beauty of silence. They are defeating the meaning of the screen."[18]

As examples of a much less negative approach, we might cite the reactions of Jean Epstein or Marcel Carné (then a journalist), both of whom accepted the advent of sound as an advance, yet insisted upon the need to return the camera's lost mobility as soon as possible.

At present, and in spite of all the nuances that must be considered in making this statement, it certainly seems that the first hypothesis—that film sound reinforces and even increases the reality effect—has gained widespread support. As a result, sound is most often considered a simple auxiliary to the scenographic analogy offered by the visual elements.

Nonetheless, there is absolutely no reason, from a theoretical standpoint, that things must remain with sound reinforcing the image. In effect, audio and visual representation have nothing at all in common. This difference, which certainly springs from the characteristics of our corresponding sense organs—the eyes and ears—is most notably evident in their very different relationships to film space. If, as we have seen, the film image is capable of evoking a space comparable to real space, sound is almost completely shut out of this spatial dimension. Thus, no definition of an "audio field" could be established to imitate the visual field, due to the difficulty in imagining what would have to be called an "out of field sound" [hors-champ sonore], which is an imperceptible sound and would seem to have to be opposed to a perceptible sound—all of which becomes quite meaningless.

All the labors of the classical cinema (and its many offshoots, which are today dominant) have therefore aimed at spatializing their sound elements, by offering corresponding visual manifestations in the image. Hence, they assure a biunique or even redundant liaison between image and sound. This spatialization of the sound, which goes hand in hand with its diegetization, is also paradoxical if one considers that film sound, coming from one or more loudspeakers that are generally hidden from view, is in fact rather minimally anchored within the real space of the theater. Instead sound seems to float out from no clearly defined source. Ironically, recent attempts at presenting directional sound that shifts realistically from one side of the screen to the other tend merely to call attention to the placement of the speakers in the theater and not to the motivating movement in the frame.

For years now there has been a resurgence of interest in cinematic forms that would not, or would no longer, make sound submit to the image. Rather, sound would be treated as an autonomous expressive film element, capable of entering into various kinds of combinations with the image. One striking example of this tendency is the systematic work accomplished by Michel Fano for the films of Alain Robbe-Grillet. In *The Man Who Lies* (1968), for instance, we hear a wide variety of sounds during the opening title sequence. Some of these noises (splashing water, rustling bushes, footsteps, and grenade explosions) will only be justified or attributed to some action seen later in the film, while still other sounds (a drum roll, whistling, and the cracking of a whip) will never be returned to or anchored in the image.

Other filmmakers have followed a completely different path, giving great importance to direct sound recording. We can cite several directors in this tradition: Danièle Huillet and Jean-Marie Straub, for instance, integrated "noise" into their adaptation of a Corneille play, *Othon* (1969), and a Schönberg opera, *Moses and Aaron* (1975); Jacques Rivette uses direct sound in *La Religieuse* (1965) and *L'Amour fou* (1968), as does Maurice Pialat in *Loulou* (1980).

Concurrently, film theorists have finally started to become much more systematic in their analysis of film sound or, more specifically, sound to image relations. We are currently in a phase that still lacks rigor, where theoretical labor essentially consists of classifying the various types of audiovisual combinations according to the most logical and general criteria possible, with the prospect of future formalization.

Thus, the traditional distinction between "sound on" and "sound off"—for a long time the sole means of classifying sound sources in relation to onscreen space and flatly imitating the opposition "on-screen"/"offscreen"—is grossly inadequate. It is in the process of being replaced by more precise analyses, which are further removed from the *a priori* of the classical cinema. While many different critics have attacked the problem, it is still too early to propose any definitive synthesis of their methods, which all remain very different from one another and still far from perfected.

Nonetheless, we may emphasize that the various classifications proposed here or elsewhere, to which we will return, seem to us (in addition to their real interest of definitively canceling out the simplistic on/off distinction), to confront a central problem: the separation between a sound's source and the representation of the emission of that sound. Whatever the proposed typology might be, it always assumes that we can recognize a sound "whose source is in the image." No matter how precise the classification, this action displaces rather than resolves the question of the spatial anchoring of film sounds. Thus, the whole issue of film sound and its relation to the image and the diegesis is another persistent question on today's theoretical agenda.

2 | MONTAGE

THE PRINCIPLE OF EDITING

As we mentioned earlier, one of the cinema's most obvious specific traits is the fact that it is an art involving both the combination and arrangement of elements. (After all, a film always mobilizes a considerable number of images, sounds, and graphic inscriptions in varying arrangements and proportions.) It is essentially this trait that the notion of editing covers, and we might also note that editing involves a concept that is very central to any theorizing of the cinema, namely, montage.[1]

As we have already explained in relation to other concepts, the idea of editing, at least in its most current definition, springs from an empirical base. For a very long time (almost since the origins of the *cinématographe*), a division of labor has existed within film production that quickly brought about the separate operation of the different phases of the production processes, just as it has in any field of specialization. Editing in a film (and more generally in the cinema) is thus first a technical activity, organized into a profession, which, during the few decades of its existence, has focused and gradually finalized certain activities and procedures.

We should briefly outline how the chain of events leading from the scenario to the finalized film is constructed, at least in a conventional production:

A first stage consists of breaking down the scenario into units of action and eventually cutting those units down still further to obtain the storyboard, which shows the units to be filmed (as shots).

These shots usually generate a number of takes during filming, and they may include some identical takes (repeated until the result is found to be satisfactory by the crew) or different takes made by covering the same action from several camera positions.

The collection of these takes constitutes the rushes upon which the actual editing work begins. This editing labor typically includes at least three operations.

1. A selection is made from the rushes to collect the useful footage, while the rejected material makes up the outtakes.

2. The assembly of the chosen shots in a certain order follows, thereby obtaining a first assembly or rough cut.

3. Finally, at a more precise stage, the exact length that will be allowed each shot must be determined, and the cutting and splicing together of the shots is accomplished. (We should point out that what we have described here is in fact current practice for editing the image track. The corresponding work on the sound track may, depending on the situation, be carried out simultaneously or after the final cut of the image track. In some cases, as in Jean-Luc Godard's *Pierrot le fou* [1965], parts of the sound track may actually be mixed and spliced *before* the image track.)

Thus, in editing's original dimension, as one specialized technique among others, it may be summarized by its three large operations: selection, assembly, and final cutting. These three operations will finally achieve a total construct, which is the film itself, made from what had originally been separate elements. In general, the concept of editing is defined with reference to the editor's labor by the theorists who have dealt with the issue. (Note that the editing process insofar as we have described it only corresponds to current practice, yet may eventually be altered in many ways.) We will retain here, for example, the definition proposed by Marcel Martin: "Editing is the organization of a film's shots according to certain principles of ordering and duration."[2] This definition broadly consolidates those characteristics proposed by most critics and is a translation in both general and abstract terms of the concrete editing process as we have described it above. Thus, it details, in a more formal way, the two given conditions that follow:

—the objects upon which the editing operates are shots of a film; hence, editing consists of manipulating the shots in order to construct another object—the film;

—there are two modes of action in editing, since editing orders the series of units that are the shots and determines their duration.

As a matter of fact, however, such a formalization makes the limited nature of this conception of editing, and its submission to technological process, quite evident. Thus, a more extensive and theoretical consideration of the collection of film phenomena leads us to consider broadening the definition. Working from the above definition, which we will label the "narrow" definition of editing, we will propose expanding it in two directions; first, the definition must embrace the objects of editing, and second, it must accommodate the modes of action. Both of these aspects of editing have already been mentioned above.

The Objects of Editing

The narrow definition poses the "shot" as the canonical editing unit, yet we have already pointed out in a previous discussion how this term can be somewhat ambiguous given its very polysemous nature. Admittedly, in the present case this ambiguity may be partially reduced because "shot" here can be understood according to only one of its many aspects—that marking the inscription of time into the film. This is to say that the shot here is characterized by a certain duration and movement and thus becomes equivalent to the expression "an (empirical) editing unit."

Yet we might also consider that the operations of ordering and splicing that define editing may also be applied to other types of objects that we will now distinguish.

PARTS OF A FILM (OR FILM SYNTAGMAS) LARGER THAN A SHOT.   This first, rather abstract formulation covers a very real problem, at least for narrative-representational film: in general, these films are composed of a certain number of large narrative units placed in sequence. We will ultimately see that the classical cinema has even established a veritable typology of these large units that has remained relatively stable throughout its history. In accordance with Christian Metz's definitions we will refer to these large units as "segments" or "large syntagmas."[3]

Beyond the problem of the segmentation of narrative films as it has been posed so far, we can give two concrete examples in regard to this first extension of the concept.

First, there is the general phenomenon of film citation. Any fragment of one film that is cited in another film will be defined there as an easily divisible unit. Its size will generally be larger than a shot and will enter into a direct relation, on this level, with the rest of the film.[4]

Second, we can cite a historic example involving a much smaller sphere. In the work accomplished by Eisenstein's students in their preparation of the filming of a fictional episode, Eisenstein proposed cutting the script into large narrative units (christened "shot complexes"). Then

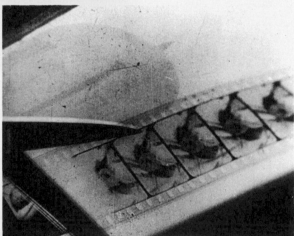

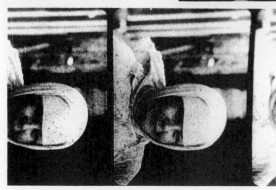

Three frames from *The Man with a Movie Camera* (Dziga Vertov, 1929). From the top, the editor, the film about to be cut, a fragment of film.

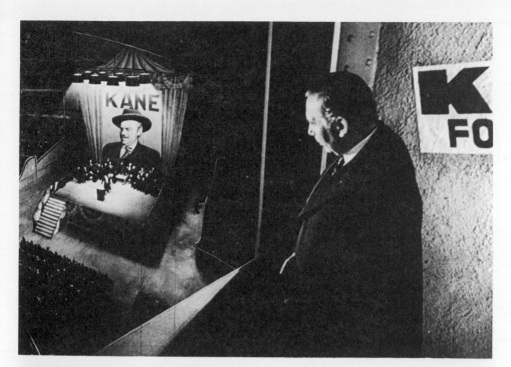

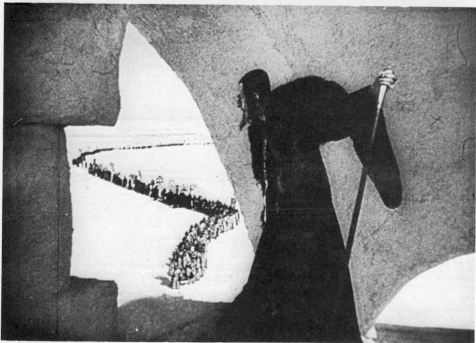

Two examples of montage within the shot: top, *Citizen Kane* (Orson Welles, 1941); bottom, *Ivan the Terrible* (S. M. Eisenstein, 1945).

he asked them to consider two levels of découpage editing: the first between the shot complexes, and the second between individual shots within these large sections. It is also necessary to include the instance of all films constructed expressly upon the alternation and combination of two or more narrative series.[5]

PARTS OF A FILM SMALLER THAN A SHOT.   Here once again this formulation incorporates figurative cases that are quite real, even banal, wherein a shot may be considered divisible into still smaller units. There are two ways to picture this "fragmenting" of the shot.

1. *In duration*: from the point of view of content, a shot may very well be seen as the equivalent of a longer segment, as in the classical case of the "sequence shot" or *plan-séquence*, whose very definition is a shot that operates as a sequence. In addition, however, there are a large number of instances of shots that are not really sequence shots, yet where some event (such as a camera movement or gesture) is sufficiently marked to play the role of a caesura, or even a true disruption, or at least to summon up some substantial transformations in the frame.

A famous example exists within *Citizen Kane* where the camera first reveals Susan Alexander singing onstage at the opera, then rises up in a long vertical crane shot until reaching the catwalk, ending up on two stagehands. During this ascending movement the image is constantly transforming itself, as much from the point of view of shifting perspective as from the actual composition in the frame (which becomes more and more abstract). While filmed in a single take, this shot is nonetheless immediately readable as the sum of successive montage effects. Welles's film is very rich in this sort of shot construction.

2. *In its visual (and particularly spatial) parameters*: in a manner that is more or less manifest, depending on the case, a shot may be analyzed as a function of the visual parameters that define it. Here the cases of imaginable figures (of which we can find examples in existing films) are quite numerous and diverse. To give a clearer idea, these cases will range from relatively succinct plastic effects (such as a violent opposition between black and white within the frame) to spatial collage effects that may, by contrast, be quite sophisticated.

Admittedly, in these two examples, as in all the other instances arising from this category, there is absolutely no isolatable editing operation. The activity of the editing principle (the assembly of different, indeed even heterogeneous pieces) is produced here inside the unit that is the shot. What this signifies, among other practical consequences, is that this sort of effect is always arranged before filming.

Obviously, it is necessary to add that in this case, as well as in the long take, montage effects, even if they can be very clear and unmistakable—as in the example we cited—can never really be formally defined with the same rigor as editing in its narrow sense.

PARTS OF A FILM THAT DO NOT COMPLETELY COINCIDE WITH THE DIVISION OF SHOTS. This is the case when we consider the reciprocal play within a film of two different instances of representation, without that play necessarily having its divisions agree with the shot divisions. In fact, the most notable case is that of montage between the image track, taken in its entirety, and the sound track. Moreover, contrary to what we have just shown in the section above, here there is, in the most common instance of the classical cinema, a process on the order of manipulation by montage because the sound track is most often constructed after filming and then custom-fitted, as it were, to the image track. The dominant conceptions concerning sound, however (which we referred to in chapter 1), pretend that this montage procedure may be denied as such and that, on the contrary, the classical film tends to present its image and sound tracks as consubstantial. In addition, classical notions of editing allow that both sound and image, working together, tend to efface the actual production process.

The only film theories that describe the sound-image relationship as an editing process and that acknowledge all the consequences (including the relative autonomy granted to the sound track in relation to the image track) are the theories directly opposed to any classical aesthetic of transparency. (We will return to this point with regard to both Bazin and Eisenstein later in this chapter.)

Obviously, in most of the cases that we have just mentioned we are more or less distant not only from the initial narrow definition of editing, but also, on occasion, from an actual editing operation. Nevertheless, if we can consider that there is always some common trait that does belong to the realm of editing, it is precisely the fact that it always involves the interrelation of at least two elements (whether on the same level or not). This placing of elements into a certain relationship produces some specific effect that was never present within any of the initial individual elements. Later in this chapter we will return to this conception of editing as montage or a productive process and then we will point out some of montage's limitations.

We could go even further in extending the definition of editing or montage by pushing it to the point of considering objects that are no longer parts of the film. This claim, even more than the three preceding categories, may seem to go beyond film boundaries. In fact, it is a rather abstract notion, and the situation to which it refers is cited only in theory, as an eventual possibility. Hence, we cannot be certain whether this might not lead to an overly broad definition that would result in stripping away all the consistency in the original concept.

From this point of view we could, for example, define entire films themselves as being part of a montage. Included might be various films by the same director, films within the same school (such as neorealism), films about a common topic, or films constituting a given genre or subgenre. We will not, however, insist on this usage.

Modes of Action in Editing

Quickly returning to the narrow definition of editing, we can now verify that it was much more complete and satisfying in relation to modes of editing than to the objects of editing. In fact, that definition assigned the process a role as organizer of the elements of film (specifically shots and the expanded area of similar film elements that we have just discussed), according to their order and duration. If we were once again to make a new inventory of the numerous and quite diverse objects discussed in the previous section, we would now see that in order to account for the group of all possible cases it is necessary to add the criticism of simultaneous composition (or the process of juxtaposition) to the criteria of order and duration. By using these three sorts of operations, which include the juxtaposition of homogeneous or heterogeneous elements, ordering in both contiguity and succession, and calculation of duration, we can account for all of the eventualities that we have encountered. Even more importantly, we will be able to confront virtually all concrete cases, whether actual or imaginable.

Montage: The Large Definition of Editing

Having acknowledged the three criteria of the actual modes of editing, we are now prepared to define editing in a larger sense, which we will label "montage." Rather than working from the simple empirical base furnished by the editor's traditional practice, we will begin by taking into consideration all the manifestations of the editing principle within the entire film domain.

We therefore propose the following definition, which we will subsequently designate as the "large" definition of editing or "montage": "Montage is the principle governing the organization of film elements, both visual and audio, or the combination of these elements, by juxtaposing them, connecting them, and/or controlling their duration."

We should note that, among other things, this definition does not contradict Christian Metz's concept of editing "in the large sense," in which editing is "the concerted organization of syntagmatic co-occurrences along the film chain."[6] He also distinguishes three principal modes of manifestation for these "syntagmatic" relations (or relations in a series). Those modes are:
—collage, as in the case of isolated shots related to one another;
—camera movements; and
—the co-presence of several motifs within the same shot.

Our own description is much larger. We should certainly reiterate here that this expansion of the definition is only of interest and use within a theoretical and analytical perspective.

THE FUNCTIONS OF MONTAGE

The large definition of editing provided above poses montage as capable of influencing diverse film objects while operating in three large modes. Now we will examine the question of montage functions, while still maintaining our same goal, which is to design the construction of a formal model, capable of accounting for all the existing film instances.

As in the preceding exposé, we will begin by outlining the traditional aesthetic approach to this issue. This approach, like the one described for the objects of editing and its various modes, is generated primarily by actual editing practice, which it reflects quite empirically. We will soon see, however, that this time the empirical approach will not result in any simple definitions.

It may be useful to begin by pointing out an ambiguity that exists on the level of vocabulary. What we designate as montage "functions" (and which thereby respond to the question "what does the montage produce in this or that particular case?") have often been called montage "effects," especially by the representatives of this empirical movement. Admittedly, the practical difference between the concept of function and that of montage effect is quite minimal. If we adhere strictly to the first term, however, it is for two sorts of reasons.

First, the word "effect" calls up connotations of things that can effectively be proven; hence, it is more adept at describing concrete cases. In contrast, the term "function" is more abstract and thus more useful for a task attempting to formalize ideas, even if the result is to assure the existence, or possibility, of real actualizations or cases that we will have to examine.

Second, the word "effect" could create some confusion (often implicit), between the "effects of montage" and the "montage-effect" [l'effet-montage], the term by which some theorists, such as Jean Mitry, designate what we have labeled the "montage principle" or editing in the large sense.

The Empirical Approach

Traditional considerations of the functions of montage are first based on an account of the historical conditions behind the appearance and then on the development of editing in the narrow sense. Without entering into a detailed description of this history, it is nonetheless very important to point out that from a very early stage the cinema placed images "in sequence" for narrative purposes.

There have been many debates between historians as to the precise date of editing's first appearance in a fiction film. The issue, like many similar questions, is difficult to settle. For example, the first films of Georges Méliès (1896) are already composed of several shots, yet it is generally agreed that while Méliès may be the inventor of narrative film, he did not really use editing principles. Instead, his early films are at best mere successions of tableaux. Among the great precursors and inventors of editing that is truly used as such, Edwin S. Porter is generally cited, particularly with reference to his *Life of an American Fireman* (1902) and especially *The Great Train Robbery* (1903).

In any case, all historians are in agreement that the development of editing had a primary aesthetic effect of liberating the camera, which, until then, had been fixed for static takes. There is, in fact, an oft-cited paradox here that while the most direct path to a more mobile camera would seem logically to have been via camera movement itself, editing actually played a much more decisive role than camera movement during the cinema's first two decades. As Christian Metz writes, "The transformation of the *cinématographe* into cinema was accomplished much more thanks to the problems involved in the *succession of a number of images* than in relation to any *supplementary modes of the image itself.*"[7]

Hence, the first function of editing (first, obviously, because it was the first to appear, but also because subsequent film history has continuously confirmed its preeminent importance) is actually its narrative function. Thus, all the classical descriptions of editing consider, more or less explicitly, this narrative function to be the normal function of editing. From this perspective, editing becomes that which assures the connection of the elements of an action according to a principle that is, quite globally, a relationship of causality and/or diegetic temporality. It always involves making certain that the drama is better perceived and correctly understood by the — spectator.

This fundamental or even founding function of editing is usually opposed to a second large editing function, "expressive montage," which is sometimes considered to be completely separate from the first. Expressive montage is a tactic that, according to Marcel Martin, "is not a means but an end . . . aiming to express by itself—and — by the collision of two images—some emotion or idea."[8]

This distinction between editing that is essentially aimed at being the instrument of concise narration and editing (or montage) that is aimed at producing aesthetic shocks or collisions that will eventually be independent of all fictionality obviously reflects an opposition within the specific issue of editing itself. This antagonism between the two kinds of editing resembles the division we have already discussed in the area of sound. Undoubtedly, when defined in this extremist manner, without referring to any specific fiction, even the concept of an expressive montage has never been actualized in its pure form, except within a few films from the silent era, and most specifically films of the French avant-garde. However, the vast majority of films, even silent ones, actually resort to using each of these two categories of editing.

The weakness and artificial character of this distinction between two types of films thus led us very quickly to consider that, beyond its central narrative function, editing also has the obligation to produce a number of other effects within a film. It is around this issue that empirical descriptions of the functions of montage, precisely because they *are* empirical, tend to differ strongly, placing emphasis alternately upon one or another of its functions and above all defining them according to a base of general ideological assumptions that

are not always explicitly clear. Later in this chapter we will return
to this question concerning the motivations behind various theories
of montage. For the moment we should simply point out the very
general and even vague character of these "creative" functions. Marcel Martin, who has devoted long and often quite useful treatises to
this question, proposes that montage creates movement, rhythm,
and the "idea": or three large categories of thought that confirm the
given narrative function and hardly permit us to go further in terms
of formalization.

Toward More Systematic Description

The empirical and descriptive approach we have just outlined does
indeed hold some interest for us. While always staying close to what
the history of film forms has confirmed, the empirical approach has,
in its best instances, recorded the essence of all imaginable montage
functions. Thus, our present task consists of trying to organize those
functions in a more rational manner.

PRODUCTIVE MONTAGE. First of all, it will be necessary to focus
briefly on this idea of a "creative" or "productive" montage (which
is also tied to the notion of possible editing effects). Let us note right
from the start that this idea is fairly old, having appeared during the
earliest attempts at systematic theoretical reflection on the cinema.

> The following definition may be found in the writings of Béla Balázs in
> 1930: montage can "be genuinely creative and convey to us something
> that cannot be seen on any of the images themselves."[9]
>
> In a larger and more concise fashion, in *Esthétique et psychologie
> du cinéma* Jean Mitry defines "productive" montage (or the "montage-
> effect") as the result of an association, whether arbitrary or not, of two
> images that, when related to one another, cause the viewer to perceive an
> idea, emotion, or sentiment in his or her consciousness that is not pres-
> ent in the individual images.

Thus, we can see that this notion is in fact presented as a true
definition of the montage principle, this time seen from the point
of view of its effects. Montage may be defined in very general fashion as "the combining of two film elements, resulting in the production of a specific effect that could not be produced by either of the
two elements." This important definition fundamentally demonstrates and justifies the central place that the idea of montage has
always been accorded in the cinema within every sort of theoretical
approach.

In fact, every sort of editing, and every use of it, is productive. Both the transparent narrative editing and the most abstract expressive montage aim to produce various effects by way of confrontation and collision between different elements. No matter what the importance, and it may be considerable, of what takes place at the moment of the montage (that is to say, of whatever the manipulation of the filmed material may add in relation to the original conception of the film), montage as a *principle* is by nature a production technique (producing signification and emotional response). To put it differently, montage is always also defined by its functions.

Let us next confront these functions themselves. We will distinguish three large types: syntactic functions, semantic functions, and rhythmic functions.

SYNTACTIC FUNCTIONS.   Montage assures formal relations between the elements it assembles, and these relations are marked as such; they are more or less independent of meaning. These relations essentially belong to two groups.

1. The relations may have the effects of liaison and/or its opposite, disjunction. In addition, they have the larger effects of punctuation and demarcation.

By way of example, we can cite the very classic case of the "dissolve," which as we know is a figure that usually marks an overlapping between two different episodes of a film. This demarcating quality is extremely stable, which becomes all the more remarkable since the figure of the dissolve has been associated with various significations throughout film history. For instance, for a long time the dissolve was associated in a rather systematic manner with the idea of the flashback, which is certainly not the only value of a dissolve today.

The production of a formal liaison between two successive shots (the particular case for this syntactic function) is, in particular, that which defines the "match" in the strictest sense of the term. With the match this formal liaison reinforces a continuity of the representation itself, as we will see in more detail shortly.

2. The relations may have effects of alternation (or, on the other hand, of linearity).

As in the case of the various historically confirmed forms of liaison or punctuation, the alternation of two or more motifs is a formal characteristic of film discourse, which does not by itself engage a univocal signification. For a very long time it has been stated (the idea having been expressed by montage theorists from Béla Balázs to V. I. Pudovkin) that, according to the nature of an involved shot or segment's content, alternation could signify simultaneity (as in the case of a true "alternating montage") or might express a comparison between two unequal terms with relation to the diegesis (as in "parallel montage").

SEMANTIC FUNCTIONS.   The semantic function is certainly the most important and most universal function, as well as the function that editing *always* assumes. In fact, the semantic function includes a large and extremely diverse number of cases. In an admittedly arbitrary fashion, we will distinguish two large sorts of semantic functions for editing.

First, there is the production of some denotative meaning, which is essentially spatial and temporal, and most fundamentally involves everything that defined the category of narrative editing. Editing in this sense is one of the great means of producing film space and, in a more general way, the entire diegesis.

Second, it produces connotative meanings, which are themselves quite diverse in nature; they include all the instances where montage places two different elements into relationships to produce some effect of causality, parallelism, comparison, etc.

It is quite impossible here to give a true typology of this montage function precisely because of the almost infinite expandability of the notion of connotation. Meaning here may be produced by placing any element in relation to any other element, even if they have completely different natures.

Classic examples certainly abound for illustrating the ideas of comparison and metaphor among others. For instance, we need only recall the shots of Kerensky alternating with shots of a mechanical peacock (a symbol of vanity) in Eisenstein's *October* (1928); the herd of sheep ironically following a shot of a crowd of people in Chaplin's *Modern Times* (1936); or the shot of clucking chickens serving as lively commentary on gossips in Fritz Lang's *Fury* (1936). Yet these are very particular cases involving the montage between two successive shots.

It is with reference to the semantic functions of editing that, as we will see, continual polemics have taken place throughout all of film history on the appropriateness and value of montage in film.

RHYTHMIC FUNCTIONS.   The rhythmic function of editing was also recognized and claimed early on—sometimes even in opposition to the semantic functions (most notably by the champions of "pure cinema" in France during the 1920s). Among other things, it was suggested that cinema be characterized as a "music of the image" or as a veritable combination of rhythm. In fact, however, as Jean Mitry has shown in a very detailed analysis,[10] film rhythm has practically nothing in common with musical rhythms. The lack of correspondence between the two is essentially due to the fact that while our sight is quite well adapted for perceiving proportions—that is to say, spatial rhythms—it is not very adept at perceiving rhythms of duration, to which the ear, by contrast, is very sensitive. Hence, film rhythm presents itself as a superimposition and combination of two sorts of rhythms, temporal and plastic, both of which are quite heterogeneous.

Temporal rhythms are primarily found to be established within the sound track, even though we should not completely exclude the possibility of working with the duration of visual forms. The experimental cinema, for instance, has often been tempted by the notion of producing such visual rhythms, perhaps the most clearcut instances being so-called flicker films such as Peter Kubelka's *Arnulf Rainer* (1958–1960).

Plastic rhythms may result from the organization of the frame's surface content or its division in terms of lighting intensities, colors, or any other compositional factors. Such plasticity in the image follows from classic issues dealt with by such theorists of twentieth-century painting as Paul Klee and Wassily Kandinsky.

Naturally, in distinguishing these three large types of montage functions we have drifted away from an immediate description of the concrete *figures* of editing. These figures present themselves as the locus of many simultaneous effects, as the example of a "match on action" demonstrates. The match on action is a rather commonplace figure that matches two different shots so that the end of the first shot and the beginning of the second shot show, respectively and from two different points of view, the beginning and ending of the same gesture, such as lifting and then drinking a cup of coffee or opening a door and entering a room. This sort of match will produce at least the following effects.

A syntactic effect of liaison is produced between the two shots, thanks to the apparent continuity of movement from one side of the splice to the other.

A semantic (narrative) effect results, in that this figure is part of a whole arsenal of classical conventions aimed at creating temporal continuity.

Eventual effects of connoted meanings will arise, depending on the extent of deviation between the framing of the two shots and on the nature of the action itself.

Finally, a possible rhythmic effect may be produced, tied to the caesura or break within the movement.

The idea of describing the various kinds of montage and grouping them into typologies is itself an old practice; it has been translated for a long time now by the construction of montage tables or grids. These tables, often based more or less directly on the practice of their authors, are always of interest; yet their goal for the most part is somewhat confused since they generally become more of a collection of recipes designed to nourish the techniques of film production than a theoretical classification of editing effects. In contrast to our classification, they define complex types of montage as combinations of various elementary traits, and they are just as concerned with the objects as with the modes of action and the desired effects. In other words, the very concept of a montage chart, which admittedly represented an important stage in the formalization of reflection upon the cinema, is largely obsolete today.

By way of conclusion we can rapidly consider several examples of such montage tables. Balázs made no attempt at being systematic when he outlined a number of montage types, including "ideological," metaphorical, poetic, allegorical, intellectual, rhythmic, formal, and subjective montage.[11]

Pudovkin offered a different nomenclature, which is undoubtedly more rational. His list included montage by antithesis, parallelism, analogy, synchronization, and leitmotif.[12]

Eisenstein also proposed a classification of montage, although admittedly constructed from a fairly special perspective. His montage grid consists of metric, rhythmic, tonal, harmonic, and intellectual montage.[13]

IDEOLOGIES OF MONTAGE

While we have tried carefully never to lose sight of the concrete reality of film phenomena, our construction of the concept of montage or editing in the largest sense—a construction implying that we are working from a perspective that is both as general and as objective as possible—has nonetheless masked an essential historical fact. If the notion of montage is so important for film theory, it is also (and perhaps essentially) because it has been the locus as well as the very stake in an extremely deep-seated and long-lasting confrontation between two radically opposed conceptions of the cinema.

The history of film, at least since the late 1910s, and the history of film theory, from its origins, demonstrate the existence of two great tendencies that, under the names of various critics, theorists, and schools and in diverse forms, have hardly ever ceased their opposition. This conflict has often taken on a very polemical nature.

One of the first tendencies includes all the filmmakers and theorists for whom montage as a production technique (producing meaning, affect, etc.) is more or less considered the essential dynamic element of the cinema. As indicated by the label *montage-roi*,[14] which often designates this tendency among many films from the 1920s and especially the Soviet films, their mere description often places a strong valorization on the very principle of montage. Indeed, there are even extreme cases involving an overemphasis on montage's potential.

In marked contrast, the other tendency is based on a devaluation of montage in and of itself and a strict submission of its effects to the narrative instance or to the realistic representation of the world, which is seen as the cinema's essential goal. This tendency, largely dominant throughout most of film history, may best be described by the notion of the transparency of film discourse, to which we will return shortly.

Let us restate the basic claim: if these two tendencies have throughout time been incarnated and specified in very different manners, the fact remains that their antagonism has, even to this day, defined two large ideologies of montage. By extension, they define two great ideological-philosophical approaches to the cinema itself, as an art of representation and as signification of a mass vocation.

It is certainly out of the question to present, within a few pages, a detailed picture of all the attitudes adopted toward this issue during the last sixty years. Hence, we have chosen to explicate and contrast the theoretical systems of André Bazin and S. M. Eisenstein here because they demonstrate in radical, almost extremist form, each of our respective montage positions. This is not to claim that either of these men is necessarily the leader of one school or the other; each of them has exerted different sorts of influence. If, however, we have chosen these two it is because both have elaborated a fairly coherent aesthetic system and theory of the cinema. In addition, they have each developed very clear assertions on their ideological assumptions; finally, each has granted the question of montage—in opposed senses—a central place within his system.

André Bazin and the Cinema of Transparency

Bazin's system is built upon a basic ideological assumption that may in turn be articulated by two complementary theses that we can state here.

In reality, or the real world, no event is ever endowed with an *a priori* meaning. Thus, Bazin designates this idea by the expression "the immanent ambiguity of reality."

The cinema's ontological vocation is the reproduction of reality by respecting this essential characteristic as much as possible. The cinema, therefore, must produce, or strive to produce, representations that are endowed with as much ambiguity as exists in reality itself.

In particular, this requirement is translated by Bazin as film's necessity to reproduce the real world within its physical continuity as well as that of its events. Hence, in "The Virtues and Limitations of Montage," he claims that "essential cinema, seen for once in its pure state [in *The Red Balloon*] . . . is to be found in straightforward photographic respect for the unity of space."[15] Such an argument helps illustrate all that is both paradoxical and provocative in relation to other conceptions of cinematic "specificity," and especially in relation to the montage theorists. Bazin further develops his assertion when, in the same text, he writes, "What is imaginary on the screen must have the spatial density of something real. You cannot therefore use montage here except within well-defined limits or you run the risk of threatening the very ontology of the cinematographic tale."[16]

The essence of these Bazinian conceptions, ideologically speaking, resides in these few principles that lead him to reduce the place allotted to montage by a considerable degree.

Without claiming to exhaust his ideas here, we will describe these conceptions in relation to montage along three major axes.

THE LIMITATIONS OF MONTAGE. The limitations of montage are admitted by Bazin himself to form a special case, yet for us they will serve to establish a sort of extreme case and thus become a unique and clear demonstration of the principles involved in Bazin's theory. The actual definition of this special case is set up as follows by Bazin: "'When the essence of a scene demands the simultaneous presence of two or more factors in the action, montage is ruled out.' It can reclaim its right to be used, however, whenever the import of the action no longer depends on physical contiguity even though this may be implied."[17]

Naturally, this definition is only meaningful if one explains what the "essence of a scene" (or "import of the action") is considered to be. We have seen that, for Bazin, what is primary is in fact the event as it appears in the real world or in an imaginary world analogous to the real one—in other words, insofar as its meaning is not "determined *a priori*." As a consequence, for him the "essence of a scene" can only designate precisely the same famous ambiguity, which is the imposed absence of signification to which he attaches such a high value. Montage for Bazin will then be "ruled out" (*interdit*) every time the real event—or rather the event that is the *referent* to the diegetic event in question—must be strongly ambiguous. It will be ruled out, for example (at least in principle), every time the event's outcome is not foreseeable.

The privileged example employed by Bazin involves the filming of two diegetic antagonists, such as a pursuer and his or her prey. These are perfect instances since the events have an undetermined outcome. (For example, the hunter may or may not capture the prey, and in some cases Bazin is further fascinated by the possibility that the pursuer may be "devoured" by the hunted game.) In Bazin's eyes, any resolution of such an event by the use of montage—as in an alternating montage between a series of shots of the hunter and shots of the hunted—is pure trickery.

TRANSPARENCY.   Naturally, in a large number (perhaps even the majority) of practical instances montage may not be strictly forbidden. The event could be represented by means of a succession of discontinuous film units (that is to say "shots" for Bazin), but only on condition that this discontinuity should also be *masked* as much as possible. This is the famous notion of the transparency of film discourse, which designates a specific (though widespread and even dominant) film aesthetic according to which film's essential function is to present the represented events to be seen, rather than presenting itself as a film. The essence of this conception is defined by Bazin in the following way:

Whatever the film, its aim is to give us the illusion of being present at real events unfolding before us as in everyday reality. But this illusion involves a fundamental deceit, for reality exists in a continuous space, and the screen in fact presents us with a succession of tiny fragments called "shots," whose choice, order and length constitute precisely what we call the film's *découpage*. If, through a deliberate effort of attention, we try to see the ruptures imposed by the camera on the continuous unfolding of the event represented, and try to understand clearly why we normally take no notice of them, we realize that we tolerate them because they nevertheless allow an impression to remain of continuous and homogeneous reality.[18]

Thus, we can see in a very coherent way that what is considered primary within this system is always a "real event" presented in its "continuity." This presupposition is certainly the place one could most profitably begin to criticize Bazin.

In concrete terms, this "impression" of continuity and homogeneity is achieved by the formal work that characterizes the period of film history often called the classical cinema, whose most representative figure is the match on action. The match, whose physical existence follows from decades of experience by classical cinema editors, may be defined as any shot transition that is effaced as such. That is to say, it is any shot change that strives to preserve the elements of continuity from one side of the splice to the other.

The language of classical cinema has isolated a large number of match on action figures, so many in fact that we cannot cite them all here. The major kinds, however, include:

—the eyeline match: a first shot shows us a character looking toward something that is generally offscreen, while the next shot shows the object; if that object is a second character looking back toward the first, then we have a "shot/reverse shot";

—the match on movement: a movement begun in the first shot and given a specific speed and direction is repeated in the second shot with the same direction and an apparently comparable speed (the same diegetic object does not necessarily have to be the moving body in each shot, as witnessed in the famous match of a spinning stick and a satellite in Stanley Kubrick's 2001 [1968]);

—the match on action: a complete gesture is begun by a character in the first shot, then finished in the second (in spite of the change of point of view);

—the match on the axis: two successive movements (eventually separated by a brief temporal ellipsis) of the same event are filmed in two shots, with the second shot filmed along the same camera-to-object axis, but the camera has now been moved closer to or farther from the object.

While this list is far from exhaustive, it nonetheless allows us to establish that the match can function just as well in organizing purely formal elements (such as movement independent of any support-object) as in organizing fully diegetic elements (like a represented glance).

We should point out, for this last issue, Bazin's system was again taken

Editing and matches: several examples from *Muriel* (Alain Resnais, 1963).

Shot 32   Shot 33

Match on action cutting on the character's gesture.

Shot 56   Shot 57

Cutting for a shot/reverse shot effect.

Shot 489   Shot 490

Cutting on a subjective point of view: Alphonse hanging up the telephone receiver.

Shot 497   Shot 498

Cutting on the axis to emphasize character movement: here Hélène throws herself into Alphonse's arms.

Shot 623   Shot 624

Cutting on a character's gesture: Bernard opens the dresser drawer violently and
then turns his head toward Hélène offscreen.

Shot 633   Shot 634

Cutting abruptly with an ellipsis to emphasize the character's gesture: Shot 633
reveals the characters preparing the meal; Shot 634 cuts suddenly to Bernard
seated and drinking.

up and amplified by a whole classical tradition of film aesthetics. In the writings of Nöel Burch, for example, we can find a very detailed description of the various functions of the match, according to whatever spatial and temporal gaps they mark.[19]

BAZIN'S NEGLECT OF MONTAGE OTHER THAN IN MATCHES. As a logical consequence of the preceding considerations, Bazin refuses to consider the existence of any instances of montage outside the passage from one shot to another. The most spectacular manifestation of this refusal can probably be seen in the way that he valorizes (especially in relation to Orson Welles) the use of film in depth and shot sequence, both of which, according to him, produce a univocal "gain of realism." If, for Bazin, montage can only reduce reality's ambiguity by forcing meaning onto it (by forcing the film to become discourse), then, inversely, filming in long takes with great depth must logically be more respectful of the "real": such shots "show more" reality in a single piece of film and place everything on an equal footing before the spectator. As Bazin writes:

> Contrary to what one might believe at first, "*découpage* in depth" is more charged with meaning than analytical *découpage*. It is no less abstract than the other, but the additional abstraction which it integrates into the narrative comes precisely from a surplus of realism. A realism that is in a certain sense ontological, restoring to the object and the decor their existential density, the weight of their presence; a dramatic realism which refuses to separate the actor from the decor, the foreground from the background; a psychological realism which brings the spectator back to the real conditions of perception, a perception which is never completely determined *a priori*.[20]

Once again we can point out that these claims are consistent with the veritable obsession with continuity that defines the Bazinian system. They nonetheless proceed from a certain blindness to anything that might directly contradict them in the films from which they take their pretext (especially *Citizen Kane*). Hence, in Welles's film, which is analyzed at great length by Bazin, depth of field is used at least as much to produce montage effects (for example, by juxtaposing within a single image two scenes that are represented along relatively heterogeneous modes) as it is to present "equally" all elements of the representation. Moreover, the long takes often offer an occasion (thanks most notably to the many camera movements) to produce transformations or even disruptions inside the shots, all of which closely resemble montage effects.

S. M. Eisenstein and the Dialectical Cinema

Eisenstein's system, while perhaps less monothematic than Bazin's, is just as coherent, yet in a way that is radically opposed to the Bazinian system. The basic ideological assumption upon which Eisenstein's system is built excludes all consideration of any supposed "reality" that could, in and of itself, contain its own meaning or that should not be manipulated. One could say that for Eisenstein at his most extreme the "real" holds no interest outside of whatever meaning it is given or whatever reading it receives. Thus, the cinema is seen as one tool among others for this reading activity. A film's duty is not to reproduce the "real" without intervening, but instead to reflect this reality while simultaneously making some ideological judgment about it (and maintaining an ideological discourse).

Certainly, this sort of approach concerns a problem that Bazin's theory never raises (or rather that it abandons), which is the question of the *criterion of reality* in a given discourse. For Eisenstein the choice is clear: that which ensures the truthfulness of the discourse uttered by a film is its conformity to the laws of dialectical and historical materialism (and sometimes, in a more brutal sense, its conformity to the political ideas of the moment). If there is a criterion of reality for Bazin, it is included within reality itself, which is to say that in the final analysis it is based on the existence of God.

Moreover, Eisenstein considers film to be less a representation than an articulated discourse, and his reflections on montage consist precisely in defining this articulation. We will next distinguish three principle axes of Eisenstein's definition.

THE FRAGMENT AND CONFLICT. The notion of the "fragment," which is absolutely specific to Eisenstein's system, designates the film unit for him. Hence, the first thing to note is that, in opposition to Bazin, Eisenstein, quite logically, never considers that this unit is necessarily equivalent to the shot. The fragment is one unitary piece of film that, in practice, will often be combined with other shots (especially since Eisenstein's films are characterized by shots that are generally very short); yet these fragments may, at least theoretically, be defined in a completely different sense since they are units of discourse rather than units of representation.

What is more, this idea is strongly polysemous and receives at least three rather different yet complementary meanings in Eisenstein's work.

First, the fragment is considered as an element of the film's syntagmatic chain. In this usage it is defined by the relations and articulations that it offers with reference to its surrounding fragments.

Second, the fragment taken as a film image is conceived as divisible into a very large number of material elements corresponding to various parameters of film representation (luminosity, contrast, "grain," graphic sound quality, color, duration, shot scale, etc.). This breaking down of the image is considered as a means of calculation or mastering of the expressive and signifying elements of the fragment. The relations between fragments are consequently described as linking certain of a given fragment's constituent parameters with other such constituent parameters from one or more fragments within a complex (and actually always uncertain) calculation.

An example of such calculation, often cited by Eisenstein himself, is the sequence of the "fog at the Odessa harbor" in *Battleship Potemkin* (1926), which takes place just before the dead sailor Vakulinchuk's burial. In this sequence the fragments are essentially assembled as a function of two parameters: the "fogginess" (to be analyzed in turn as varying degrees of grayness and focus) and "luminosity."

Finally, the concept of fragment includes a certain kind of relationship with the referent. The fragment, extracted from the real (a real already organized in front of and for the camera), operates as a *break* or *cut* within the real, which is the exact opposite of the Bazinian "window onto the world." Thus, Eisenstein's frame always has more or less the value of a clean cut between two heterogeneous worlds—those of the onscreen and offscreen space.

The notion of the offscreen has practically never, except for several minor exceptions, been used by Eisenstein. Bazin, however, in spite of the normative strength of his own options, had fully grasped the crux of the problem and accordingly wrote about the two opposing conceptions of the frame. One stance held that the frame acted in a "centrifugal" manner, which is to say that it opened out onto an assumed exterior or offscreen space. The second approach saw it as "centripetal," denying any kind of exterior and defining itself purely as an image.[21] It is obviously this second tendency to which Eisenstein's fragment belongs.

Thus we can see how this notion of the fragment demonstrates the same conception of film as an *articulated discourse* at every level of its definition. The enclosing of the frame focuses attention on the meaning that is isolated there, and this meaning, constructed analytically by taking the material characteristics of the image into consideration, begins to combine and articulate in an explicit and tendentiously *univocal* manner. (Roland Barthes has observed that Eisenstein's cinema is not polysemous, but instead *"devastates ambiguity."*)[22]

Similarly, Eisenstein considers that the production of meaning from the sequencing of successive fragments is built on a model of conflict. If the notion of conflict is not entirely original (since it derives very directly from the concept of contradiction as posited in Marxist philosophy's dialectical materialism), Eisenstein's use of the idea is nonetheless rather surprising because of its extensive and systematic nature. Conflict for him is the canonical mode of interaction between *any* two units of film discourse. There is not only conflict between fragments, but also "within montage fragments," which are then specified according to various individual parameters. Let us cite, among numerous examples, an extract from "A Dialectical Approach to Film Form," written in 1929:

> In my opinion, however, montage is an idea that arises from the collision of independent shots—shots even opposite to one another. . . . We can list examples of types of conflict within the shot:

1. Graphic conflict.
2. Conflict of planes.
3. Conflict of volumes.
4. Spatial conflict.
5. Light conflict.
6. Tempo conflict . . .
7. Conflict between matter and viewpoint (achieved by spatial distortion through camera angle).
8. Conflict between matter and its spatial nature (achieved by *optical distortion* by the lens).
9. Conflict between an event and its temporal nature (achieved by *slow-motion* and *stop-motion*); and finally
10. Conflict between the whole *optical* complex and a quite different sphere.[23]

Naturally, as an outline of the analytical decomposition of the fragment into all its consistent parameters, such a list cannot hope to be exhaustive, even though Eisenstein does occasionally make

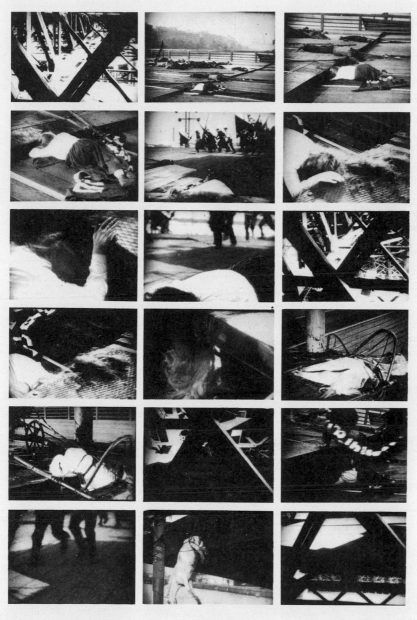

A particularly pertinent example of Eisenstein's theories of montage in action: *October* (1927).

October (S. M. Eisenstein, 1927).

utopian claims that the list is complete. This list is primarily valuable in its ability to show the "down shifting" of montage's productivity; in other words, the idea of productive montage that we cited above is operating here in full force.

EXTENDING THE CONCEPT OF MONTAGE. As an immediate consequence of the preceding discussion, montage in this system becomes the single and central principle controlling all production of meaning. Moreover, this definition of montage organizes all the partial signification produced within any given film. Eisenstein never ceases to return to this point and even devotes an entire section of his important treatise on montage (written between 1937 and 1940) to demonstrate that framing is only one particular case involving montage's general problematic in that framing and the frame's composition aim above all to produce meaning.[24]

The ultimate phase of his theorizing, from this perspective, is that of "audiovisual counterpoint," an expression that attempts to describe sound cinema as a contrapuntal play generalized among *all* the elements or film parameters—including the image (which has already been considered in the definition of the visual fragment), as well as parameters of sound. The idea, in and of itself, is not new in relation to his own analytical image manipulation, but it is nonetheless very important historically because this is perhaps the only systematic attempt to theorize a film's sound elements other than according to the redundancy and submission of the soundtrack in relation to the scenic-visual dimension. In Eisenstein's theory (but not in his films since the only film where he pushed this idea to the limit was *Bejine Meadow* [1935–36] which was banned and its original version lost), the various sound elements (words, sound effects, and music) participate on an equal footing with the image in a manner that remains relatively autonomous in terms of both the image and the production of meaning. The sound constituents may, according to the instance, reinforce the image, contradict it, or simply maintain a parallel discourse.

MONTAGE'S INFLUENCE ON THE SPECTATOR. Finally, the last consequence of all these considerations of film form (which, for Eisenstein, is immediately analyzable as a vehicle of predetermined, desired, and mastered meaning) has as its task to influence or "shape" the spectator. On this point Eisenstein's vocabulary varied enormously over the years, with the variations following the models of spectator psychology that he successively adopted. Yet his preoccupation with the spectator has always remained central and essential. The important thing here, with regard to the coherency of the system, is to demonstrate that all the models he uses to describe the spectator's psychic activity have a common hypothesis, in spite of their wide diversity: all the models propose a direct analogy between a film's formal processes and the functioning of human thought.

During the 1920s, Eisenstein readily refers to "reflexology," which considers that all human behavior arises from the composition of a great number of elementary "stimulus → response" phenomena. While he did not believe it possible to calculate *all* the parameters making up a fragment, Eisenstein was tempted by the idea that one could calculate the elementary effect of all these stimuli and thus master the psychological effect produced by the film.

Later he would search for a functional analogy between film and more global, less mechanical, representations of thought. This research would lead Eisenstein to defend the concept of film "ecstasy," which involved, in a very organic sense, an "out of self" experience by the spectator that would carry his or her affective and/or intellectual participation in the film.

Thus, as theorists, Bazin and Eisenstein oppose one another at every level, not just concerning the issue of montage. Moreover, while one might have expected that there would be point to point disagreements between the two that followed from their opposing stances on common issues, their antagonism is actually much more radical, since their two systems have practically nothing in common. Not only are their opinions opposed on issues such as the role of montage, among others, but they are literally not speaking about the same things. What interests Bazin is almost exclusively the faithful, "objective" reproduction of a reality that carries all its meaning within itself; Eisenstein does not conceive of film except as an articulated and assertive discourse that can only maintain a figurative reference to reality.

These two ideological positions are certainly not the only conceivable examples. Nonetheless, for several decades now they have been at the center of a polemic that is occasionally diffused but always bitter, between "those who put their faith in the image" and "those who put their faith in reality," to use Bazin's own words.[25] While Bazin's system is perhaps less refined conceptually than Eisenstein's, it does nonetheless possess a sort of evidential component (in our society anyway), which may explain the very great influence that it has exerted upon a whole generation of theorists. For example, one finds very "Bazinian" themes and arguments in the impassioned writings of Pier Paolo Pasolini during the late 1960s.

By contrast, Eisenstein's system, for a long time poorly understood, had remained a sort of museum piece until the last decade or so. Its rediscovery accompanied, in a very significant fashion, the great ideological film movement of the early 1970s, which is often interpreted as a lively attack on Bazinian theories. At that point a materialist cinema was actively promoted in opposition to the cinema of transparency.

3 CINEMA AND NARRATION

NARRATIVE CINEMA

The Cinema Encounters Narration

In the vast majority of instances, going to the movies means going to watch a film that tells a story. This assertion may appear to be an obvious point or truism, since cinema and narration seem to be consubstantial, yet our opening statement should not be glossed over. The joining of these two realms was far from obvious in the beginning; during the first days of the cinema's existence, movies did not seem immediately destined to become so overwhelmingly narrative.

The cinema could very well have become nothing more than an instrument for scientific investigation, a tool for reportage and documentary, an extension of painting, or simply a short-lived object of amusement at the fairgrounds. It had been conceived as a means of visual recording that did not have any special vocation or specific techniques for telling stories. If, however, there was no special predestination involved in the meeting of cinema and narration, and if this encounter was partially accidental, like some chance occurrence of civilization, there are nonetheless several reasons behind this union. We will outline three of these reasons—two of which involve the very material of cinematic expression itself: the moving representational image.

The Moving Representational Image. The cinema, as a recording device, offers a representational image wherein, thanks to a certain number of conventions, the filmed objects are recognizable (for more on this specific point see chapter 1). The simple process, however, of representing and displaying an object in such a way that it may be recognized is an act of *presentation* implying that one wishes to say something in regard to that object. Thus, the image of a revolver is not only equivalent to the term "revolver," but it implicitly conveys an *énoncé* such as "here is a revolver" or "this is a revolver." As a result, there is evidence of an expositional quality in the image and of a desire to make the object signify beyond its simple representation.

Moreover, even before its reproduction, every object already carries (at least for the society in which it is recognizable), a whole array of values that it represents and "narrates." Every object is already, in itself, a discourse. It is a sort of pattern-book or sampler of its own social realm, which, by its very status, becomes a shifter between discourse and fiction since an object (or more correctly any person who observes an object) tends to recreate its social milieu. Thus, by the weight of the social system to which the represented object belongs, and by its visible presence, every figuration and representation calls forth narration, or at least an embryonic form of it. To prove this point it should be sufficient to think of the first photographic portraits and recall that they can instantly become small narratives for us.

The Moving Image.   While the cinematic restitution of movement has often been cited for its role in contributing to the cinema's realism, less mention has been made of the fact that the moving image is an image in perpetual transformation that permits us to see the represented object's passage from one stage to another. (This movement thereby requires a temporal dimension.) The represented object in the cinema, therefore, is always in the process of *becoming* represented. By the simple fact of being filmed, every object and every landscape, no matter how static, is inscribed within a specific duration and is thus a subject of transformation.

Literary structural analysis has demonstrated that every story and every fiction can be reduced to the progression from an initial state to a final situation. Fiction may also be diagramed as a sequence of transformations, linked together in a series such as the following: misdeed to be committed—misdeed committed—act to be punished—punishment process—act punished—good deed accomplished. It becomes evident, moreover, that, thanks to the nature of the moving image, cinema can offer both duration and transformation to narrative fiction. It is thus partially through these common points that the encounter between cinema and narration was accomplished.

Search for Legitimacy.   The third reason that may be proposed for cinema joining with narration involves a more historical explanation of the cinema's status in the beginning. "An invention with no future," as Louis Lumière claimed, the cinema was at first a rather vulgar spectacle, a carnival attraction justified primarily, but not completely, by its technical novelty.

To escape from this relative ghetto required that the cinema place itself under the auspices of the "noble arts," which, during this pivotal point between the nineteenth and twentieth centuries, were the theater and novel. The cinema had to prove that it too could tell stories that were worthy of interest. While Georges Méliès's shows were already simple stories, for instance, they still lacked the developed and complex forms of a theatrical play or novel.

Thus, it was partially in order to be recognized as an art form that the cinema began to develop its faculties for narration.

It was to this end, in 1908, that France's Société du Film d'Art was created. Its goal was to "react against the popular and mechanical side of the first films" by calling upon renowned stage actors to adapt literary subjects, such as *The Return of Ulysses, La Dame aux Camélias, Ruy Blas,* and *Macbeth,* for the cinema. The best-known film of this series was *L'Assassinat du Duc de Guise* (with a scenario by French academician Henri Lavedan and a musical score by Camille Saint-Saëns). The film boasted the actor Le Bargy, who also took credit as director (1908).

Non-narrative Cinema: A Difficult Boundary

NARRATIVE/NON-NARRATIVE. Narrating consists of relating an event, whether real or imaginary. This definition implies at least two things. To begin with, it assumes that the unfolding of a story is at the discretion of whoever is telling it; therefore, this narrator can produce any number of ploys to achieve the desired effects. Second, it implies that a story's unfolding is regulated simultaneously by both the narrator and the story's controlling models.

Narrative cinema is certainly dominant today, at least on the level of consumption. On the level of production, however, we must not forget the important positions occupied by films in the industrial, medical, or military realms. The narrative cinema, therefore, must not be equated with the essence of the cinema itself, because such a reduction would further underestimate or ignore the role that the so-called non-narrative avant-garde, underground, or experimental cinema has played, and is still playing, in film history.

The commonly held distinction between narrative and non-narrative cinema, even if it does recognize a certain number of the differences between their products and modes of production, may not be entirely foolproof. In effect, the NRI (narrative-representational-industrial) cinema cannot be directly contrasted with experimental cinema without falling into fruitless caricature. There are two opposing reasons for this difficulty.

Not every film element is necessarily narrative-representative. \
Narrative cinema actually makes use of visual materials that are not representational, such' as fades, swish-pans, or aesthetically motivated manipulation of color or composition.

A number of recent film analyses have called attention to sporadic moments in Lang, Hitchcock, and Eisenstein that escape both narration and representational images. Thus, one may find a sequence that works much like a flicker film (a film playing on the extreme brevity of the appearance of images out of blackness and on the opposition of a very bright image to a very dark one), in the midst of a classic period. Such scenes exist, for instance, near the end of two Fritz Lang films noirs: *Ministry of Fear* (1945) and *Scarlet Street* (1945).

Second, however, while the self-proclaimed non-narrative cinema avoids relying on certain traits of the narrative film, it still retains a number of narrative characteristics. For one thing, it occasionally differs only in its systematic use of a process that was merely used temporarily by so-called classical filmmakers.

Films like those of Werner Nekes (*T.WO.MEN* [1972], *Makimono* [1974]) or Norman McLaren (*Neighbors* [1952], *Rhythmetic* [1956], *Chairy Tale* [1957]) may play with the progressive multiplication of elements (no plot, no characters) and the acceleration of movement. In the end, however, these films reassert a traditional characteristic of narration—they give the spectator the impression of a logical development before necessarily inserting an ending or resolution.

Finally, in order for a film to be truly non-narrative, it would need to be nonrepresentational. This is to say that one would not recognize anything in the image and that temporal, sequential, or cause-and-effect relations could not be perceived between the shots or the elements of the image. In fact, these perceived relations would inevitably engage the notion of an imaginary transformation or of a fictional evolution controlled by a narrating activity.

> Nonetheless, even if such a film were possible, the spectator, being accustomed to the presence of fiction, would still have a tendency to re-inject narrative where it does not exist; any line or any color may serve to engage fictionality.

SUBSTRUCTURE OF A POLEMIC. Much of the criticism aimed at classical narrative cinema is based on the idea that the cinema was led astray in following the Hollywood model. The Hollywood cinema may be considered to have three major flaws: first, it is American, and thus politically marked; second, it is narrative in the strictest nineteenth-century tradition; and finally, it is industrial, which is to say that its products are all tightly calibrated.

While these arguments are partially accurate and justified, they do not take into account all of classical cinema. To begin with, they assume that the classical narrative cinema is a cinema of the signified with neither work nor reflection on the signifier. These criticisms also pretend that the non-narrative cinema is a cinema of the signifier without a signified and without content.

That the American cinema is a distinctly marked cinema is obvious, yet the same is true of all film production. In addition, it is not only a film's content that is political, since the cinematic apparatus itself is equally engaged in both the narrative and non-narrative film (for more on this point, see chapter 5).

The notion that the narrative cinema can be isolated from novelistic and theatrical models rests on a double misunderstanding.

First, it assumes that there is a nature or specificity in film that should not be spoiled by mixing it with alien languages. Thus, there is a return to the belief in an "original purity" of the cinema, which is far from having been proven.

Second, it forgets that the cinema carefully forged its own tools and its own precise figures by trying to tell stories and by making them understandable for the spectators.

Alternating montage only took form in order to show that two episodes that follow one another in the film (since they cannot be represented simultaneously within the frame) are actually contemporaneous in the story.

Editing and systems of camera movement only have meaning as functions of narrative effects and their comprehension by the spectator. It can certainly be objected that non-narrative cinema no longer has recourse to these cinematic means, in that it is no longer narrative. Yet we just mentioned that experimental film always retains some traits of the narrative cinema, since narrative cannot always be reduced to simply "having a plot." Moreover, all of this does not prevent these means from being the same ones that come to mind during typical discussions of the cinema in general.

As far as the cinema's typical industrial production is concerned, standardization is admittedly quantitatively important and even dominant within the cinema. However, it is not certain that the standard industrial films are those being referred to when we speak of the analysis of film and cinematic language since these studies often draw their examples from *nonstandard* industrial films, such as *Citizen Kane*.

The denunciation of the film industry can be seen as a valorization of artistic and artisanal creation. The adjective "independent," which is often applied to this other cinema, also expresses this privileging of the artistic element. This glorification of the artist, however, risks becoming, or reactivating, the overly romantic conception of a creator, struggling in isolation under the guidance of some inspiration about which s/he can say nothing.

In conclusion, therefore, if it is not justifiable to cast experimental film beyond the bounds of the cinema, it is also not permissible to dismiss classical narrative cinema as old hat, about which nothing more could be said. That dismissal of the classical cinema is based on the belief that those films simply repeat the same old story in the same old way, which ends up reducing the cinema to novelistic plot while ignoring both its plastic effects and its effects on the spectator.

This repetition is, however, one of the most important elements of the cinematic institution and one of its functions that still remains to be analyzed today. The notion of "submitting to ideology" alone is not sufficient for understanding the fact that spectators go to the movies to see stories whose basic scheme is repeated from film to film (for more on this point, see chapter 5, on identification).

Narrative Cinema: Objects and Objectives of Film Study

OBJECTS OF STUDY.   To study the narrative cinema requires that one begin by clearly defining the difference between the two terms "narrative" and "cinema." As we saw in the preceding section, neither term should be confused with the other: narrative is not equivalent to the cinematic, and all cinema is certainly not narrative.

The "cinematic" can be defined, following Christian Metz, not as everything that appears in films, but rather as that which is capable of appearing *only* in films.[1] It involves, therefore, in a specific manner, cinematic language in the narrowest sense of the term.

The first *films d'art* were content, to a large extent, to record theatrical performances. Other than the mechanically recorded moving image, they contained very few specifically cinematic elements. The filmed material in and of itself had little or nothing cinematic about it. By contrast, analyzing the kinds of relations between the onscreen and offscreen space of

Jean Renoir's *Nana* (1926), as Noël Burch has done, involves leaning much more toward the cinematic.[2]

Narrative, by definition, is extracinematic since it concerns the theater, novel, and even daily conversation, as well as films. The systems of narration were elaborated outside the cinema and, for the most part, long before its birth. This distinction explains how the functions of various film characters can be analyzed with the critical tools forged in literature by Vladimir Propp (prohibition, transgression, departure, return, victory, etc.), or A. J. Greimas (actant, opponent, etc.). These narrative systems operate with other systems in films, but properly speaking they do not constitute the cinematic. They are the objects of narratology, whose domain is much broader than the mere cinematic tale.

As necessary as this stated distinction may be, it should not make us forget that the two elements have areas of interaction and that it is possible to establish a model specific to the cinematic narrative. This film model will be different in certain respects from novelistic and theatrical narratives (see, for example, Francis Vanoye's *Récit écrit—Récit filmique*).

On the one hand, there are film subjects, such as plots or themes, which, for reasons springing from the film apparatus and performance, are given preferential treatment by the cinema. On the other hand, a specific sort of action calls, in a more or less imperative way, for a certain sort of cinematic treatment. Inversely, the way a scene is filmed affects its meaning.

> Filming the function of a chase (a narrative unit) by an alternating montage of the shots pursuers-pursued (a signifying cinematic figure) will have a different narrative effect than filming the same action from a helicopter in a single sequence shot (another cinematic figure). In Joseph Losey's *Figures in a Landscape* (1970), this second type of treatment displays the effort and fatigue of the pursuers, and the foolishness of their attempts, while the first type of figure, when used in D. W. Griffith's *Intolerance* (1916), leaves the suspense more open.

OBJECTIVES OF STUDY. Interest in the study of narrative cinema rests primarily in the fact that narrative film is still dominant today. Moreover, it is through the narrative film that one can grasp the essence of the cinematic institution—its position, functions, and effects—in order to situate these elements within the history of cinema, art, and even history itself.

Nonetheless, it is also necessary to take into account the fact that film-makers like Michael Snow, Stan Brakhage, and Werner Nekes use their films to direct critical reflection toward the elements of classical cinema (its fiction, apparatus, etc.). Through their work it is also possible to isolate certain essential aspects of cinematic operations.

The first goal here is, or was, to bring to light the signifying figures (relations between a signifying ensemble and a signified ensemble) that are unique to the cinema. It was this particular goal that the "first" semiology (based on structural linguistics) fixed upon the partially attained, notably with Metz's *grande syntagmatique*. Metz analyzed the different modes of shot ordering that were possible for representing an event in film (see chapter 4).

This *grande syntagmatique*, which is the model for a construction of a cinematic code system, offers an example of the necessary interaction of the cinematic with narrative. It is only applicable, however, to the classical narrative cinema. The cinematic units are, in effect, isolated as functions of their form, but also as functions of the narrative units they are shaping.[3]

The second goal is to study the relations existing between the moving narrative image and the spectator. This is the objective of the so-called second semiology, which emphasizes "metapsychology" (a term borrowed from Freud, designating the psychic states and processes common to all individuals). This second semiology strives to demonstrate both the similarities and differences between dream, fantasy, and hallucination, and the *film state* in which the spectator of the fiction film finds himself or herself. This investigation into certain psychoanalytic concepts allows the semiologist to retrace some of the psychic processes necessary for, or induced by, the viewing of a film.

This sort of research, which today is being pursued along many axes, will allow an understanding of the psychic functions and benefits peculiar to the spectator of a fiction film.

Because many of these issues will be brought up in chapter 5, we will not enter into much detail concerning them here. We should note, however, that this sort of analysis allows one to escape the psychologism that too often pervades film criticism. Instead, metapsychology reconsiders notions such as identification or conceived benefit, along the lines of "living vicariously" or "changing one's ideas."

The third objective derives from its predecessors. The social functioning of the cinematic institution both springs from and cuts across the first two goals. We can distinguish two levels of this social functioning.

3a *Social Representation.*   This level involves an almost anthropological dimension wherein the cinema is considered to be the vehicle of representations that a society gives of itself. One could say, insofar as the cinema is capable of reproducing systems of representation or social articulations, that films took the place of great mythical tales. The typology of a character or a string of characters need not only be taken as representing a film period, but a period of society as well. Thus, the American musical comedy of the 1930s is not without ties to the Depression.

Through its romantic love stories set in luxurious settings, these comedies made very clear allusions to the Depression and the social problems it created. (For example, one need only look at the three films made under the *Gold Diggers* title by Busby Berkeley and Lloyd Bacon in 1933, 1935, and 1937, and at Fred Astaire and Ginger Rogers comedies like *The Gay Divorcee* [1934] or *Top Hat* [1935].) A film like *Tchapaiev*, by S. Vassiliev and G. Vassiliev (1934), also has connections with a certain moment of Stalinism since it promotes, by its very construction, the image of the positive hero or social actor proposed as a role-model.

One must not conclude too rapidly, however, that narrative cinema is a transparent expression of social reality, nor its exact opposite. Such hasty decisions have allowed Italian neorealism to be taken for a "slice of reality" and have led to seeing the euphoric atmosphere depicted in musical comedies as an opiate, pure and simple.

Things are never as simple as all that, and society cannot be read directly from its films. Moreover, this sort of analysis of the cinema must not be restricted to film alone, but instead requires an in-depth preliminary study of social history itself. There is, after all, a complex network of interactions between the procedures and organization of film representation and social reality (insofar as historians can reconstitute it). It is only by studying the connections, inversions, and disparities between these two realms that this analysis can be accomplished. (See, in this connection, "The 'Real' and the 'Visible' " in Pierre Sorlin's *Sociologie du cinéma*.)

3b *Ideology.*   The analysis of ideology springs from the two preceding points to the extent that it is simultaneously directed at the control of the spectator's psychic play and the circulation of a certain social representation. It is this route, for example, that the team of *Cahiers du Cinéma* critics followed in their approach to John Ford's *Young Mr. Lincoln* (1939).[4] They examined the relations existing between a historical figure (Lincoln), an ideology (American liberalism), and a film *écriture* (John Ford's fiction). Their work revealed a complex weaving of phenomena that was only perceptible within the subtle stitchwork of Fordian fiction. As they prove, once again, film analysis must be very detailed in order to be fruitful or even accurate.

THE FICTION FILM

Every Film Is a Fiction Film

The dominant characteristic of the fiction film is that it represents something imaginary, a story. If one breaks down the process, it can be seen that the fiction film consists of a double representation: the setting and actors represent a situation that is the fiction, while the film itself, in the form of juxtaposed images, represents this first representation. Thus, the fiction film is doubly unreal: it is unreal because it represents the fiction and because of the way in which it represents the fiction (using images of objects and of actors).

Due to its perceptive richness, film representation is undoubtedly more realistic than other modes of representation (such as painting or theater), but at the same time it only shows effigies, as the re-corded shadows of objects that are themselves absent. In effect, the cinema has this power to "make absent" that which it shows. Cinema makes it absent in both time and space since the filmed scene has already taken place and only later is that scene unfurled on the screen where it then inscribes itself. In the theater, that which represents or signifies (actors, setting, accessories) is indeed real and exists even though what it represents is fictional. In the cinema, both the representer and the represented are fictional. In this sense, every film is a fiction film.

The industrial film and scientific film, like documentary, fall un-der the law requiring that every film, by its materials of expression (moving images and sounds), "unrealizes" what it represents, trans-forming it into a spectacle.[5] The spectator at a scientific documen-tation film does not behave any differently than a spectator at a fic-tion film: s/he suspends all activity since the film is not reality and by virtue of this suspension is allowed to suppress any action or any conduct. As his or her label indicates, the documentary spectator is also attending a spectacle.

From the first moment when a phenomenon is transformed into a spectacle, the door is opened to reverie (even if it takes on a serious form of reflection), because the spectator is not required to do anything beyond receiving sounds and images. The film spectator is especially inclined toward reverie since, by the cinematic apparatus and its materials, film approaches the dream world without actually becoming confused with it.

Aside from the fact that every film is a spectacle and always presents the slightly fantastic character of a reality that may not reach me and from which I may be exempted, there are other reasons that scientific and documentary films cannot escape fiction. To begin with, every object is already a sign of something else and is already held within a social imaginary.

Thus, every object is offered as the support for a small fiction (see pp. 70–71).

In addition, the interest in scientific and documentary films often rests on the fact that they show us previously unknown aspects of reality, calling more attention to the imaginary than to the real. Whether this involves molecules invisible to the naked eye or exotic animals with surprising behavior patterns, the audience members find themselves submerged in the fantastic world of phenomena that are different from those normally accepted as belonging to reality.

André Bazin wrote two remarkable analyses of the documentary paradox in his articles "Cinema and Exploration" and "The Silent World."[6] He notes, in regard to the film of the *Kon-Tiki* expedition: "Does the killer whale, that we can barely see refracted in the water, interest us because of the rarity of the beast and of the glimpse we get of it, slight as it is? Or rather is it because the shot was taken at the very moment when a capricious movement of the monster might well have annihilated the raft and sent the camera and cameraman seven or eight thousand meters into the deep? The answer is clear. It is not so much the photograph of the whale that interests us as the photograph of the *danger.*"[7]

Moreover, aesthetic concern is not absent from scientific or documentary films, and it tends to transform the bare object into an object for contemplation. The object is transformed into a "vision" that brings it still closer to the imaginary. An extreme example of this vision could be found in several "documentary" shots from F. W. Murnau's *Nosferatu* (1922), wherein the professor demonstrates to his students that vampirism exists within nature.

Finally, scientific and documentary films often resort to narrative techniques to maintain interest. Among other examples we can cite dramatization, which can make a small suspense film out of a series of reports. (A surgical operation, whose outcome is portrayed as uncertain, could thus be reassembled into a story whose episodes lead toward a happy or sad ending.) In addition to dramatization, a voyage or itinerary approach is frequently used in documentary; as in any story, it immediately sets up linear development, continuity, and temporal limits ("So the hot summer sun returns to the Amazon delta"). Within documentary, short stories often serve to retell a life or various adventures by using a character who gives a semblance of coherence to information gathered from quite heterogeneous sources.

Thus, there are several reasons (modes of representation, content, method of exposition, etc.) why every film, no matter what its genre, may be dependent upon fiction.

The Problem of the Referent

In linguistics there is a distinction between the concept (or signified), which is part of the functioning of the language system (la langue) and therefore internal to it, and the actual referent, to which the signifier and signified of the language system refer. The referent, as opposed to the signified, exists outside the language system and can roughly be likened to reality or the world.

Without entering into a discussion of the different meanings given to the word "referent" in linguistics, we must specify that the referent cannot be understood as a single, unique object. Instead, the referent is more like a category or class of objects. It consists of abstract categories that are applicable to reality, yet are just as apt to remain potential as to become actualized in a particular object.

As far as cinematic language is concerned, the image of a cat (iconic signifier + signified "cat") does not have as its referent the specific cat that was filmed, but rather the entire category of cats. In effect, it is necessary to distinguish between the act of filming, which requires a specific cat, and the attribution of a referent to the image seen by the individual or group watching the film. If we put aside the case of the family portrait or home movie, an object is not generally photographed or filmed without becoming a representative of the category to which it belongs. It is to this larger category that the image refers and not to the representative object used for the filming.

The referent of a fiction film, therefore, is not the actual filming, that is to say, the people, objects, sets, and locations actually placed in front of the camera. In The Black Stallion (Carroll Ballard, 1979),

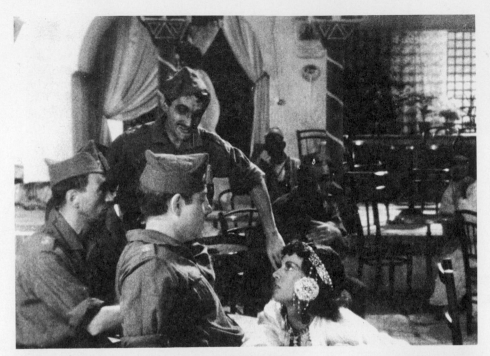

Four representations of history in the cinema: top, *La Bandera* (Jules Duvivier, 1938); bottom, *Gone with the Wind* (Victor Fleming, 1939).

Top, *The Prisoner of Shark Island* (John Ford, 1936); bottom, *The Leopard* (Luchino Visconti, 1963).

for instance, the referent for the horse is not the collection of several real horses that were undoubtedly necessary to make the film. Instead, for the majority of the spectators, the referent was a credible type of wild horse.

The distinction between the fiction film and the home movie allows us to grasp the fact that there is more than one referent for an image. Instead of a single referent, there are varying degrees of reference that are determined by any personal knowledge and information available to the spectator with regard to the image. These degrees of reference lead from very general categories to categories that are smaller and more complex. Moreover, these latter categories are no more "true" than the former, since they may just as well rest on a true understanding as on a "vulgate," whether common sense or a system of plausibility.

In American detective-thrillers of the 1930s, the referent is not so much the real historical epoch of Prohibition as it is the imaginary universe of Prohibition that was created in the spectators' mind out of the string of articles, novels, and films that they have read or seen.

Thus, for a fiction film, part of the referent may very well be composed of other films by way of citations, allusions, or parodies.

In order to naturalize its labor and duties, the fiction film has often displayed a tendency to choose as its subject matter historical eras and true stories around which a common discourse already exists. Thus, it pretends to be submitting to reality while it is only trying to make its fiction realistic. What is more, it is by this same process that the fiction film transforms itself into an ideological vehicle.

Narrative, Narration, and Diegesis

There are three different instances to be distinguished in the literary text: narrative, narration, and diegesis. These distinctions, which are very useful in analyzing narrative films, require several qualifications before being used in the study of the cinema.

NARRATIVE AND THE NARRATIVE TEXT.   The narrative is the *énoncé* in its material state or the narrative text that takes charge of telling the story. But this *énoncé*, which is only formed by language in a novel, is different in the cinema, where it includes images, spoken words, written words, sounds, and music—all of which make the organization of the film narrative more complex. Music, for example, which does not in and of itself have any narrative value (it does not signify events), becomes a narrative element of the text only by its co-presence with elements such as dialogue or images placed in sequence. Music's participation in the structure of the film narrative must therefore be taken into account.

With the advent of sound cinema, a vast polemic developed around the roles that would be attributed, respectively, to dialogue, sound, and music within the functioning of narrative. Would they be used for illustration, repetition, or counterpoint? Within the larger debates over cinematic representation and its specificity (see chapter 1, on audio representation), this new polemic involved specifying the place these new elements were to be awarded in the narrative structure. Moreover, it can be seen that until recently, and for quite complex reasons, the attention of film analysts has been directed toward the image track, to the detriment of the sound track. The role of the latter, however, is quite fundamental for the organization of the narrative.

The film narrative is an *énoncé* presented as a discourse, since it implies an enunciator (or at least a locus of enunciation) and a reader-spectator. These elements, therefore, are organized and ordered in terms of several requirements.

To begin with, the simple readability of a film requires that a grammar be more or less respected so the spectator may understand both the order of the narrative and the order of the story. (The use of the term "grammar" here is a metaphor since it does not involve the grammar of the language system [*la langue*].) This principle of ordering must first establish the basic level of the reading of a film or its denotation, that is, the recognition of objects and actions shown in the image.

Next, an internal coherence within the narrative as a whole must be established. This coherence is itself a function of widely diverse factors such as the style chosen by the director, the rules of the genre to which the narrative belongs, and the historical era that produced it.

Thus, for example, the use of irises to begin and end the sequences in Truffaut's *Two English Girls* (1971) is both an anachronistic and nostalgic use of an expositional technique that was typical of the silent film, but has since disappeared. Similarly, the use of pretitle sequences (the narrative beginning even before the presentation of the film's titles), which is a tactic widely employed by television to hook the spectator into the show, had its hour of glory during the late 1960s.

The systematic use of the mismatch, as in Godard's *Breathless* (1959), marked an evolution in the conception and status of the narrative during the 1960s. Film narratives became less transparent with relation to their story, readily displaying themselves *as* narrative.[8]

Finally, the order and rhythm of the narrative are established as functions of the directed reading that is imposed upon the spectator. This reading is also conceived, therefore, in view of its narrative effects (suspense, surprise, temporary appeasement, etc.). Also concerned are the arrangement of the parts of a film (the linking of sequences and relation between the sound and image tracks) as well as the mise-en-scène itself, by which we mean the composition within the frame.

> Alfred Hitchcock was referring to these sorts of relations during a discussion of *Psycho* (1960): "I was directing the audience. You might say I was playing them like an organ. . . . I don't care about the subject matter; I don't care about the acting; but I do care about the pieces of film and the photography and the sound track and all of the technical ingredients that made the audience scream."[9]

Because fiction only allows itself to be read according to the order of the narrative itself, one of the first chores for the analyst is to describe this construction process. The order, however, is not purely linear: it does not allow itself to be decoded with a single projection of the film. Instead, the order is also made up of foreshadowing, recall, connections, slippages, and transitions, which, above and beyond the narrative's unfolding, make the narrative into a signifying network. It becomes a fabric of interlaced threads in which a single narrative element may belong to several schemes. It is for this reason that we prefer to use the term "narrative text" instead of "narrative" alone, since the latter perhaps places too much emphasis on the notion of the linearity of the discourse. (For more discussion of the concept of text, see chapter 4.)

Not only is the narrative text a discourse, but it is also a *closed discourse* since it inevitably includes a beginning and an end, being physically limited. Within the cinematic institution, at least in its current form, film narratives rarely exceed two hours, no matter how extensive the stories they have to convey. This enclosure of the narrative is important to the extent that, on the one hand, it acts as an organizing element of the text that is conceived as a function of its finality; on the other hand, it allows the elaboration of the textual system(s) that make up the narrative.

One must be careful to distinguish clearly between a story, which is said to be "open" (in which the end is left suspended or allows several possible interpretations or continuations), and a narrative [*récit*], which is always finished and closed.

Finally, it should be mentioned that it is sufficient that an *énoncé* recount an event, or a real or fictive action (and the quality of that retelling hardly matters), in order to be considered some sort of narrative. From this perspective, a film like Marguerite Duras's *India Song* (1974) is no more or less a narrative than John Ford's *Stagecoach* (1939). These two narratives do not relate the same sort of event and they do not "tell" them in the same way, yet each of them is, nonetheless, a narrative (see pp. 70–71).

NARRATION.   Narration may be defined as "the productive narrative act, and, by extension, the totality of the real or fictive situation in which it takes place." It concerns the relations that exist between the *énoncé* and the *énonciation*, insofar as they are evident in the narration. These relations are therefore only analyzable as functions of the traces left within the narrative text.

Without giving a detailed typology of the relationships between *énoncé* and *énonciation* (what Gérard Genette calls "voice"), we must nonetheless explain several points here that concern the cinema.

1. *Narrative study is relatively recent* in literature, yet is even more recent in the cinema, where these sorts of issues have only been raised of late. Until now, analyses have been concerned for the most part with the *énoncé* or with the films themselves.

This sort of approach, moreover, is parallel to that followed by linguistics, which has only begun during its second phase to lean toward analyzing the relations between *énoncé* and *énonciation* phases, that is, the traces of the latter in the former.

2. *Narration regroups both the narrating act and the position* in which this act is inscribed. This definition implies at least two things: narration puts into play the workings (of the acts) and the frame in which they take place (the position). It does not, however, return us to physical people or real individuals. Thus, it may be assumed from this definition that the narrative position may contain a certain number of determinations that modulate the narrative act. It is then quite useful to distinguish between the terms "author," "narrator," "narrative instance," and "character-narrator" as clearly as possible.

Author/narrator: literary and film criticism alike have promoted the notion of author. *Cahiers du Cinéma*, for example, tried to establish and defend the "politique des auteurs" between 1954 and 1964.

This auteur theory assigned itself a double task. First, it wanted to bring certain filmmakers into the limelight, filmmakers who had been considered second-rate by most critics, and who were for the most part American studio directors. Second, it wanted these directors awarded the status of total artists, rather than being considered uncreative assembly-line workers or technicians simply drawing a weekly salary from the Hollywood industry.

Beyond promoting a certain cinema (which would have ties with the essence of the French New Wave), this "politique" was founded on the notion of a film auteur, conceived as the equal of the literary author, as an independent artist, gifted with a personal genius and style.

Today the word "author" is too tainted with psychologism to allow continued use of the term within analyses whose aims have now changed so radically. In effect, the notion implies that the author has an individuality, a personality, a real life, a personal psychology, and even a world view, all of which center that author's function around his or her actual person and the "desire for personal expression." The temptation is therefore quite strong for a number of critics to consider, on the one hand, that the director is the only artist and creator of his or her oeuvre; and, on the other hand, that one can (and must) begin analyzing and explaining this oeuvre or collected work by considering the director's declared or assumed intentions. This approach, however, imprisons the functioning of language within fields of psychology and the conscious mind.

The "real" narrator is not the author, because his or her function cannot be confused with an actual person. The narrator is always a fictive role since s/he pretends that the story preceded its representation (while it is the narration that constructs it). Similarly, the narrator pretends that s/he and the narrative are completely neutral before the "truth" of the story. Yet even in the case of autobiography, the narrator must not be confused with the actual person of the author.

The function of a narrator is not to "express his or her essential preoccupations," but rather to select from among a certain number of techniques for his or her story's treatment. (The narrator may or may not be the creator of these chosen procedures and is most often a simple user of them.) For our purposes, the narrator will be the director, in that s/he chooses a certain sort of narrative sequencing or construction, a certain type of découpage, and an editing style, in opposition to other options offered by film language. The concept of narrator, thus understood, does not, however, exclude the idea of narration and invention: the narrator certainly produces both a narrative and a story and may invent certain narrative strategies or plot constructions. However, narrative production and innovation are not born *ex nihilo*, but instead develop as functions of preexisting figures. Above all, they consist in a labor upon film language.

Narrator and narrative instance: one may wonder whether it is even possible to speak of *a* narrator under these institutional conditions wherein a film is always the product of a crew and its filming requires that a wide range of choices be made by the technicians (including the producer, script writer, camera operator, chief electrician, and editor, among others). It seems preferable to speak of a film's "narrative instance" to designate the abstract place where the choices for the story and narrative treatment are worked out, and where the film codes are at play, as well as where the parameters of film narrative production are defined.

> This desire to distinguish theoretically between people and functions owes much to structuralism and psychoanalysis. Structuralism considers the individual to be a function of the social system in which s/he is inscribed; psychoanalysis considers the subject to be submitting unconsciously to the symbolic systems s/he is using.

This abstract place that is the narrative instance, and to which the narrator belongs, not only incorporates the narrative functions of the collaborators, but also includes the position in which these functions operate. Similarly, this concept covers the "real" narrative instance (which follows below), the budgetary figures, the social period during which the film is produced, and the cinematic language as a whole. It also involves the narrative's genre in the measure that it imposes some choices while prohibiting others: in a western, for instance, the hero must not order a cup of hot chocolate, just as the heroine of a musical cannot murder her lover in order to steal his money. And the narrative instance incorporates the film itself by operating as a system or structure that imposes a form upon the elements that compose it.

The "real" narrative instance involves that which usually remains offscreen in the classical narrative film. In the classical film, the real instance tends to efface every mark of its existence as much as possible from the image track and sound track, but it will never completely arrive at this goal. It is only detectable as a principle of organization.

When the real narrative instance does mark its presence within the narrative text in an obvious manner it is to give the effect of distancing, aimed at breaking the narrative's transparency and the supposed autonomy of the story. This presence may take many very diverse forms. The range of examples runs from Alfred Hitchcock, who stealthily reveals himself in his films via some banal shot, to Jean-Luc Godard, who in *Tout va bien* (1972), for example, shows the checks that he had to sign to gather actors, technicians, and material.

The "fictive" narrative instance is internal to the story and is explicitly assumed by one or more characters. The example from Akira Kurosawa's *Rashomon* (1950), in which the same event is "retold" by three different characters, is well known. Yet this device is also used quite frequently in standard detective films. Billy Wilder's *Double Indemnity* (1944) is presented as the confession of a principal character, Walter Neff. In Orson Welles's *Lady from Shanghai* (1948) and Otto Preminger's *Laura* (1944), the narrative is attributed, from the very first images, to the hero, who announces right away that he is going to tell a story in which he was involved. In Joseph Mankiewicz's *All About Eve* (1950), this role is attributed to a secondary character placed in a position as ironic observer.

Robert Montgomery's *Lady in the Lake* (1946) is the most extreme exploitation of this procedure. The hero is the character-narrator for the entire film, which is in turn filmed almost completely with a "subjective" camera. Similarly, in a much more general sense, many films use flashbacks that are attributed to a character-narrator, again serving as examples of fictive narrative instances.

STORY OR DIEGESIS.   Story can be defined as "the signified or narrative content, even if, under the circumstances, this content turns out to be lacking in dramatic intensity or strong events."

This definition has the advantage of freeing the concept of story from the dramatic and action-oriented connotations that usually accompany it. The narrated actions may very well be quite banal, even bleak and barren—as in certain Antonioni films of the early 1960s; they still, however, constitute a story. Needless to say, the cinema, and in particular the American cinema, has often presented fictions based on spectacular events. Victor Fleming's *Gone with the Wind* (1939) is a canonical example, to which must be added all the Hollywood superproductions that were aimed at fighting against the growth and competition of television from 1955 to the present. Similarly, there are the spectacular war films, as well as the many disaster films of the 1970s. However, this does not necessarily imply a sort of natural union between thrilling stories and the cinema. In fact, huge spectacle films devote themselves more to the prestige of the cinema itself as an institution than to the beauty or perfection of their stories.

In contrast, the more refined films of Yasujiro Ozu (*Tokyo Story* [1953], *An Autumn Afternoon* [1962]) or Chantal Akerman (*Jeanne Dielman* [1975], *Les Rendez-vous d'Anna* [1978]) also tell stories, but about the daily life of the petite-bourgeoisie.

The concept of story, therefore, does not presuppose struggle, but rather the involvement of fictional elements, proceeding from the imaginary. These fictive elements are ordered, each in relation to the others, through a development, an expansion, and an ultimate resolution, finally to form a coherent whole in which the elements are usually linked together. There is a sort of phrasing of the story, at least in that it is organized into sequences of events.

> By speaking of the phrasing of a story to designate the logic of its development, we do not wish to say that a story can be compared to a sentence or that it can be summarized by the sentence's form. Only an action, insofar as it is a story "brick," can be summed up or diagramed like a sentence, on a level equivalent to Claude Lévi-Strauss's analyses of the mytheme.[10]

It is this completeness and coherence of the story, however relative, that seems to render it autonomous and independent of its own narrative. The story appears to be endowed with its own existence that constitutes it as a simulacrum of the real world. In order to take into account this tendency of the story to present itself as its own universe, the term "diegesis" has been substituted for "story."

> "Diegesis," according to both Aristotle and Plato, was, along with "mimesis," one of the modalities of "lexis," which is to say it is one of several ways to present a fiction. It is a specific technique of narration. The contemporary meaning of "diegesis" is therefore slightly different from the original sense of the term.

First of all diegesis is the story understood as a pseudo-world, as the fictional universe whose elements fit together to form a global unity. Thus, it is necessary to understand diegesis as the ultimate signified of the narrative, since it is fiction at the moment when the latter not only takes shape but *gives* shape as well. As a result, the sense of diegesis is larger than that of story, while the story ends up being the subset of diegesis because the diegesis is that which the story evokes or provokes for the spectator. Similarly, one may speak of a diegetic universe incorporating the series of narrative events, and their assumed frame (geographic, historic, or social), as well as the emotional atmosphere and motivations surrounding those events. The diegesis for Howard Hawks's *Red River* (1948) covers the story (a herd of cattle is driven to a railway station with an accompanying rivalry between a father and his adopted son), as well as the fictive universe that underlies that story (the conquest of the West, the pleasure of open spaces, the assumed moral code of the characters, and their life styles).

> This diegetic universe has an ambiguous status: it is simultaneously what produces the story, what the story is built upon, and what it refers to. For this reason we can claim that the diegesis is indeed larger than the story. Every specific story creates its own diegetic universe, yet the opposite is also true: the diegetic universe (outlined and created by preceding stories, as in the case of genre films) helps in the constitution and comprehension of the story.
>
> For these various reasons, one will occasionally find the expression "diegetic referent" in place of "diegetic universe." "Diegetic referent" is used to designate the fictional framework that serves, explicitly or implicitly, as a realistic background for the story. (For more detailed discussion of the referent, see pp. 79–82.)

Finally, we may understand diegesis as the story caught up in the dynamics of reading the narrative, which is to say that it is elaborated within the spectator's mind from the impression left by the film's unfolding. We are no longer speaking of the story only insofar as it can be reconstructed once the reading of the narrative (or the viewing of the film) is completed, but instead the story that I, as spectator, have formed and composed from the elements that the film has provided me bit by bit—the story as my own current fantasies and the memory of preceding film elements allow me to imagine it. Diegesis, therefore, is the story taken within the plasticity of reading and thus includes its false leads, temporary expansions, or imaginary ellipses, as well as brief dismemberments and re-memberments, before it finally solidifies into a story that I can retell in a logical order from start to finish.

It is thus necessary to distinguish between the terms "story," "diegesis," "scenario," and "plot." "Scenario" can be understood as the description of the story within the order of the narrative. "Plot," on the other hand, is a summary, given in the order of the story's telling, of the setting, relations, and actions that tie together the various characters.

In his famous *Dictionary of Films*, Georges Sadoul gives the following brief account of the plot of Nicholas Ray's *Johnny Guitar:* "Johnny Guitar (Hayden), a reformed gunfighter, defends Vienna (Crawford), a saloon owner, against the Marshal (Bond), a jealous female banker (McCambridge) who hates her and wants her run out of town, and an attempted lynching."[11] It is worth noting that what Sadoul means to relay to us in this summary is both the film's plot and its diegetic universe (1800s, American West, gunfighter, female saloon owner, Marshal).

There is still one subordinate point to be covered before moving on. Occasionally the term "extradiegetic" is used, but not without raising a few problems. It is used most often in regard to music that intervenes in order to emphasize or to express characters' emotions, without its actual production ever being localized or even imagined within the given diegetic universe. For instance, there is the typical and even caricatured use of violins erupting in a western during a scene when the hero is about to join the heroine out by the corral at night. During this scene the music plays a role within the diegesis by signifying love, yet without really being part of the diegesis in the same way that the night, the moon, and the sound of the wind in the trees would be.

RELATIONS BETWEEN NARRATIVE, STORY, AND NARRATION.
Relations between Narrative and Story. There are three kinds of relations between narrative and story that are labeled here to coincide with Gérard Genette's terms "order," "duration," and "mood."[12]

Order includes the differences between the unfolding of the narrative and that of the story. Quite frequently, for reasons of suspense, mystery, or dramatic interest, events within a narrative are not presented in the same order in which they are supposed to have happened. Thus, these cases involve instances of anachrony between the two series of events. Moreover, it is possible that an event may be mentioned after the fact in the narrative while it has already occurred earlier in the diegesis or fictional time frame. The flashback is a prime example of such manipulation of narrative order, as is any narrative element or strategy that demands reinterpreting an event that has already been presented or understood previously in another form. This process of inversion is used very frequently in the case of a detective or psychological mystery, where the scene constituting the reason behind a given character's behavior is shown by "delayed action."

In Alfred Hitchcock's *Spellbound* (1945), for instance, it is only after many episodes and numerous attempts that the crazed doctor, John Ballantine (played by Gregory Peck), successfully remembers the day when his younger brother was impaled on a spiked fence. The two boys had been playing together and the death was partially John's fault.

In Robert Siodmak's *The Killers* (1946), nearly the entire film is a flashback. Within the first minutes of the film we are shown the death of the hero, Swede (Burt Lancaster), while only afterward are we shown the inquest that searches through his past to learn the reasons behind his murder.

The opposite strategy also exists, in which elements of the narrative tend to evoke some future diegetic event by anticipation. This instance obviously involves the flashforward, but also any sort of announcement or indication permitting the spectator to anticipate the unfolding of the narrative by imagining a future diegetic event.

The flashforward is a fairly rare technique in film. In a strict sense it designates the appearance of an image (or a series of images) whose position in the story's chronology is situated *after* it is shown. This cinematic figure occurs particularly in films that play with the fiction's chronology, such as Chris Marker's *La Jetée* (1963), in which the main character realizes at the end of the film that the image of the quay that has obsessed him from the beginning is the scene of his own death. Similarly, Alain Resnais's "science fiction" film *Je t'aime, je t'aime* (1968) is built on related principles.

The flashforward is also found in modern films tending toward "dysnarration": Godard's *Weekend* (1967) uses brief flashforwards to the eventual car crash of Roland and Corinne, while during another scene (the garbage workers' dialogue) images of the rebel band, the FLSO, are presented far in advance of that group's appearance in the story. Alain Robbe-Grillet's *L'Immortelle* (1962) presents a unique instance of sound flashforward since we hear the sound of an accident at the beginning of the film even though that crash will occur later in the film. Moreover, this technique is even commonly used in genre films that strongly introduce structures of suspense: in Roman Polanski's *Rosemary's Baby* (1968), for example, the heroine perceives a painting of a city on fire during her ear-

liest nightmares, while she will later discover that painting in the Caste-
vets' apartment at the end of the film. Similarly, the shot under the title
sequence of Howard Hawks's *The Big Sleep* (1946) represents two burning
cigarettes on the edge of an ashtray, foreshadowing the eventual love relations of the film's central couple.

Thus, it is obvious that if the flashforward is indeed rather rare, the
construction that it implies is, by contrast, rather common, most often
employing objects that function as announcements of what will eventually happen.

According to Jean Mitry, this sort of announcement by the narrative of later diegetic events arises from a *logic of implication* that is
understood and put in motion by the spectator during the film's
projection.[13]

Hence, it is possible that in a western a shot from high atop a mountain
looking down on a stagecoach preparing to enter a mountain pass is adequate, without any further clues, to inform the spectator of an impending
Indian ambush (see the section on the genre effect in this chapter).

The narrative strategies of recall and foreshadowing may each
evoke either a great expanse of time (over twenty years in the case
of *Spellbound*) or a very minuscule period (as in the case of sound
overlapping from one shot into the preceding or subsequent shot)
and may operate in both the diegetic and fictional time schemes.

In Robert Bresson's *The Ladies of the Bois de Boulogne* (1945), for example, the heroine lies in her silent bedroom after an encounter with her
former lover. Suddenly there is the sound of castanets. This sound actually belongs to the following sequence, situated in a nightclub.

The second type of time relation, duration, concerns the agreement or disagreement between the imagined duration of the diegetic
action and the time of the narrative as it presents that action. It is
very rare that the narrative's duration agrees precisely with the duration of the story being told: Hitchcock's *Rope* (1948) pretends to
unfold "in a single shot," while *The Set-Up* (Robert Wise, 1949) and
The Twelve Angry Men (Sidney Lumet, 1957) are famous instances
of films whose story time coincides with their screen time (even
going so far as to reveal the diegetic time by inserting shots of a
clock on the wall at the beginning and end). Generally the narrative

is shorter than the story, but certain sections of the narrative may occupy more time than the story events they narrate.

There are involuntary examples of narrative time exceeding story time in certain films by Méliès, since the technique of matching on action had not yet been established. For instance, the passengers of a train might disembark in a shot filmed from inside the train, then we might see them descend the same steps in a following shot from a camera on the platform. More frequently, time may be extended by slow motion, such as the representation of memory in Sergio Leone's *Once upon a Time in the West* (1969) or the many step-printed scenes in Godard's *Every Man for Himself* [*Sauve qui peut (la vie)*] (1980). Time may also be extended by repeating actions or portions of actions, such as the repeated takes on the Russian sailor breaking a plate in Eisenstein's *Battleship Potemkin* (1925).

The category of duration also includes the case of narrative ellipsis. In *The Big Sleep*, Philip Marlowe is on a stakeout in his car: one shot shows him getting settled for a long wait; a brief fade to black follows; next we fade up on exactly the same shot of Marlowe, except he has shifted his position slightly, the cigarette that he was smoking only seconds before has disappeared, and the rain has stopped abruptly. These slight changes in the setting indicate that several hours have passed in the story time.

Finally, the third category, mood, is determined by the point of view that guides the relating of the events and controls the quantity of information given about the story by the narrative. For our purposes here we will only discuss the concept of focalization in considering the relations between these two narrative instances. It is necessary when determining narrative mood to distinguish between focalization *by* a character and focalization *on* a character; however, focalization may not always be singular, but instead may vary, fluctuating considerably during the course of the narrative. Focalization *on* a character occurs quite frequently since it springs rather naturally from the organization of every narrative involving a protagonist and secondary characters: the protagonist is simply the one that the camera isolates and follows. In film this procedure allows a certain number of effects so that, for instance, while the protagonist occupies the image and thus monopolizes the screen, the action may continue elsewhere; such events are thus revealed later to surprise the spectator.

Focalization *by* a character is just as frequent and manifests itself most often in the guise of what is known as a subjective camera position, yet it often appears in a rather dazzling form, fluctuating dynamically within the film.

At the beginning of *Dark Passage* (Delmer Daves, 1947), the spectator can only see what is in the immediate field of vision of the escaping prisoner, while the police alert is set in motion around him.

A more typical strategy of the narrative film is the sporadic presentation of shots that are attributed to the vision of a specific character (see chapter 5, on primary and secondary identification).

Relations between Narration and Story. Genette designates the relations between narration and story with the term "voice."[14] We will restrict ourselves to asserting that the organization of a classical narrative film often leads to the phenomenon of diegetization of elements that belong exclusively to narration. Thus, the spectator may be led to consider diegetic an element that is actually a prominent intervention of the narrative instance into the development of the narrative.

There is an example of this phenomenon in Truffaut's *The Wild Child* (1969), wherein the succession of shots is quite often motivated by the characters' attention. Hence, when Dr. Itard prepares for the arrival of the child he is seen approaching a window where he then stands daydreaming. The next shot shows the imprisoned child in a barn, trying to reach a skylight from which light is streaming in. The mise-en-scène manages to relay the impression of having followed the doctor's thoughts during the shot change.

THE EFFICIENCY AND EFFECTIVENESS OF THE CLASSICAL CINEMA. The phenomenon of diegetization, mentioned above, is an effect of the general functioning of the cinematic institution that seeks to efface the traces of its labor, and even its presence, from the film spectacle. In the classical cinema the impression often created is that the story "tells itself" and that its narrative and narration are both neutral and transparent. The diegetic universe pretends to offer itself without any intermediary and without the spectator having the feeling that s/he must posit a third instance or presence to understand what is seen and heard.

The fact that the fiction film is offered to the viewer's comprehension without overt reference to its own enunciation is homologous to Emile Benveniste's proposals to analyze linguistic *énoncés* by dividing them into *histoire* (story) and *discours* (discourse).[15] According to Benveniste, discourse is a narrative that can only be understood as a function of its conditions of enunciation, from which it retains a number of markers (the pronouns "I-you" that refer to the speakers, present tense verbs, future tense, etc.). A story, however, is a narrative without marks of enunciation and without overt reference to the situation that produces it (the pronouns "he-she" and verbs in the past tense).

> We can see that the term "story" in Benveniste's sense, where it designates an *énoncé* without marks of enunciation, is quite different from Genette's conception, which he defines as the narrative content of an *énoncé*.

The classical fiction film is a discourse (since it is the product of a narrative instance) that is disguised as a story (since it acts as if the narrative instance did not exist). This disguising of film discourse as story has indeed made it possible to explain the common rule requiring that the actor avoid looking into the camera: diverting one's glance means pretending that the camera is not present and also denying both the existence and intervention of the apparatus. Moreover, this diverting of the actor's glance prevents direct address to the spectator, who remains, as it were, a secret voyeur sitting in the darkened theater, hidden from view.

By offering itself as story (in Benveniste's sense) the fiction film gains certain advantages. For one thing, it presents us with a story that seems to tell itself and thus acquires an essential value by being as unforeseeable and surprising as reality itself. As a result, the film seems to be nothing more than the delivery of unfolding events that do not appear to be guided by anyone. This "realistic" trait allows the masking of the arbitrariness of the narrative and the concealment of both the narrating's constant intervention and the conventionally controlled nature of the interconnected events.

This story that no one seems to narrate has events that appear naturally, much like the images that surface on the screen only to be chased off by others. But it is also a story that no one guarantees and thus it must "play without a net." By attending such films one is subjected to a surprise that will be either agreeable or disagreeable, depending on whether the outcome is found to be wonderful or disappointing. Thus, the story is always caught between all or nothing. It is constantly at risk of falling short and disappearing into insignificance just like the fleeting images on the screen that may in turn disappear without warning as they fade to black or white, putting an end to what the spectator had thought could be organized into a durable fiction. The uncertain character of the fiction film, which may be compared to the minimal reality of the film material—a strip of film wavering between being a money maker or a total flop—allows it endlessly to revive the spectator's attention. Finally, the viewer is left attentive yet uncertain about what will follow within a story and hence remains dependent upon the movement of the images.

It is, therefore, quite certain that the narrative cinema draws much of its fascination from its ability to disguise its discourse as story. Nevertheless, the importance of this phenomenon should not be exaggerated since it remains the case that the spectator often goes to the movies in search of the marks of enunciation and narrating. In other words, film pleasure involves much more than the little fears that I experience from not knowing (or pretending not to know) the outcome of the film. Pleasure is also found in the appreciation of the methods used to propel the narrative forward and establish the diegesis.

Thus, cinephiles (and all film spectators are to some extent cinephiles) may enjoy a particular editing strategy or a given camera movement because those techniques seem to be a sort of signature, thereby becoming something special. The pleasure we feel at a fiction film, therefore, springs from the mixture of story and discourse, wherein both the naive spectator (which we always remain) and the connoisseur (which we may gradually become) may find simultaneous satisfaction in spite of the permanent gulf between them. The classical cinema draws its effectiveness from this duality. By very strong and careful regulation the cinematic institution wins on two opposing planes: if the spectator is taken into and carried away by the story, the institution asserts itself behind the scenes; but if the audience is made aware of the discourse level, the institution boasts about its own creative skill and spectacle.

Narrative Codes, Functions, and Characters

THE PROGRAMMED STORY: PREDESTINED PLOTS AND HERMENEUTIC PHRASES. When we go to see a fiction film, we always go to see both the same film and a different film. This contradiction comes from two sorts of activities. On the one hand, all films tell the same story in spite of differing episodes and appearances—they all deal with the confrontation of desire and the law and the expected surprises from their dialectic clash. Thus, while always being different, every story is always the same.

On the other hand, every fiction film follows the same path in giving the impression of a steady development and then an eruption that is supposedly due only to chance rather than predictable formulae. Hence, spectators find themselves in a paradoxical situation: they can foresee and yet not foresee what will follow in the story, while they want to know and yet do not want to know what is about to happen. Both the programmed plot development and unexpected occurrences are actually controlled in all their intricate maneuvers by the cinematic institution and even become part of that institution in the form of narrative codes.

The fiction film thereby has the character of a ritual since it must lead the spectator to the revelation of some truth or final solution by first achieving a certain number of obligatory stages and necessary detours. Some narrative codes serve, accordingly, to control this gradual progression toward the conclusion and the resolution of the story. This delayed progression is described by Roland Barthes as the paradox present in every narrative, since all narratives lead the reader toward an eventual resolution while simultaneously pushing back that same ending. As Barthes writes, "'Suspense' is clearly only a privileged—or 'exacerbated'—form of distortion . . . it offers the threat of an uncompleted sequence . . . [thus] becoming a disturbance which is consumed with anxiety and pleasure."[16] As a result, the progression in a fiction film as a whole is modulated by the two codes of predestined plot and hermeneutic phrase.

A predestined plot consists of giving away, in the first few minutes of a film, both the essence of the plot and its resolution, or at least its desired resolution. Thierry Kuntzel has shown the affinity between the predestined plot and the dream-prologue, which presents in a very condensed and allusive manner what a second dream will later reveal.[17]

Contrary to what is generally believed, this narrative process is fairly frequent in mystery films since, far from killing the suspense, it may often enhance it. In Billy Wilder's *Double Indemnity* (1944), the protagonist, Walter Neff, gives away the solution to the mystery right at the start since it is he who killed a man. Neff killed him to obtain a woman's love and money, neither of which he will finally receive.

The predestined plot gives direction to both the story and the narrative as a whole, and it even partially fixes their programming. This sort of foreshadowing of the plot may figure explicitly (as in the case of *Double Indemnity*), allusively (in the form of several shots during the title sequence), or implicitly. The implicit type would include films that begin with some sort of catastrophe that nevertheless makes it clear right from the start that the cause will be found and the evil effects will be repaired. (We will return to this final point during our discussion of narrative functions.)

Once a solution is proposed, the story is laid out, and the narrative is programmed, an entire arsenal of delays may intervene to slow down the plot. This system of delays operates within what Barthes labeled the "hermeneutic sentence [phrase]";[18] it consists precisely of a sequence of relay-points, which may lead us from the establishment of the plot to its resolution, but by way of a series of false leads, suspensions, decoys, revelations, detours, and even omissions.

> From the very moment the hired killer penetrates the victim's apartment in Hitchcock's *Dial M for Murder* (1954), for instance, the succession of shots is designed to give the impression that there is a perfect agreement between diegetic time and the time of the narrative. Next, however, the editing, which had followed conventional rules for showing the passage to the door, thereby maintaining continuity, suddenly skips over a gesture by the murderer. That missed gesture will later hold the solution to part of the mystery.

These strategies apply a brake to the story's progress and serve partially as a sort of "antiprogram" program. It is a program in that it needs to be regulated in its development,[19] so as to reveal gradually the information needed for the disclosure of the final solution. In this case the staggered arrangement of the delaying actions constitutes a kind of syntax that controls the placement of these brakes or barriers—hence the word "sentence" in Barthes's expression. It becomes an antiprogram in the sense that its function actually involves restraining the story's progression toward the solution fixed by the predestination of the plot or its equivalent. Predestination of the plot and the hermeneutic phrase are both programs, yet each is the antiprogram of the other.

Thus, by the interplay of these constraints and oppositions, a film can give the appearance of a progression that is never guaranteed and is effected by chance, while constantly pretending that it must submit to "cold reality," which is beyond the film's control. The narration's labor, therefore, involves standardizing and naturalizing the programmed stop-and-start construction of the plot in order to give it the look of pure chance or fate at work. The entire notion of plausibility also plays a part in this construction; we will return to that aspect of narrative construction in more detail shortly.

In Marcel Carné's *Quai de brumes* (1938), Jean the deserter tries to avoid detection by leaving his uniform with Panama, the manager of a bar where "discretion is the rule." As a measure of caution, Panama sends the clothes to the bottom of the harbor. This gesture thereby inscribes itself within the development of one of the first programs, which is Jean's eventual escape on a boat.

But the clothes are dragged up by the police along with a body, and Jean is accused of a murder. Hence, the first program is thwarted and replaced with a second: will Jean be arrested before he can sail away? In the end, of course, Jean will be defeated by a jealous thug.

Within the cinema the very impression that the programs are both temporary and fragile is further accentuated by the cinematographic signifier itself, since one shot is driven out by the next, just as one image replaces another without the next one being foreseen. Tenuous and faltering, the moving image lends itself particularly well to this sort of interplay between two narrative programs.

> If the detective genre is among the most prolific of genres in the cinema it is certainly not due to chance alone. It is dominant because the intrigue rests upon a material of expression that fits it so well, which is the moving image and hence the "unstable" image.
>
> Moreover, we could signal the relationship between the narrative code of suspense and fetishism: both of them center around the "just-before" or the delay of uncovering the truth.[20]

The economy of the narrative system (economy since it aims at controlling the delivery of information) is remarkably efficient in the extent to which it is strictly ambivalent. It allows the system to see to it that the spectator can both hope and fear at the same time. In a western, for example, if the hero is wounded by the bandits, that scene can act as a barrier to the direct plot line requiring his eventual victory. Thus, the failure scene is an element of the antiprogram. At the same time, however, that scene is the logical notification to the audience of the opposite scene, which will follow later when the hero will get revenge on the attackers: thus, the scene is also an element of the positive program.

The system also allows pathos to develop by way of the "scotch bath" principle. John Ford, for instance, set up a strategy of alternating happy scenes with violent scenes so that the audience would be subjected to extreme emotions (helping them lose sight of the narrative's arbitrariness). But the technique has a second effect, which is that the audience is made impatient to know the images that are

Two examples of predestination taken from the title sequence of *The Big Sleep* (Howard Hawks, 1946) announcing the ultimate formation of the couple.

More examples of predestination from *The Most Dangerous Game* (Ernest B. Shoedsack, 1932): the opening images of the door knocker and the mural announce the final hunt.

going to follow and whether those images will confirm or undercut what is currently being seen. Film spectators, unlike readers of novels, cannot reassure themselves by skipping to the end of the episode to verify the outcome of the narrative program.

THE FUNCTIONS. We have just shown that the fiction film has a certain ritualistic aspect, at least to the extent that the story obeys set programs. It is also a ritual in that it perpetually renews the same story, or at least we might say that the plots it builds from may quite often be reduced to a limited number of circuits. The fiction film, much like myth or folktales, is built upon a finite number of base structures whose number of possible combinations is limited.

To become convinced of this one need only consider four very different films within the classical American cinema: *Swing Time* (George Stevens, 1936), *Spellbound* (Alfred Hitchcock, 1945), *The Searchers* (John Ford, 1956), and *The Big Sleep* (Howard Hawks, 1946). The action in all four films unfolds within quite different situations and circumstances, while it also concerns different sorts of themes with very diverse characters. Nevertheless, their plots may be summarized or diagramed according to a model common to all four: the protagonist must rescue another character from the hold of a hostile setting. One may, therefore, regard the fiction film, in spite of its infinite variations, as being composed of invariable elements, by using the model of functions derived by Vladimir Propp for Russian folktales or the model of mythemes defined by Claude Lévi-Strauss's study of myth.[21]

Vladimir Propp defines functions in the following manner: "Functions of characters serve as stable, constant elements in a tale, independent of how and by whom they are fulfilled."[22]

In the examples we just cited above, a character was abducted or kidnapped (by the Indians, gangsters, a rival lover, or the unconscious). The protagonist must then perform a counterabduction in order to restore the other character to a "normal" environment (by ridiculing the rival or rendering the unconscious conscious). Thus, the situations, characters, and course of events may vary, but the functions, for their part, remain constant.

All this is not to say that the functions of a fiction film would be strictly the same as those of a fairy tale. While the film's functions have some of the same characteristics as those in a fairy tale, and may quite often resemble them, they nonetheless have been "secularized" or rendered specifically for film use.

The functions combine with one another within sequences that constitute miniprograms since one sequence sweeps away another, and so on, until the closure that finally represents a return to the initial condition or gives access to some desired situation. The "evil deed" (murder, theft, separation, etc.) implies at the outset of the story an initial situation that is offered as normal and good and, at the story's end, a destiny that is the eventual "reparation of the evil deed." In the same way the narrative "departure" function demands the "return" function.

Taken from this stance, every story is homeostatic since it simply retraces the disruption left by disorder and returns everything to its proper place. More fundamentally, however, stories may be analyzed in terms of disjunctions and conjunctions, or separation and reunion. In the end, a story is made of nothing more than unwarranted disjunctions that then give way, via transformations, to normal conjunctions, or it may consist of unwarranted conjunctions that demand normal disjunctions. This structural schema, which could serve in analyzing or at least diagraming any kind of plot, can also function alone, in a purified fashion, without the trappings of traditional fiction (see pp. 70–71).

> From this sort of analysis it is easy to feel all the ideological weight represented by this kind of fiction. These narratives involve staging a given social order as normal, and that order must then be maintained, no matter what the cost.

Thus, the history of the fiction film, like that of the Russian folktale or myth, is built from the assembling of sequences of functions.

> In order to avoid confusion over the technical film term "sequence," which designates an ensemble of shots, we prefer to employ the term "program-sequence" to describe what Propp meant as a literary "sequence."

These program-sequences may follow one another, with each new misdeed, lack, or need leading into a new program-sequence, as in the case of serials or films compiled of sketches. Much more commonly, however, a new program-sequence will begin before the preceding one is finished. In that case there would be an interlocking construction among the units that could produce no foreseeable completion, except perhaps by looping back to the first link in the narrative chain, thereby closing off the original program-sequence.

> This process of interrupting one program with another is obviously an occurrence that belongs to the workings of the hermeneutic phrase and

is a strategy widely used by suspense or mystery films in particular. *The Enforcer* (Raoul Walsh, Bretaigne Windust, 1950), for example, juggles three different diegetic time periods (present, recent past, and distant past), while the D.A.'s inquest, the police reports, and the gangster's confessions never stop interrupting one another. The story in *The Enforcer*, therefore, steadily unravels level after level until finally winding back to the very first program-sequence.

Yet this procedure can just as easily benefit comedy. In the well-known gags of Buster Keaton and Jerry Lewis, for instance, the character intends to fix up one blunder, but commits a second mistake in the process, which then must be rectified and hence leads to a third, etc.

Finally, two different program-sequences may have a single common resolution. This is the case in adventure films, for instance, where the hero not only defeats his or her adversaries, but simultaneously wins the heart of the desired woman or man.

The story told by a fiction film, therefore, takes on the appearance and form of an erector set. Its parts are determined once and for all and are also limited in number, but they can enter into a very large number of different combinations since their selection and placement remain relatively free. However, while the narrative instance has only a very restrained freedom for its internal organization and sequence-program ordering, it does, by contrast, maintain complete freedom in choosing the manner in which the preset functions will be fulfilled and in deciding the attributes and qualities of the characters. It is this freedom that allows the controlled and limited play with an erector set to take on its perpetually new appearance.

CHARACTER.   Propp proposed calling characters "actants," and this allowed him to define them in terms of their "sphere of action" rather than their psychology or social status. Specifically, "sphere of action" implies the cluster of functions that the characters fulfill within the story. After Propp, A. J. Greimas suggested defining an "actant" as any character who fulfills only one function, while proposing the label "actor" for those characters who accomplish many functions throughout the story as a whole.[23] Propp, in fact, had already written that one character could carry out any number of functions and that one function could be accomplished by any number of characters.

Greimas ended up establishing an actantial model with six terms. His model includes the subject (which corresponds to the protagonist); the object (which may be the character for whom the protagonist is searching); the sender (the *destinateur* who sets the mission, task, or action to be accomplished); the receiver (the *destinataire* who will benefit from the subject's mission); the opponent (who arrives to block the subject's action); and the helper (who brings assistance to the subject). It should be clear from this list that a single character could simultaneously, or alternately, be sender and receiver, object and receiver, etc.

Within film noir the female character is quite often the object of the quest; the helper, since she aids the hero in his task; and the opponent, since she is usually the one who has undertaken some scheme and messed up the detective's trail. At the other extreme, *Rio Bravo* (Howard Hawks, 1959) has a subject represented by four different characters—the sheriff and his three deputies. In that case one might consider the four as a single actant.

While the actants are finite in number and remain invariant, the characters are practically infinite in number because their attributes and qualities can vary without their sphere of action being modified. Conversely, they may also apparently remain identical when their sphere does change.

Thus, a gangster (opponent) may be characterized as a brutal and savage product of the ghetto, or he may be distinguished and refined.

The character of the Indian has seen its sphere of action evolve relatively far during the history of the western, yet still retains its basic attributes and values. The Indian has, as a result, shifted from being a simple "massacre machine" in some films to becoming a positive subject in others. Particularly revealing in this respect is the contrast between two John Ford films—*Stagecoach* (1939) and *Cheyenne Autumn* (1964).

What we normally label as the psychological richness of a character very often arises only from the modification of the cluster of functions that it fulfills. This modification does not operate in relation to reality so much as in relation to a preexistent model of the character, wherein certain generally accepted actantial connections find themselves abandoned in favor of unusual combinations.

On the level of actant models, the fictive character is therefore an operator since it assumes (in accordance with the functions it must fulfill) the transformations needed to advance the story. In addition, the character thereby assures a certain unity beyond the diversity of functions and actant poles. As a result, the fiction film character is a bit like a "guiding line" with its role of homogenization and continuity.

If the actant model, originally elaborated for literature, can be applied to a fiction film character, there is still at least one point at which the film character differentiates itself from the novelistic and even theatrical character. A character in a novel is only an empty proper name on which attributes, character traits, feelings, and actions will crystallize. The theatrical character is situated between the novel's character and that of the cinema—it is only a being written on a piece of paper, but it finds itself incarnated periodically by one actor or another. It may happen, however, that certain theatrical characters retain the mark of a specific actor. Hence, in the United States, the Count of Monte Cristo was inscribed with the traits of James O'Neill, Eugene's father, throughout the period of his life.

In the cinema the situation is quite different, and for several distinct reasons. First of all, the script does not usually have any existence on its own. If it does become well known, it is generally after the film's initial run, and the character only exists on the screen.[24] Second, the character only exists one time in a film, which, once recorded, never knows any variation. In theater, by contrast, the incarnation varies from actor to actor or even, for a single actor, from performance to performance. Third and finally, the fictional film character does not exist on its own, being dependent upon the traits of a given actor (except in the case of remakes like the James Bond series, which is still relatively rare in film production), and even then it depends upon a single performance that has been shot and then preserved in the final cut of the distributed film.

Thus, if it comes to mind to say "James O'Neill" for the Count of Monte Cristo, it is also quite common to refer to the actor's name when speaking of a given film character. For example, I remember quite well that it is Lee Marvin who throws the boiling coffee into the face of his accomplice Gloria Grahame in *The Big Heat* (Fritz Lang, 1953), yet I have completely forgotten the names of the characters.[25] This example helps show that the fiction film character has no existence beyond the physical traits of the actor interpreting it, except in the case where a character is named and discussed before appearing in the image.

In the cinema, the status of the character ultimately belongs to the star system, which, in and of itself, functions within the cinema's institution. As Edgar Morin has pointed out,[26] the star system has been pushed to the limit by the American cinema, but is also present in all commercial cinemas. It may be defined by its interrelated economic and mythological aspects, each of which connects with the other. Since the cinema is an industry that makes use of large amounts of capital, it aims at maximizing the profit on its investments. This economic fact leads to a double practice: on one hand, the industry retains actors under contract for a specific production company; on the other hand, it then reduces its risks by allowing only a consistent image of that actor to be used. During the days of the Hollywood studio system, these contracts generally ran seven years.

Moreover, if a given actor shows himself or herself particularly competent at portraying a certain kind of role or character, the tendency is to repeat the project in other similar films to profit once again from the same recipe. This process is precisely where the mythological aspect enters into the star system since it forges a sort of brand name image of the actor, packaging him or her as a star. This image simultaneously builds from the actor's physical traits, past or future film performances, and "real" or supposedly real life. The star system tends to consider an actor a character already, even outside actual production. Finally, a film character only comes into existence by way of this other character, the star.

> If the fictive character indeed gains from reality by basing itself both on the character of the star and on that star's previous roles, that actor may actually lose touch with reality. Without even speaking of the obvious case of Marilyn Monroe, we may consider Bela Lugosi, who ended up taking himself really to be the satanic character of his films, or Johnny Weissmuller, who supposedly entered a psychiatric hospital exhibiting traits of Tarzan.

As a result, the star system promotes the organization of the fiction around a central character or couple, setting all the others back in the shadows. It is consistent with this system, therefore, that a number of scenarios are written for a specific actor, as a function of that individual. The character is then tailored to fit the actor. We know, for instance, that certain actors have contracts that not only stipulate the number of shots that will be devoted to them in the film, but also certain qualities in the characters they will interpret. Buster Keaton, for example, was forbidden to laugh, and Jean Gabin's contracts before World War II required that he die at the end of every film. The star's own image always feeds into the character's traits, but in return the character feeds the image of the star.

REALISM IN THE CINEMA

To start this discussion of realism in the cinema it is necessary first to distinguish the realism of the materials of expression (image and sound) from the realism of the film subject.

Realism and the Materials of Expression

Among all the arts and modes of representation, cinema seems to be among the most realistic because it can reproduce the movement and duration of an event or place, while simultaneously restoring its sound ambience. But the simple formulation of this hypothesis should reveal that realism in the cinema is only being considered here in relation to other modes of representation rather than to reality itself. Today this notion that film effectively captures reality is considered passé—the era of believing in the objectivity of the cinematic techniques of representation has passed, along with the enthusiasm of theorists like André Bazin who saw the model itself within the image of the model. This faith in the objectivity of the apparatus was based both on an unfortunate wordplay in French surrounding "objective" (*l'objectif* being the name for the lens of the camera as well) and on a confidence in the essential neutrality of the camera as a scientific tool. This question, however, was sufficiently examined in chapter 1, so it is unnecessary to take up all the pertinent arguments again here.

It should suffice to recall that cinematic representation does not involve the camera alone and submits to a whole series of constraints, ranging from technical necessities to aesthetic ones. In fact, it is subordinate to the type of film stock used, the kind of light source available, and the lens selection and quality, as well as to the necessary selection and mixing of sounds, the editing choices, the ordering of sequences, and their mise-en-scène. All these procedures require that a vast ensemble of codes be assimilated by the public so that the presented image resembles a perception of reality.

The "realism" of the cinematic materials of expression is merely the result of a large number of conventions and rules, all of which vary according to the specific period and culture in which the film is made. We must recall that the cinema did not always have syncsound and was not always available in color, and even when sound and color were available their particular degree of realism was modified through the years. The color schemes of the films of the 1950s seem excessive today, while the color style of the films of the 1980s, with their systematic use of pastels, seems quite fashionable. Actually, at every stage of film history (silent, black and white, and color), the cinema was considered realistic. Realism always seemed to be a gain of reality in relation to a previous mode of representation (see chapter 2, on editing and reality). Yet, while this gain is infinitely renewable in terms of technical innovations, it will also be infinite in that reality can never be attained.

The Realism of Film Subject Matter

When speaking about cinematic realism we must also consider the realism of subject matter and its treatment. It is according to this sort of realism that traditions such as "poetic realism" (a specific group of 1930s French films) or Italian "neorealism" (films from the liberation era) are defined. Neorealism is a particularly striking example of the ambiguity inherent in the term "realism" itself.

It should be noted that neorealism, like the labeling of most film schools, was created by critics who established a theoretical model for the convergence of what today looks like a relatively limited number of films. The differences found today between the films of Robert Rossellini (*Rome Open City* [1946], *Paisan* [1946]), Vittorio DeSica (*Shoeshine* [1946], *The Bicycle Thief* [1948]), Luchino Visconti (*La Terra Trema* [1948], *Bellissima* [1950]), and Federico Fellini (*I Vitelloni* [1953], *Il Bidone* [1955]) are primarily stylistic ones.

For André Bazin, the movement's discoverer and defender, neorealism could be defined as a cluster of specific traits, yet these traits actually relied more on the ensemble of conventional film production than on reality itself. According to Bazin, this school was characterized by the following: location shooting in natural settings (as opposed to the artifice of studio production); the use of nonprofessional actors (as opposed to the "theatrical" conventions of professional actors' performances); recourse to scripts based on techniques from 1930s American novels, along with a concern for simple characters (as opposed to the carefully woven classical plots and their extraordinary heroes); and a reduction of the action per se (in contrast to the spectacular events staged in the conventional commercial film). Finally, the neorealist cinema was to have been low budget, thereby escaping all the rules set by the cinematic institution and directly opposing the American and Italian superproductions of the prewar era.

This is the network of elements making up neorealism for Bazin; yet each of these points, taken separately or together, is open to criticism. The degree of outdoor or location shooting in these productions was limited. Many neorealist films contain scenes that were in fact shot in the studio, but when mixed with location scenes they passed for real locations themselves. Moreover, shooting on location and in a natural setting is not, in and of itself, a function of a scene's realism. One must add social factors to the settings before they can truly become natural, producing such places as ghettos, deserted neighborhoods, fishing villages, or suburbs. Yet the studio set for Erich von Stroheim's *Greed* (1924) is just as realistic as any of the location sets in these Italian films.

The recourse to nonprofessional actors is believed to be as "natural" as location sets since these characters are felt to truly live, yet their use is also limited and manipulative. Their status as nonprofessionals still does not cancel the fact that they must act, which is to say that representing a fiction still involves bowing to the constraints and conventions of film representation, even if that fiction resembles the actor's real life. Moreover, their voices were generally dubbed over at the studio by professional actors, which serves to illustrate that their "realistic" expression was apparently not realistic enough. In addition, these nonprofessional actors only represented part of the cast since the films often included some professionals.

Finally, the process of auditioning actors at the actual locations, combined with the numerous rehearsals and the many retakes that their inexperience required, helped to raise the cost of production. This final point, along with the other elements such as use of studios for postdubbing and even shooting, would seem to contradict the last point in the Bazinian definition of neorealism, concerning the economical nature of the production techniques used in these films. They only gave the desired appearance of economizing on production, just as they only produced a more real image thanks to the use of studios. Neorealism, therefore, concerned itself with erasing the cinematic institution as such by effacing the marks of enunciation. This is actually a fairly classical procedure that we have already referred to above in several examples from the traditional fiction film.

As for the lack of conventional drama in their stories, it is certainly true that neorealism films avoid substantial amounts of spectacle, adopting instead a slower pace for the action. Nonetheless, they resort to a fiction in which the individuals are characters that arise out of certain social stereotypes such as the lumpenproletarian, the idyllic worker, or the Sicilian fisherman, none of which is strictly realistic. What is more, even if the portrayal of these characters has changed, their functions still remain the same. Whether the hero departs in search of his stolen bicycle or attempts to recover an atomic secret that a spy is about to hand over to the enemy, the story still involves a "quest" that follows a "misdeed" that upset the "initial situation." The fiction only appears more realistic in that, first, it tries to be less rosy by being more populist and featuring social issues while building toward a deceptive or pessimistic

Neorealism and its leg-
acy: top, *Open City*
(Roberto Rossellini,
1945); middle, *Shoe-
shine* (Vittorio De Sica,
1946); bottom, *The
Bicycle Thief* (Vittorio
De Sica, 1948).

Top, *Umberto D.* (Vittorio De Sica, 1952); bottom, *Salvatore Guiliano* (Francesco Rosi, 1961).

ending; and second, it refuses to follow certain conventions. But this abandonment results in the installation of new conventions.

Bazin's enthusiasm for this "new" film form pushed him to an excessive stance. In writing about *The Bicycle Thief*, for instance, he wrote, "No more actors, no more story, no more sets, which is to say that in the perfect aesthetic illusion of reality there is no more cinema."[27] One must interpret this "no more cinema" against the pejorative sense of "it is cinema," which is to say a representation whose conventions have become too apparent to be acceptable or "naturalized." From this perspective, the time would quickly come when neorealism would also appear as "cinematic."

Another claim by Bazin seems much more justified: "One might group, if not classify in order of importance, the various styles of cinematography in terms of the added measure of reality. We would define as 'realist,' then, all narrative means tending to bring an added measure of reality to the screen."[28] This definition nonetheless requires that one specify that this "added measure of reality" may only be considered in relation to a system of conventions that will hereafter be considered out of date. The "added measure of reality" pertains exclusively to the denunciation of conventions; yet, as indicated above, this denunciation goes hand in hand with the installation of a *new* system of conventions.

The Plausible

The plausible simultaneously involves the relationship between a text and commonly held opinion, its relation to other texts, and also the internal functioning of the story being told.

THE PLAUSIBLE AND PUBLIC OPINION.   To begin with, the plausible may be defined in its relation to public opinion and proper standards of behavior. Plausibility is always defined as a function of propriety, and this is why one judges an action plausible only if it can be recounted as a maxim. In other words, it must fit one of those deeply rooted forms that express public opinion under the appearance of a categorical imperative. Thus, one is never startled to see the hero of a western devote himself obsessively to the pursuit of the person who killed his father, all in the name of family honor, just as we are never surprised that a private eye in a detective film will work desperately, against all odds, to discover the guilty party simply because "you have to finish what you start."

As a result, the plausible constitutes a *form of censorship* since it restrains the number of narrative possibilities and imaginable diegetic situations, all in the name of preserving the rules.[29] Thus, the critics and public alike found two of Louis Malle's films unrealistic for presenting paradoxical characters: in *Murmur of the Heart* (1971), a young well-balanced mother initiates her son into the world of sexuality, while in *Pretty Baby* (1978) a naive yet cunning young girl prostitutes herself. Such paradox is often implausible since it runs contrary to common opinion or the accepted *doxa*, even though both public opinion and the plausible may vary across time.

THE SYSTEMATIC ECONOMY OF THE PLAUSIBLE. The plausible also consists of a certain number of rules that affect character actions in terms of the maxims by which those very actions may be conditioned. These rules, which are tacitly recognized by the public, yet never explained, are applied so well that the relationship between a story and the system of plausibility to which it submits is essentially a silent one. The final gunfight in a western responds to strict rules that must be respected or else the audience will judge the director inept and the situation unrealistic. Still, nothing in the western or reality itself explains why the hero must walk alone to the center of the main street and wait there until his adversary draws.

On the other hand, whatever is foreseeable is considered to be plausible. By contrast, the implausible is judged to be that which the audience cannot possibly foresee, whether from the angle of the story or that of its maxims, and the implausible will suddenly appear as a show of force of the narrative instance trying to achieve its goals. If, for example, one does not want to make the cavalry's last minute rescue of a ranch under Indian attack appear too implausible, one would have to introduce several earlier scenes indicating that the ranch was not far from the fort and that the cavalry commander had been informed of the attack. The plausible, therefore, is tied to the motivation of the actions undertaken within the story. Thus, every diegetic unit always has a double function, one of which is immediate, while the other is long-term or delayed. Its immediate function may vary, but its delayed function is discreetly to prepare the arrival of another unit for which the first will have served as motivation.

In Jean Renoir's *La Chienne* (1931), Maurice wants to have it out calmly with Lulu, the woman he supports but who deceives him. While Maurice reasons with her she undoes the pages of a large book with a paper-knife. This action is plausible since Lulu has been presented as an idle person; in other words, her idleness motivates the fact that she reads in bed and thus uses a paper-knife to cut apart the pages.

But the obsessed Maurice kills her with the paper-knife. The murder becomes plausible to the extent that the character Maurice has his psychological and moral motives, while, in addition, the weapon was found "naturally" and "by chance" in this setting. Thus, cutting apart the pages of a book has the immediate function of signifying Lulu's casual manner and futility, while its delayed function is to lead "naturally" to her murder.

If, within the diegesis, it is the causes that seem to determine the effects, within the narrative construction it is the effects that determine the causes. In our example, Maurice does not kill Lulu with a paper-knife because she uses one; rather, she uses one because Maurice is going to kill her with it. When seen from this angle, the narrative gains in economy, and this economy comes in many forms. First of all, the narrative gains from the double function of the diegetic element, which, in a way, serves twice instead of only once. It also profits because one unit can be overdetermining or overdetermined: that unit may, in effect, act as a sounding board for a number of other elements disseminated later within the narrative or it may have been referred to itself by other earlier elements. It thereby profits from the reversal of the narrative determination of the cause by the effect, into a diegetic motivation of the effect by the cause.

Thus, the narrative is able to transform the artificial and arbitrary relations established by the narration into a plausible and natural relationship established by the diegetic facts. From this perspective, the plausible becomes only one means of naturalizing the arbitrariness of the narrative and then realizing it (in the sense of making it pass for real). To repeat a formula set by Genette, if the function of a diegetic unit is what it is used for, its motivation is whatever it needs to conceal its function.[30] In the most successful instances of transparent narratives, the plausible is an implicit motivation that costs nothing, since, belonging to commonly held opinion and accepted maxims, it does not have to be inscribed within the narrative.

THE PLAUSIBLE AS AN EFFECT OF THE CORPUS.   If the plausible is defined in relation to common opinion or maxims, it is also necessarily defined in relation to other texts to the extent that the latter always tend to disseminate a commonly held opinion by their very convergence. Thus, a film's plausibility owes much to previous, already produced films, since plausibility will be judged as that which has already been seen in a previous work. As we have already shown, in many cases paradox was implausible, but only in its very first film instances. Once that same situation has been recreated in several films, it will appear both realistic and normal.

If we consider the plausibility of character as an example, we can build upon our earlier observations that, within the play of interference between actor and character, the plausibility of the latter owes much to the previous work of the former, so the new character is also in debt to the already forged star image. For example, the combination of brash independence and potential sensitivity of the Clint Eastwood character in *Tightrope* (1984) does not really work or seem plausible except in that Eastwood has already played this kind of character in many earlier films. Similarly, the young asocial characters that proliferate in late 1970s French films owe part of their success and plausibility to the social conditions that accompany that period of economic crisis. But this cinematic avatar of the young, the anarchist, the unemployed, the misfit, and the posthippie leftist is especially realistic thanks to its recurrence within a substantial number of films of the period. Its success does not depend on its plausibility—it is the plausibility that depends on the success, and all this can, undoubtedly, be analyzed more in terms of ideology than of reality.

One may argue, therefore, that the plausible is established not as a function of reality, but as a function of already established texts (or films). It owes more to discourse than to the real, hence, it is an effect of the corpus. In this way the plausible is founded upon the reiteration of discourse, whether at the level of public opinion or of an ensemble of texts. It is for this reason that the plausible is always a form of censorship.

Consequently, it becomes clear that a work's content is decided much more in relation to previous works (whether to copy or oppose them) than in relation to any more detailed or more correct observation of reality. The plausible, therefore, must be understood as a form, which is to say an organization, of the standardized content of a string of texts. Its changes and its evolution then become functions of the earlier plausible's system. The character of the asocial young man is merely a new avatar of the street punk from past decades, and the importance of such characters to the cinema has always been stronger than their real sociological influence. Within this evolution of the plausible, the new system only appears "real" because the old one is declared out of date and hence denounced as conventional, even though the new system is obviously just as conventional.

The Genre Effect

If, therefore, the plausible is an effect of the corpus, it will accordingly be more solid within a long series of films that are closely related in their expression and their content, as is the case within a genre. Hence, insofar as the plausible is concerned, there is a genre effect. This genre effect has a double impact. First, thanks to the permanence of the same diegetic referent and the recurrence of typical scenes, it allows the plausible to reinforce itself from film to film. In a western, for instance, the hero's code of honor and the Indians' modes of action seem plausible, on the one hand, because they are fixed (during a considerable period these genre films knew only one code of honor and one way for the Indians to behave), and, on the other, because they are ritually repeated, being brought back in film after film.

The second major characteristic of the genre effect is that it allows the establishment of a plausible that is specific to a given genre. Each genre has its own plausible—what is plausible in a western will not be realistic in a musical comedy or a detective film. It would certainly be implausible if, in a western, the protagonist's enemy admitted defeat after being ridiculed in public, even though this would be quite realistic and even typical in a musical comedy. Similarly, it would be implausible if the adversary in a musical comedy tried to kill the protagonist for having ridiculed him or her. Thus, the famous "generic rules" are only pertinent inside a given genre and only carry the full weight of plausibility within the group of films produced as part of that particular genre.

This double impact of the genre effect is only effective in the instance of maintaining the plausible, since the plausible maintains the necessary cohesion of the genre. This is not to say that the plausible aspects of a genre are permanently determined and never vary. Instead, they are susceptible to evolution at a number of points, on the condition, however, that a certain number of other points be respected and maintained. This explains how, since its origins, the western has come to witness the particular modification of its plausible. Yet these modifications tend to serve more for the survival of the plausible than to produce any new, more correct approach to reality. All of this is equally true for any other genre.

In *Ride the High Country* (Sam Peckinpah, 1962), the two protagonists, both bounty hunters, have a contract drawn up in due process by their employer, but are obligated to put their glasses on in order to read it carefully. This bureaucratic care and the heroes' aging seem more realistic and more plausible than does the simple "trust in a man's word" or the eternal youth of the more traditional hero. But all of this does not prevent the protagonists of Peckinpah's film from following the same schemata (code of honor, personal panache, pursuit of justice, etc.) that their pre-

The genre effect: three looks at film noir. *Scarface* (Howard Hawks, 1932).
High Sierra (Raoul Walsh, 1941).

The Enforcer (Bretaigne Windust and Raoul Walsh, 1951).

decessors followed. Several years later, the Italian western would take its turn at challenging the conventions of "metawesterns" like *Ride the High Country*, only to establish new rules and conventions.

THE IMPRESSION OF REALITY

It has often been observed that what distinguishes the cinema from other modes of representation is the impression of reality that arises from viewing films. The impression of reality, whose mythical prototype is the terror that supposedly seized the first spectators at Louis Lumière's *Arrival of a Train at the Ciotat Station* (1895), has been the nucleus of a number of reflections and debates on the cinema. These discussions have generally attempted to define the cinema's specificity, as distinguished from painting and photography, while also establishing the technical and psychological foundations for the impression of reality itself and analyzing its effects on the spectator's attitude during film viewing.

The impression of reality experienced by the spectator while viewing a film results first of all from the perceptual richness of the film materials—the image and sound. As far as the film image is concerned, this richness is due to both the high definition of the photographic image and the restitution of movement. The high degree of definition (as we know, a photograph is much sharper and richer in information than the television image) presents the spectator with luxuriously detailed effigies of objects, while the restitution of movement in turn grants those effigies a certain weight and volume that they would lack in a still photograph. Everyone has experienced this flattening of the film image and squashing of depth when a projected film is suddenly stopped in a freeze-frame, turning the film world into a flat still photograph.

The restitution of movement, therefore, occupies an important place in the impression of reality, and that is why movement was so carefully investigated by psychologists such as A. Michotte van den Berck and Henri Wallon at the Institute of Filmology. Movement is the result of the technological regulation of the film apparatus, which allows a certain number of still images (frames) to pass through the film gate at a set rate each second (18 frames per second in a silent, 24 fps for sound). This procession of images permits certain psycho-physiological phenomena to take place, producing an impression of continuous movement. The phi-phenomenon, which is of prime importance among these operations, involves our perception of apparent movement in certain instances when there is no actual motion. The phi-phenomenon may be illustrated by setting up a system of lightbulbs in a series or line and then flashing them one after the other in rapid succession. The resulting effect, often produced on older movie theater marquees or in discotheque lighting designs, is perceived as one continuously moving spot or streak of light rather than a succession of individual flashes. Hence, the spectator has mentally established a continuity and movement where there was technically only discontinuity and stasis. This same effect is produced in the cinema between two still frames when a spectator covers over the gap existing between two successive images of two successive positions by a character.

One must not confuse the phi-phenomenon with persistence of vision. The former pertains to the mental activity of covering over a real gap, while the latter is due to the relative inertia of the retina's cells, which briefly retain the trace of any luminous impression. This process can be observed when you close your eyes after having stared at a clearly lit object and the object's shape or impression remains visible. It is also illustrated by watching someone "write" in the dark with a lit cigarette or flashlight, while you "see" an arabesque of light. Contrary to widely held notions, persistence of vision plays virtually no role in cinematic perception.

It is also worth noting that reproducing the appearance of movement is, in effect, equivalent to reproducing its reality: a reproduced movement is a "real" movement, since its visual manifestation is identical in both cases.

The perceptual richness proper to the cinema depends equally upon the co-presence of image and sound. Sound restores a scene's sonic dimension, which painting and the novel lack, and thereby supplies the impression that the perceptual elements present in the original scene have all been maintained. The impression is therefore stronger when the sound reproduction has the same "phenomenal fidelity" as the perceived movement.

If the perceptual richness of the film materials is one of the foundations of the cinema's impression of reality, it is further reinforced by the psychic position occupied by the spectator during the actual projection. This position, insofar as it concerns the impression of reality, may be defined by two of its aspects. First, spectators experience a lowering of their threshold of vigilance: conscious of being in a movie theater, we suspend all action and partially renounce the solidity of reality. Second, the film bombards the audience with visual and audio impressions (the richness of perceptual cues mentioned above), in a continuous and rapid wave (see chapter 5, on double identification).

There are still other factors pertaining to the impression of reality, however, besides the phenomena of perception linked to the film material and the particular state into which the spectator is thrust. The impression of reality is also based upon the coherence of the diegetic universe constructed by the fiction. The diegetic universe takes on the consistency of a possible world, because it is strongly supported by the system of the plausible and is organized so that every element of the fiction seems to respond to some organic necessity by appearing essential to the imagined reality. Moreover, it becomes a world whose constructed nature, artifice, and arbitrariness are erased for the benefit of an apparent neutrality. This neutrality, as we have already noted, owes a great deal to the mode of film representation and to the image's procession across the screen, which then gives the fiction the appearance of a natural surfacing of events as well as the "spontaneity" of reality.

> The surfacing of the real, due in part to the procession of images and sounds, does not necessarily contradict the coherence and consistency of the fictional universe. It is actually an integral part of the fiction's construction. The fictional universe becomes consistent, yielding an impression of reality, precisely because the world springs up in front of us and seems to obey chance itself. If this world is too predictable or too carefully controlled, it will only appear to be a fiction—an artifice with no depth.

What is more, the system of iconic representation, the "scenic" or theatrical apparatus specific to the cinema, and the phenomena of primary and secondary identification (with the camera and characters, see chapter 5) all see to it that the spectators find themselves included within the represented scene, thereby becoming, in a way, part and parcel of the fictional situation. It is precisely this inscription of the spectator into the scene that Jean-Pierre Oudart defined as *l'effet de réel* (the real effect), distinguishing it from *l'effet de réalité* (the reality effect). For him, the reality effect concerns the system of representation, more specifically, the perspective system inherited by the cinema from Western painting. The real effect, however, according to Oudart, depends on the fact that the subject-spectator's place is marked or inscribed by that same representative system as if s/he belonged to the diegetic space. This inclusion of the spectator means that s/he no longer perceives the elements of the representation as such, but rather perceives them as being the profilm things themselves.

The mutual reinforcement of the various factors involved in the impression of reality has, for a long time, made that impression appear to be a basic issue in defining the cinema's specificity. Consequently, certain theoreticians and aestheticians of the cinema, such as André Bazin and Amedée Ayfre, have believed they could elevate it to an aesthetic norm that could not be transgressed without betraying the "ontology of the film image" or the cinema's "natural vocation."[31] It is this ideology of film's transparency in particular that led Bazin to become so enthusiastic over neorealism (for more on transparency, see chapter 2). This same belief in the cinema's transparency has, more generally, implicitly founded the major part of traditional critical discourse or the notion that film images and language offer faithful and natural doubles for reality, except for a few secondary details.

It was to combat this sort of privileging of the impression of reality and the supposed transparency of film representation that a critical wave favoring deconstruction was set in motion around 1970, especially by the journal Cinéthique.[32] The stakes involved showing, on the one hand, the artificiality of the impression of reality, and, on the other, the ideological importance that this camouflage (hiding the labor of production and its presuppositions) had for the cinema of transparency. The winnings involved displaying the mechanisms of this naturalism. This critical current called for a materialist cinema, which, in opposition to the realist-idealist cinema, would manipulate the spatial structures of the image in order to thwart the perspectival effects produced by the camera's lens itself. In addition, these critics demanded the use of "textural" matches to break away from the linear ordering of shots that is obtained from the classical cinema's use of "invisible" matches on action.

In spite of the obvious limitations of this wave of deconstruction (the impression of reality cannot be reduced to perspective or the fluidity of shot changes), these critics were valuable in reactivating discussions on the impression of reality and idealist conceptions of the cinema. They also avoided two potential pitfalls: first, the exclusivity of content (the reduction of a film's meaning to explicit ideological themes); and second, the threat of formalism (considering the signification process to be autonomous in relation to any content or ideology).

This reflection upon the impression of reality in cinema must be considered in all its ramifications, such as its technological, physiological, and psychological determinations, as they relate to a system of representation and its accompanying ideology. Such reflection remains pertinent today to the extent that, on the one hand, it allows us to dismantle the notion, still widely held, that the cinema is transparent and neutral in relation to reality. On the other hand, this discussion remains fundamental in understanding the functioning and control of the cinematic institution, conceived as a social machine for representation.

Having said all this, we must note that this consideration of the cinema's impression of reality has partially covered over the attention that the spectator pays to the film image's "lack of reality," which is another fundamental, yet not necessarily contradictory, aspect of the cinema. It is partly because the image oscillates between a "full" representation (representing something in a realistic manner) and the extreme transience of its material (shadows and flashes) that it fascinates and holds the audience. The image demands that the spectator be more than a simple witness, but also someone who strongly invokes the "represented," since s/he is already convinced of the representation's minimal consistency.

4 | CINEMA AND LANGUAGE

FILM LANGUAGE

The preceding chapters have made little reference to the notion of film language, and admittedly that absence may appear rather paradoxical. Indeed, the concept of film language stands at the intersection of all the problems that an aesthetics of the cinema poses, and has posed, since its beginning. The notion of a film language has served strategically to propose the cinema's existence as a means of artistic expression. In order to prove that film was a true art form, it was first necessary to provide it with a specific language that was different from that of literature or theater.

Granting film a language, however, risked fixing its structures and slipping from the level of language to that of a static grammar. Thus, the use of "language" with reference to cinema gave way to a multitude of misunderstandings simply because of the imprecise nature of the term. These misunderstandings have, unfortunately, marked the trail of the history of film theory right up to the present, as can be witnessed in such labels as "cinelanguage," "film grammar," "cinestylistics," and "film rhetoric."

Moreover, the theoretical stakes of these debates are far from academic. The entire issue involves understanding how cinema functions as a means of signification as compared to other languages and expressive systems. Thus, film theorists must constantly struggle to oppose any attempt at assimilating film language with verbal language. But if the cinema functions very differently from verbal language, as almost everyone concedes, is it necessarily a "language of reality," as Pier Paolo Pasolini describes it? In other words, is the cinema deprived of any instance of language; and, if not, is it possible to specify any such instance without stumbling ineluctably onto the mistaken path of normative grammar?

An Ancient Notion

The expression "film language" not only appears before the application of semiology to the cinema, but even predates Marcel Martin's *Le Langage cinématographique,* originally published in 1955. References to film language can be found in the work of the cinema's first theorists, Ricciotto Canudo and Louis Delluc, as well as in writings on cinema by the Russian formalists. For French aestheticians in particular, it was important to contrast the cinema with verbal language by defining film as a new means of expression. In fact, this opposition between the cinema and verbal language is central to Abel Gance's manifesto "The Music of Light":

> I continue to argue that words no longer contain truth in our contemporary society. Prejudices, morality, chance, and physiological depreciation have all stolen away the true significance of the spoken word. . . . It was thus necessary to be silent for a long time in order to forget the ancient, worn, and obsolete words, even the most beautiful of which no longer leave their mark. Only then could we allow the entrance of the tremendous influx of modern forces and learning, so as finally to find the new language. The cinema was born of this necessity. . . . As in the formal tragedies of the eighteenth century, it became necessary to assign strict rules, or an international grammar, to future films. Only by being encased in such a corset of technical difficulties could the geniuses finally break forth.[1]

The essential characteristic of this new language was its universality, permitting one to bypass the barriers posed by the various national languages. It seemed to realize the ancient dream of a "visual Esperanto." As Louis Delluc writes in *Cinéma et Cie,* "The cinema goes everywhere and is a great means of allowing people to converse." Hence, this "music of light" need not be translated since it is understood by everyone and allows the return to a sort of "natural" state of language, preceding the arbitrariness of language systems:

> The Cinema, by multiplying the human meaning of *expression by the image* (a meaning that Painting and Sculpture had before maintained for us), will form a truly universal language system

out of characters that are still beyond suspicion. As such, it will be necessary for it to redirect all the "figuration" of life, which is to say art, toward the sources of all emotion, searching all the while for life within itself via movement. . . . New, young, and proceeding cautiously, it seeks out its own voice and words. And it brings us, with all our acquired psychological complexity, to the great language which is true, primordial, synthetic: visual language, outside the analysis of sounds.[2]

Most important here is that Canudo, Delluc, and Gance are, above all else, critics or filmmakers. Their perspective is a promotional one since they want to prove the complexity of film. They baptize cinema "the seventh art" and undertake a qualitative overvaluation, complete with a campaign that systematically proclaims cinema's distinct boundaries. As Canudo writes, "Do not search for analogies between cinema and theater. There are none." For him, cinema is the total art form toward which all other arts have strived. Similarly, Gance writes, "the language of images that leads us toward the ideography of primitive writing is not yet in focus, because our eyes are not made for it."

In a strict sense, of course, none of these claims involve a serious attempt at theorizing the cinema. While the allusions to language do in fact sound prophetic, they are also deliberately metaphorical. Thus, it will eventually prove more fruitful to look toward Béla Balázs and the Soviet theorists for the first substantive foundations of a reflection upon the cinema as language.

Nonetheless, while confining our discussion to the French realm for the moment, the drive toward a theorization of the cinema is quite evident in the writings of Jean Epstein, author of a great many aesthetic essays that continually champion the need for the formation of a true "philosophy" of the cinema. In *Bonjour, cinéma* (1921), he announces, "The philosophy of cinema is still to be accomplished."[3] Most importantly, Epstein takes up Louis Delluc's notion of *photogénie*: "I will label as possessing *photogénie* every aspect of things, beings, or souls that gains in moral quality by its cinematic reproduction. Similarly, any aspect that is not enhanced by the cinematic reproduction lacks *photogénie* and does not belong to cinematic art."

It is quite obvious here that the normative perceptive still reigns supreme. Moreover, Epstein's philosophy involves more of an aesthetic of the auteur or a poetics of film creation than a general theorization.

The language of images in the silent cinema of the 1920s: *The Last Laugh* (F. W. Murnau, 1924). *Faust* (F. W. Murnau, 1926).

L'Inhumaine (Marcel L'Herbier, 1924). *Fall of the House of Usher* (Jean Epstein, 1928).

The birth of film aesthetics during an epoch when cinema was silent is not without consequences for the most commonly held conceptions concerning film expression. Cinema remains above all an art of the image, while its other elements (dialogue, written words, sound effects, and music) must accept its priority. The most "cinematic" silent films, according to these criteria, were those that completely did without the written language of intertitles, such as *The Last Laugh* (F. W. Murnau, 1924). In such films the characters must be made to speak as little as possible, which obviously limits their choice of subject matter and situations. However, these constraints posed fewer problems for "avant-garde documentaries." The label "pure cinema" has often been applied to films without intertitles in order to designate clearly their originality.

The advent of sound greatly disturbed this unshared sovereignty of the image, but on an aesthetic plane the newcomer was perceived for a long time as an intruder who must be domesticated, and this point of view was held by directors as diverse as Chaplin and Eisenstein, as well as by many critics.

The First Theorists

There is certainly not enough space here to develop a complete history of film theories—that would require an entire volume of its own. However, before beginning a discussion of the writings of Béla Balázs and the Soviets (whose studies play a decisive role in establishing fundamental conceptions of cinematic language), we must mention Hugo Münsterberg's *The Film: A Psychological Study*, which was first printed in New York in 1916. With an insight that is both rare and intense, Münsterberg analyzes the psychological mechanisms of film perception, including problems of depth and movement, as well as the role of the spectator's attention, memory, imagination, and emotions. He also strives to define the cinema's specificity by how it causes the outside world to lose its concrete limitations: "Motion pictures, which [are] freed from the physical forms of space, time, and causality, are adjusted to the free play of our mental experiences."[4] Münsterberg concludes by claiming that cinema, more than any other art, is "destined to overcome outer nature by the free and joyful play of the mind."[5]

It was the Hungarian aesthetician Béla Balázs, however, who first undertook the direct study of film language in his essay "Der Sichtbare Mensch" (The Visible Man, 1924).

Béla Balázs developed his analyses in subsequent books, including *Theory of the Film*, first published in Moscow in 1945.

In a chapter entitled "A New Form-Language," Balázs begins with the question, "When and how did cinematography turn into a specific independent art employing methods sharply differing from those of the theater and using a totally different form-language?" He responds by listing three principles basic to the cinema but lacking in the theater:

"1. Varying distance between spectator and scene within one and the same scene; hence varying dimensions of scenes that can be accommodated within the frame and composition of a picture.

"2. Division of the integral picture of the scene into sections, or 'shots.'

"3. Montage, that is, the assembly of 'shots' in a certain order in which not only whole scene follows whole scene (however short) but pictures of smallest details are given, so that the whole scene is composed of a mosaic of frames aligned as it were in chronological sequence."[6]

The Soviet theorists and filmmakers who assembled within the VGIK (State Film School, directed by Lev Kuleshov—the first film school) would systematize this editing function. V. I Pudovkin summarizes this conception of editing: "By the junction of the separate pieces the director builds a filmic space entirely his own. He unites and compresses separate elements, that have perhaps been recorded by him at differing points of real, actual space, into one *filmic* space."[7]

Admittedly, there will be differences of analysis and even antagonistic contradictions between Pudovkin, Eisenstein, and Vertov, but they remain unanimous in their recognition of montage's dominant role since "presenting something as everyone sees it does not accomplish anything at all" (see chapter 2 for Eisenstein's conception of montage).

However, it is in *Poetika Kino*, which is a collection of five essays published in 1927 by six members of OPOYAZ (Society for the Study of Poetic Language) that the hypothesis of "cinelanguage" is most explicitly formulated. In his article "Fundamentals of the Cinema," Juri Tynianov explains that "within the cinema the visible world is presented not as is but within its semantic correlation, otherwise film would be nothing more than a living photograph. The visible man and visible object are only elements of cine-art once they become devices of the semantic sign."[8]

This "semantic correlation" is given as a stylistic transfiguration: "The correlation of characters and objects in the image, the correlation of characters between themselves, of the totality and its parts, of what it is conventional to label 'composition of the image'—the shooting angle and the perspective in which they are shot and finally lighting, all have a colossal importance." It is by the mobilization of these formal parameters that the cinema transforms its base material—the image of the visible world—into a semantic element of its own language. Tynianov also outlines a conception of the cinema which resembles that of Pasolini when he writes, "As strange as it may seem, if we establish an analogy between the cinema and the verbal arts, the only legitimate analogy will be that between cinema and poetry rather than cinema and prose."

In Boris Eichenbaum's "Problems of Cine-Stylistics," he declares that it is "impossible to consider the cinema as a completely non-verbal art. Those who wish to defend cinema from literature often forget that in film it is the audible word that is excluded and not thought, which is to say internal language."[9] According to this hypothesis, reading a film necessitates a simultaneous labor of perception, with this labor being the functioning of internal language that characterizes all thought: "Cinematic perception is a process that goes from the object, from visible movement to its interpretation, to the construction of internal language. . . . The spectator must accomplish a complex labor to connect the shots (by constructing cine-sentences and cine-punctuation)." All of this leads Eichenbaum to the following definition of film: "In the end, cinema, like all other arts, is a particular system of figurative language" (since it is often employed as a language system or *langue*). This statement assumes that any determination of whether the cinema is or is not a signifying system depends on the intentions of the user.

Nevertheless, for the Russian formalists there is only art and hence a "cinematic language system" when there is a stylistic transformation of the real world. This transformation can only intervene when allied with the use of particular expressive procedures that result from the intent to communicate a signification. "Cine-sentence," "cine-semantic," "cine-stylistic," "cine-metaphor"—all these terms indicate the general movement of extrapolation that characterizes the approach taken by these theorists. This movement will then be amplified with attempts to elaborate various film "grammars."

The Film Grammars

Film grammars were essentially developed in Western Europe after the liberation as artistic promotion of the cinema became more recognized worldwide. Thus, film was granted status as an art form possessing a language. In order to understand this language more fully, it seemed necessary to explore its principal figures. In fact, the proliferation of didactic manuals that resembled scholarly textbooks was a direct result of both the amazing proliferation of film clubs and the expansive shifts in popular education. Film, the sheer size of whose audience made it the first truly popular art, had to be explained to its large public, supposedly watching films in complete innocence, though not without intuitively following its language.

Above all, this movement is characteristic of French and Italian film theory, yet its actual initiator seems to have been Raymond J. Spottiswoode, author of *A Grammar of the Film*, first published in London in 1935. Spottiswoode's contribution was to systematize (from a rather didactic perspective) the then recent writings of Eisenstein and Rudolf Arnheim (*Film as Art*, 1932).

Spottiswoode draws up a table of analysis for film structures and a grid for the synthesis of their effects; then he separates the specific elements into optical and nonoptical, divides the latter into static and dynamic, and so forth. Yet his goal is to define the aesthetic principles that serve a "correct" cinematic language: "It is the aim of this book to make as precise as possible the language and grammar which the film, as a prospective art-form, has to acquire."[10]

In France, the two best-known writers on film grammar are certainly André Berthomieu (*Essai de grammaire cinématographique*, 1946) and Dr. Robert Bataille (*Grammaire cinématographique*, 1947). As Roger Odin has pointed out, the model used in these film grammars was constituted from the normative grammars of scholastic practice.[11] Thus, cinematic language was not being compared to a language system, but only to literature, and film language was being made to conform to the practice of the "great writers." The goal of such film grammars was to allow the acquisition of a good cinematic style or even a harmonious style by understanding the fundamental laws and fixed rules that govern film construction. These grammars supply a list of errors and serious mistakes that may be made, unless, of course, the director is trying to create a particular stylistic effect.

"For example," writes Berthomieu, "jumping from an establishing shot to a close-up may constitute a voluntary error designed to capture the spectator's attention by way of an unexpected visual shock."

Bataille's definition sums up this impulse: "Cinematic grammar studies the rules that preside over the art of correctly transmitting ideas by the succession of animated images that comprise a film."

Thus, these grammars function in the normative manner of traditional grammars of verbal language. They convey an analogous aesthetic involving transparency ("the best technique is that which is not noticed") and realism ("the image must preserve the impression of reality"), and, as we know, this aesthetic of transparency based on the invisibility of the technique plays a fundamental role in the cinema. Furthermore, the analyses of film language proposed by these grammars draw very closely from grammars of natural languages. Film grammars have, therefore, borrowed both terminology and approach: they begin with shot (as an equivalent of the word), set up a nomenclature (shot scale), specify the way they should be organized into sequences (like a cinematic sentence), and label the punctuation marks.

Nevertheless, the authors of these grammars are also very conscious of the *analogical* nature of their analyses. Robert Bataille, for instance, specifies that it is not necessary to make a precise parallel between typographical punctuation marks and optical conjunctions because the selection of one of these conjunctions does not have the same obligatory status as a punctuation mark. He is wary of assimilating the shot with the word, yet he certainly compares them: "Just as every word evokes an idea, every shot shows an idea." However, he also insists upon their differences: "The word is essentially intellectual while, by contrast, the shot is essentially physical." These oppositions are often presented in debatable terms, yet Bataille offers a definition of the shot that is less naive than it may first appear: "The shot is a visual representation of a simple idea." This definition places the shot on the level of the effect produced on the spectator, who is only expected to perceive a single idea during the shot's time on the screen. On the other hand, however, Bataille insists on the fact that the shot cannot be studied in isolation because "its role in the thought process essentially depends on the place it will occupy among other shots."

Ultimately, as Roger Odin observes, these normative grammars are no better or worse than many scholastic grammars of verbal language. It must be understood that their perspective is more stylistic than purely grammatical. While practicing an abusive metaphorization of the concepts, they occasionally contributed elements in their descriptions of film language that have served as the basis for many later analyses.

For a long time these film grammars have served as a scapegoat and have been blamed for every attempt to formalize cinematic language during the entire period dominated by Bazin's notion of transparency. At the moment, however, when more critics have become convinced of the arbitrariness of the assumptions behind the similarly normative conceptions in Bazin's theories, it is logical that researchers will once again take an interest in the elaboration of grammatical models of film language that are now based on textual linguistics.

The Classical Conception of Language

The rejection of these film grammars implies an empirical conception of film language, and it is necessary to go into details concerning film language before considering the theoretical specifications set forth by Jean Mitry and Christian Metz. Marcel Martin's book *Le Langage cinématographique* can serve here as a useful point of reference for outlining this "indigenous" conception of film language as it existed before the application of semiotics to the issue.

Strangely enough, one does not find a very unified definition of film language in Martin's introduction; he only confronts it directly in the work's conclusion. Martin ties the appearance of film language to the gradual discovery of the processes of film expression. For him, as will be the case for Mitry and Metz, film language was constituted historically by the artistic contributions of filmmakers like Griffith and Eisenstein. Thus, the cinema was not gifted from the start with a language; instead it began as the mere recording of an already existing spectacle or as the simple reproduction of reality. Only when the cinema wanted to tell stories and convey ideas did it perfect a whole array of expressive techniques. For these theorists, film language constitutes the collection of these techniques.

Film language, therefore, is doubly determined: first, by history, then second, by narrativity. This conclusion amounts to claiming that primitive films have no language and that non-narrative films also lack a language, or if they do have one then it must be structurally identical to that of narrative films. Christian Metz shares this position in his earliest articles when, for example, he writes, "A film by Fellini differs from an American Navy film—made to teach the art of tying knots to new recruits—through its talent and through its intention and not through its most intimate semiological workings. Purely vehicular films are made in the same way others are."[12] As we will see later, Metz completely changes positions in *Language and Cinema*.

This classical conception of language also presupposes two other hypotheses—one equates language with traditional film language, the other completely dilutes the instance of the language act, thus making cinema the locus for the direct apprehension of the real. The former hypothesis is the more rigorous interpretation, while the latter may be considered the more casual approach.

TRADITIONAL FILM LANGUAGE.   While it seemed strategically decisive to the pioneers of film theory that they affirm film language's existence, such an acknowledgment has certainly generated caution ever since. For instance, Marcel Martin could not refrain from mentioning that "the concept of language is fairly ambiguous when applied to the cinema. Is it necessary to see what I have labeled the grammatical and linguistic arsenal as essentially connected to the processes of film expression?"[13] Earlier in his book, Martin stated that when "cinema-language" confines itself to being a simple conveyor of ideas and emotions, it ends up internalizing the seeds of its own destruction as an art form by becoming a means that no longer contains its own purpose. It is here that Martin notices that traditional film language is capable of disguising any real instance of language: "Far too often traditional film language appears as a sort of childhood disease of the cinema, especially when it limits itself to being a collection of prescriptions, processes, and devices that anyone may use, and which are automatically guaranteed to provide clarity and efficiency to the narrative while simultaneously supplying its artistic purpose." This conclusion leads Martin to write about films that are "impeccably efficient on the level of language usage, but completely worthless from an aesthetic point of view or in terms of their really being filmic."[14]

It should be obvious from Martin's use of the term "language" that there is a slippage operating between the level of pure language and that of style. This confusion becomes even more noticeable when he writes about "*cinema-language* being overtaken by *cinema-being*." While Martin is indeed correct in mentioning that most important contemporary directors have practically abandoned the entire grammatical and linguistic arsenal that he lists and analyzes, he nonetheless makes a mistake in concluding that it is the language that has actually aged and become outdated. Instead, what has evolved is the directors' stylistic selection, such as the dominant shooting conventions that characterize a given film period. Martin himself raises the issue later in his book when he writes, "In order to avoid any ambiguity we should give preference to the concept of *style* rather than language."[15]

TOWARD A DISAPPEARANCE OF LANGUAGE? By reducing film language to a list of narrative and expressive processes, however, and

Toward a disappearance of language? *The Eclipse* (Michelangelo Antonioni, 1962).

The Red Desert (Michelangelo Antonioni, 1964).

then freezing it forever in the form of such a list, we risk denying the very existence of film language, or at least making its importance merely relative. Moreover, this gradual bypassing of language in its traditional sense in favor of "the sublimation of writing [*écriture*]" results in a confirmation of the Bazinian theory of transparency that we outlined in chapter 2. When the role of film language is minimized, film ceases to be language and spectacle and becomes instead style and contemplation. As a result, that which appears on the movie screen once again becomes similar to whatever was filmed, since "découpage and editing are decreasingly playing their usual role of analysis and reconstruction of the real." According to this Bazinian interpretation, the spectator is no longer the prisoner of this découpage and analytical editing, and thus the viewers find themselves once again "before a window from which they participate in events that have all the appearances of objectivity and reality, events whose existence seems to be completely independent of that of the audience."

Here it becomes obvious that the classical definition of language, with all its internal distortion and hesitation, can only hinder any real consideration of film language's status within the cinema. Instead we need to mobilize the linguistic-semiotic approach, enlarge the notion of language, and then, in as precise a manner as possible, confront it with what film language is *not*, in order to give support to all the desired clarifications within this traditional debate.

A Language without Signs

Credit must be given to Jean Mitry for having both reaffirmed the existence of film language and expanded its base, all within the third chapter of *Esthétique et psychologie du cinéma*. Mitry begins with the traditional conception of the cinema as a means of expression in order to add quickly that a means of expression like the cinema must be a language: "Any means of expression capable of organizing, constructing, and communicating thoughts, or which can develop ideas able to change, take form, and transform, thus becomes a language, and *is* what we know as a language." Mitry continues, defining the cinema as "an aesthetic form (like literature), that employs an *image* that is, in and of itself, a *means of expression* whose sequence (which is to say its logical and dialectic organization) is a *language*."[16]

This definition is important in that it places the emphasis on the cinema's signifying material (here the image in its largest sense) while it also stresses its sequential nature. Both of these traits are characteristic of a language. For Mitry, language is a system of signs and symbols (thus he begins from a very Saussurean stance), and this system allows the designation of things by naming them, the signification of ideas, and the translation of thoughts. Further on Mitry specifies that it is not necessary to reduce language to the only medium that allows the exchange of conversation, that is, verbal language. He explains that verbal language is only one particular form of a very general phenomenon. There is in fact a film language, even if it is based on significations that spring from "the reproduction of the concrete real," which is to say the analogical reproduction of the visual and audio real, rather than the conventional abstract figures of verbal language.

It was quite clear to Mitry that the error of previous theorists—an error underlying the dominant conception of film language—rests in the fact that those theorists posed verbal language *a priori* as the exclusive form of language. Hence, they concluded that, since film language is necessarily quite different from verbal language, film language is *not* a language at all.

> Mitry clearly summarizes the dialectic involved in the elaboration of film language out of its representation of the image of things: "Obviously a film is something very different from a system of signs and symbols. At least it does not present itself *exclusively* as such a system. A film is *first* of all images, and images *of something*. It is a system of images whose goal is to describe, develop, and narrate an event or a sequence of various events. However, depending upon the chosen narrational strategy, these images *are* organized into a system of signs and symbols; they become symbols or may become symbols in addition. Thus, unlike words, the images are not uniquely signs, rather they are first objects or concrete reality and as such they are objects that take on (or are given) a definite meaning. In other words, the cinema *becomes* language in that it is *first* a representation, but becomes meaningful under cover of these same representations. Film is, if you will, a language in the second degree."[17]

Mitry's theoretical positions thus allow him to avoid a potential contradiction between film as a representation of the real and as a language. He clearly demonstrates film language's level of existence by insisting on the fact that, even while the cinema is a representation of the real, it is nonetheless not a simple copy of the world. Hence, the freedom of the filmmaker in creating a pseudo-world or universe similar to the real one does not contradict the existence or process of language. Instead, it is language that allows film creation to be accomplished at all.

Every film requires both combination and arrangement, yet these two activities in no way imply an alignment with conventional linguistic structures. Instead, film's importance derives precisely from its insistent proposition that it is a new type of language and is thus different from verbal language. Hence, film language clearly distinguishes itself from spoken language. The semiological undertaking that was initiated by Christian Metz endeavors to measure the disparities and areas of possible agreement between spoken and film language, and all this with a level of precision never before known in the field of film theory.

THE CINEMA: LANGUAGE OR LANGUAGE SYSTEM?

As mentioned earlier, one occasionally finds the term "cinelanguage system" rolling off the pens of certain film aestheticians. For instance, filmmaker and theorist Jean Epstein spoke of film as a universal language. Empirical use of the concept of film language leads to the confusion between the two levels of language: grammatical and stylistic. In fact, the main conclusion that can be drawn from our preceding sidetrip through the history of film language is surely that most of the treatises devoted to cinematic language are actually just catalogues of the dominant figures in whatever film *écriture* or "writing style" typifies a certain period in film history.

A great number of historians and theorists, right up to Jean Mitry, have tried to connect the terms "means of expression," "language," and even "language system" with film. Yet they have done so without ever appealing directly to the study of language itself. In other words, they tried to sidestep *linguistics*.

By contrast, the point of departure for Christian Metz's work is based on a very different assumption: the cinema is postulated as a language, yet it is immediately studied as a verbal language system. Inspired as he is by the fundamental tripartition of Saussurean linguistics in which language is understood as the sum of the verbal language system and speech-act, Metz details the status of cinematic language by contrasting it with the traits characterizing a language system [*langue*]. The result is an attempt at a negative description that defines everything that film language *is not*.

This confrontational approach can be found primarily in the third chapter of *Film Language*, "The Cinema: Language System or Language?"[18] This essay originally appeared in the French review *Communications* 4

(1964) along with Roland Barthes's famous essay "Elements of Semiology," which pointed the direction for semiological studies during the rest of that decade.

Semiology, which Ferdinand de Saussure defines as a "science that studies the life of signs within society,"[19] would entail the study of various language systems and has still never been fully developed, at least not as of this date. Semiology may be summarized as the application of the processes of analysis originating in linguistics to other languages. Hence, it managed to provoke a great number of disputes in a number of different fields. For instance, during its initial phase (1964–1970), semiology was primarily preoccupied with the narrative aspects of languages in order to move in the direction of the study of enunciation and discourse. During this period, French literary studies by Gérard Genette, Claude Brémond, and Tzvetan Todorov were particularly influential.

During the next stage, Metz's articles in *Film Language* (which is a translation of parts of his two-volume *Essais sur la signification au cinéma*) began to direct these discussions toward the specific problems posed by film narration. His *Language and Cinema* (originally published in France in 1971) marks a radical new phase in linguistic-inspired methodology by directly applying concepts from Danish linguist Louis Hjelmslev's *Prolegomena to a Theory of Language*. It was only by Metz's gradual progression from working on film devices to working on the spectator that the linguistic heritage was further complemented by the psychoanalytic illumination that gained more and more acceptance after his *Imaginary Signifier* (1974).

In fact, it is not really possible to draw up a unified chart of semiology because it has had to adapt itself differently for every field of study. If, for instance, one can recognize a certain degree of homogeneity within literary studies, the semiology of painting (exemplified in the work of Louis Marin) or music (as in Jean-Jacques Nattiez's writings) has little or nothing in common with the writings of Metz,[20] save an initial body of reference works that has then been retooled for each discipline.

Film Language and Language System(s)

In his *Course in General Linguistics*, Saussure begins by distinguishing "language system [*langue*]" from "language [*langage*]." He explains that *langue* is only a specific part of *langage*: "*Langage* is both a social product of the faculty of speech and a collection of necessary conventions. . . . *Langue*, on the contrary, is a self-contained whole and a principle of classification. . . . *Speaking*, on the contrary, is an individual act. It is willful and intellectual."[21]

**THE MULTIPLICITY OF LANGUAGE SYSTEMS AND THE UNITY OF FILM
LANGUAGE.** The fact is that "language system" is multiple by definition since a great number of different language systems exist. If,
however, films can differ greatly from one country to another because of variations in their sociocultural modes of representation, it
should nevertheless be obvious that each cultural community cannot be said to possess its own cinematic language. It is precisely the
vast nature of film language that allowed the notion of cinema as
"visual Esperanto" to grow up in the first place, particularly during
the silent era.

Admittedly, the sound cinema records every specific verbal language via the words of the characters; yet when cinematic language
is considered at a global level we do not find film systems that are
as organized and different from one another as those of each verbal
language system.

> During the cinema's silent era written language was presented in the
> form of intertitles that could be quite numerous. Yet in films with no
> intertitles writing nonetheless intervened right on the photographic im-
> age. Thus, when the doorman is fired in F. W. Murnau's *The Last Laugh*
> (1924), the manager hands him a letter of dismissal that is shot as an
> insert. In another film with no intertitles, Dziga Vertov's *Man with a
> Movie Camera* (1929), a number of words from posters, slogans, and signs
> invade the film. Within Godard's films as well, one can see the same
> profusion of written letters, from advertising posters to frames from
> comic strips to the extreme close-ups of a newspaper being read by Fer-
> dinand in *Pierrot le fou* (1965). Nonetheless, this diversity of language
> systems inserted within the films does not challenge the larger unity of
> cinematic language per se.

LANGUAGE, COMMUNICATION, AND THE PERMUTATION OF POLES. A
natural language system allows the continual permutation of the
poles "speaker" and "listener," since each may change roles during
a conversation. The cinema, however, does not allow this exchange
of speaking roles since one cannot directly enter into dialogue with
a film, except perhaps in a very metaphorical sense. In order to "respond" the spectator must produce an entirely different discursive
message that will always have to be produced *after* the appearance
of the initial film message. In this way cinema differentiates itself
radically from verbal communication. Moreover, this distinction
certainly has many consequences for any of the cinema's social uses
that may require immediate communicative exchanges, such as propaganda or instructional use.

Writing within the filmic image: top, *The Cabinet of Dr. Caligari* (Robert Wiene, 1919); middle and bottom, *October* (S. M. Eisenstein, 1927).

The Blue Angel
(Josef von Stern-
berg, 1930).

Hôtel du Nord
(Marcel Carné,
1938).

Citizen Kane
(Orson Welles,
1941).

The Maltese Falcon
(John Huston,
1941).

In the cinema the space of the actual enunciation is always radically heterogeneous to that of the spectator, which is why direct address to the spectator can never be anything more than mimetic and illusory. The spectator can never respond to a character, even if the address involves a commentator who speaks directly without any fictional relay. The television apparatus, by contrast, functions differently in the case of direct address since there is simultaneity between the emission and reception, and there is also the possibility of a communicative exchange by the intervention of the receiver (especially in the case of two-way cable systems).

In the theater, however, the actors and the public share the same space and time, only being separated by a conventional boundary. Yet the boundary imposed by the movie screen, as Metz points out, is completely hermetic: "Whether or not the theatrical play mimes a fable, its *action*, if need be mimetic, is still managed by real persons evolving in real time and space, *on the same stage or 'scene' as the public.* . . . At the theater, Sarah Bernhardt may tell me she is Phèdre or, if the play were from another period and rejected the figurative regime, she might say, as in a type of modern theater, that she is Sarah Bernhardt. But at any rate I should see Sarah Bernhardt. At the cinema, she could make the two kinds of speeches too, but it would be her shadow that would be offering them to me (or she would be offering them in her own absence).[22]

THE ANALOGICAL ASPECT OF FILM LANGUAGE. When theorist Jean Mitry insists on the fact that film is first and foremost images, he is privileging the analogical aspect of cinematic language. In fact, the fundamental signifying material in the cinema, which is obviously the image but also recorded sound, presents itself as a "double" of reality or as actual mechanical duplication. Translating this into more linguistic terms, we could say that the relationship between the signifier and signified of the sync-sound image is strongly *motivated* by resemblance.

By contrast, there is no analogical connection between the acoustic signifier and its signified; nor is there a strict relation between the phonetic sound of verbal language and whatever it signifies, at least not beyond the strict case of onomatopoeia.

Obviously, it is this analogical relation between signifier and signified that allows the existence of all the theories that define cinema as a *direct* reproduction of reality without any language or arbitrary code system as intermediary. However, "analogy" should not be seen as the opposite of "arbitrary," but rather as a specific form of motivation, even if, in the case of the film image, it is an unusually faithful form of motivation.

As Marcel Martin writes, "Who would not be struck by the degree to which the cinema becomes essential at this stage of the research on the perfect language? With film, in effect, the beings and things themselves appear or speak; there is no middle term between them and us and hence the exchange is direct. The sign and the thing signified are one and the same."[23]

LINEARITY AND THE EXISTENCE OF DISCRETE UNITS. One thing that characterizes our perception of a film is the linearity of its movement. In fact, the impression of continuity created by this linear movement is basic to the grasp film exercises over the audience. As a result, viewers never have the impression that they are actually perceiving various discontinuous units. Nevertheless, as Metz has noted, there exist a number of "differential" units at the heart of cinematic language. These units are equivalent to the discrete units in linguistics; the traditional definition of such units is that they have the property of being meaningful (or valuable) only in their presence or absence or in their being markedly similar or different in relation to one another. It is obvious, therefore, that these discrete units as they exist in cinematic language are quite distinct from those of a language system.

A discrete unit is always differential within a particular code, as we will see later, and in fact it is *only* so within this code. In the case of film, what distinguishes these differential units is that they are intimately connected to the first level of film signification, or that signification created by the photographic analogy. As a result, these units do not appear to be the discontinuous, discrete units that they in fact are.

"Even with respect to the significant units, the cinema is initially deprived of discrete elements. It proceeds by whole 'blocks of reality,' which are actualized with their total meaning in the discourse. These blocks are the 'shots.'"[24]

It has become common to try to define the minimal unit of cinematic language by way of the shot. Such research, however, is built on the confusion between language and code. A distinct unit never belongs to a language, but instead belongs to a code: the shot may thus be considered the unit of the code of editing, while the individual photographic frame will be the unit of the technological code for reproducing movement. Most distinguishing cinematic codes intervene independently of the borders of the shot, whether they be smaller than the shot, as in color codes, or larger units, such as narrative codes.

Such studies of the distinguishing units of film language proceed by the double criticism of the notion of "cinematic sign" and of the shot as language unit. (These issues are discussed in detail by Metz in both *Film Language* and chapter 9 of *Language and Cinema*.)

THE PROBLEM OF ARTICULATIONS WITHIN FILM.   The most extreme difference between film language and natural languages lies in the fact that cinema offers nothing resembling linguistic double articulation. Double articulation, however, plays a central role in the mechanics of natural language.

Linguistic double articulation is the means by which the arbitrariness of language establishes itself and even structures the relation of signification, allowing for the phonetic chain to be segmented into two groups of units. The first level of units includes the significant units, or morphemes, each of which possesses a signified that belongs to it alone. The second sort, the distinctive units, or phonemes, do not have their own unique signified; instead they serve to distinguish the significant units from one another.

One will not find this same sort of two-tiered segmentation with cinematic language, yet this is not to deny that the cinema has any articulation. In "The Cinema: Language or Language System," Metz proposes that the total cinematic message "brings five main levels of codification into play, each one of which would be a kind of articulation." His five levels include the following:

(1) Perception itself . . . to the degree that it already constitutes a system of acquired intelligibility, which varies according to different "cultures";

(2) Recognition of and identification of visual or auditive objects appearing on the screen. . . .

(3) All the "symbolisms" and connotations of various kinds that attach themselves to objects (or to relationships between objects) outside of films—that is to say, in culture;

(4) All the great narrative structures . . .

(5) The set of properly cinematographic systems that, in a specific type of discourse, organize the diverse elements furnished to the spectator by the four preceding instances.[25]

In writing about visual codes, Umberto Eco proposes his own hypothesis on articulation in the cinema. He asserts that film language may have a triple articulation.

"It seems to me that the only instance of third articulation can be found in cinematographic language. Suppose (even if it is not that simple) that in a cinematographic frame there are visual nonsignificant light phenomena (*figurae*) whose combination produces visual significant phenomena (let us call them 'images' or 'icons' or 'super-signs'). And suppose that this mutual relationship relies on a double articulation mechanism."[26]

According to Eco, these "discrete kinesic *figurae*" are low-level, potentially significant units of kinesic signs. He claims that everyday life also has these tiny figures, yet only a motion picture camera can isolate them fully. Nonetheless, Eco adds that "kinesic *figurae* are indeed significant from the point of view of an 'iconic' language (i.e. they are significant when considered as photographs) but are not significant at all from the point of view of kinesic languages."[27]

What these citations reveal is that articulation is actually a very general concept forged by linguistics, but only the specifically linguistic form of double articulation via morphemes and phonemes is tied to the code of natural language. Yet other forms of articulation certainly exist and can be applied with some degree of success to film code systems.

Film's Intelligibility

If a language system [*langue*] is one of the internal codes of language (and certainly the most structured code), and if the language system is the code that establishes the relation of signification by double articulation, then it follows that certain aspects of cinematic perception must exist that permit the spectator to "read" and understand a film. It is precisely the existence of these traits that justifies our use of the term "language." It is Metz who has most carefully distinguished the question of film language.

"Contrary to what many of the theoreticians of the silent film declared or suggested . . . the cinema is certainly not a language system [*langue*]. It can, however, be considered as a *language*, to the extent that it orders signifying elements within ordered arrangements different from those of spoken idioms—and to the extent that these elements are not traced on the perceptual configurations of reality itself (which does not tell stories). Film manipulation transforms what might have been a mere visual transfer of reality into discourse."[28]

"As soon as there are substitutes for objects that are more mobile and more workable than the objects themselves (and which are also, perhaps, *closer to thought* than the referent objects), and once these substitutes are organized into a discursive continuity, then a language is present, in spite of all its differences from verbal language."[29]

The intelligibility of film passes through three principal instances:
—the perceived analogy;
—the codes of iconic designation that serve in naming objects and sounds;
—and third, the signifying figures that are specific to the cinema (or the specialized codes that constitute cinematic language in the strict sense). These figures structure the two preceding groups of codes by functioning above the photographic and phonographic analogy.

This complex and overlapping articulation between the cultural codes and the specialized codes has a function homologous to that of language, without, of course, being perfectly analogous to it. Hence, it is a sort of functional equivalent to language.

THE PERCEPTUAL ANALOGY.   Vision and hearing cannot identify an object based on the totality of its perceptible sphere. For example, we recognize a flower in a black and white photograph because its color does not constitute a pertinent trait of its identification. Furthermore, we understand someone speaking to us on the telephone in spite of the narrow audio range used by the mode of transmission. Similarly, all the visual objects reproduced on film are visible in spite of the absence of the third dimension, depth; their flatness poses no major problem of identification. In practice, visual as well as audio recognition is based on certain of an object's perceptible traits (or certain traits in its image), to the exclusion of others.

This phenomenon explains how very schematic representations of objects, wherein most of their discernible traits have been deliberately suppressed, may be just as recognizable as representations that are much more complete on the level of their physical reality. Furthermore, the traits retained by a successful schematic sketch correspond precisely with what Umberto Eco labels the pertinent traits of codes of recognition. Various degrees of schematization also exist, which is to say, there are different proportions of pertinent traits of recognition and, inversely, varying degrees of resemblance or iconicity. For example, the film image has a higher degree of iconicity than does the television image.

There are also a number of counterexamples whose mere existence serves to illustrate this mechanism. For instance, a black and white photographic reproduction of an object whose color is one of its criteria of identification will break the code of recognition. Similarly, an absence of three-dimensionality can also interfere with the perception of the actual size of some objects, such as a hill, when represented in the cinema.

Schematization aside, it is only because certain perceptible traits alone may allow identification that visual manifestations, which are different in every other respect, can be perceived as multiple examples of the same object, and not as distinctly varied objects. As we wrote earlier about the referent, the photographic image of a cat does not have as its referent the specific cat that was filmed, but rather the entire category of cats. In this example, the spectators immediately select the pertinent traits of recognition (which include size, fur, shape of ears, etc.), but they do not have to consider hair color as a characteristic for basic recognition.

As a result, we can see that "schematization" is a mental perceptive principle that extends far beyond the field of the schema alone, in the current usage of the term. The most concrete vision is in fact a process of classification. The film or photographic image is not readable, or hence intelligible, unless one recognizes objects. Moreover, one must recognize objects, that is, sort them into some classification in such a way that the cat as a concept (which is not explicitly present in the image) may be reintroduced by the spectator's vision.

This question of visual analogy and resemblance is a standard issue in theories of the plastic arts and in the sociology of painting. Pierre Francastel in particular has shown that people do not judge the same images as equal likenesses during all eras or in all places.[30] Images are informed by very diverse systems, some of which are clearly iconic, while others appear just as well from nonvisual messages, as Erwin Panofsky's "iconology" has demonstrated.

Within the field of semiotics, it is mainly Eco who has analyzed this phenomenon. By way of illustration, we will cite his classic example in which we identify a zebra in contrast to a horse by perceiving the appropriate "recognition codes": "If at the zoo we see a zebra in the distance, the elements which we recognize immediately (and remember) are its stripes, and not its profile, which vaguely resembles that of an ass or mule. . . . But let us suppose that there exists an African community where the only known quadrupeds are the zebra and the hyena, and where horses, asses, and mules are unknown. It is no longer necessary to see stripes in order to recognize the zebra . . . and when drawing a zebra, it would be more important to emphasize the shape of its muzzle and length of its legs in order to distinguish it from the hyena (which also has stripes, so that the stripes no longer constitute a differentiating factor)."[31]

Despite the very high level of iconicity proper to the cinema's signifiers, it just so happens that the initial comprehension of audiovisual elements is equally assured by the collection of these basic codes of analogy. These latter codes permit the recognition of audible and visible objects that only appear in films thanks to the very resemblance that they themselves make possible.

CODES OF ICONIC DESIGNATION. The codes of iconic designation were labeled by Metz in the wake of Eco's iconic analyses and Greimas's semantic analyses. As such, they concern the process of "designation" or the act of naming visual objects.[32] Hence, a person's vision selects the object's pertinent traits, thereby assimilating the object with a social classification. Every recognized visual object is thereby named with the aid of a lexical unit, which, in most instances, is a word.

This designation, which seems to function by a correspondence between objects and the words that designate or label them, is actually a very complex process that relates the distinctive visual traits to the distinctive semantic features or traits. Designation is a process of transcoding between these traits, but it is also a selection of any traits that are considered pertinent and the corresponding elimination of all those considered to be irrelevant. The concept of a pertinent semantic trait corresponds to the notion of sememe, defined by Greimas as the signified of a single acceptance of a lexeme. For example, the sememe "woman" is composed of a number of meaningful semes such as individual, female, adult. As Metz writes in "The Perceived and the Named,"

Each *sememe* (specific unit on the level of the signified) outlines an entire class of cases rather than any single occurrence. For example, thousands of "trains" exist, even with the unique sense of a "railroad train," and they each differ greatly from one another in respect to their color, height, number of cars, etc. However, the cultural taxonomy, which includes the language system, has decided to consider these variations irrelevant and instead assumes that they all belong to the same object or class of objects. The language system has also decided that other variations would indeed be pertinent and hence sufficient to "change the object," as would be the variant between riding on rails and riding on rubber tires.[33]

Due to the specific nature of the language system, this transcoding process is accompanied by another relation that Metz labels the "metacoding" operation. A metacode is a code that is used to study another code, just as a metalanguage is a language to study other languages. The language system [langue] is the only language in a position as universal metalanguage because it must necessarily be used to analyze all other languages. Thus, the language system occupies a privileged position since it alone can say what all the other codes are saying (even if it is occasionally only an approximate process).

As a result, the language system does much more than translate vision or simply "verbalize" it, thereby translating it into a different signifier on the same level. Rather, designation concludes perception insofar as it translates perception, and thus an insufficiently verbalized perception is not fully "perception" at all in the social sense of the word.

If, for example, I think of an object that I know very well yet which I cannot manage to sketch on a piece of paper, people will consider me incompetent at drawing. If, however, this same object is drawn on a piece of paper but I cannot recall the word to name it, people will think that I have not understood the sketch and that I do not know what it represents. In Truffaut's *Wild Child* (1969), Dr. Itard struggles to teach the boy to name the daily objects he handles: a pair of scissors, a key, etc. Since the child lacks the language system's code, it is his capacity for visual identification that is actually being put to the test.

These codes illustrate the narrow interdependent bond that unites visual perception and the use of a verbal lexicon. Hence, it is these codes that continue to relativize the opposition between the visual language and the language system, making more explicit the language system's role at the interior of perception.

SIGNIFYING FIGURES SPECIFIC TO THE CINEMA. So far we have only considered the process of recognition in relation to a single aspect of meaning, that of literal or denotative meaning. However, the codes of designation do not themselves account for all the meanings that a figurative image can produce.

Literal meaning is also produced by other codes. For example, editing may simultaneously combine the relations between objects and the internal composition of an image—even in a single image. It should be understood that in a film an object may always be presented several seconds after some other object, or, by contrast, two objects may always be shown together. In either case the placement goes beyond a simple identification of the objects; instead their association by sequence or simultaneity becomes meaningful.

In Vincente Minnelli's *Some Came Running* (1959) the gambler Bama, played by Dean Martin, never removes his hat; he claims the hat brings him luck. This systematic co-presence of the hat and character certainly serves more functions than simply identifying the character. In fact, the hat connotes the unconventional lifestyle Bama leads—he is something of a contemporary cowboy—and reinforces his refusal to submit to any social or even personal compromises. Moreover, he clings to the hat even in the hospital when he refuses to change his lifestyle to prolong his life. Bama only removes it in the very last scene during the burial of the "fallen woman," Ginny Moorhead. Thus, when he finally takes off his hat at the funeral of Ginny, whom he had earlier mocked and criticized, we learn that Bama is deeply moved.

The denotative meaning produced by the figurative analogy is thus the base material of film language, becoming the foundation upon which film superimposes its combinations and specific organizations. These combinations may be present within the image in the form of framing, camera movements, and lighting effects, or they may involve the relations between images produced by editing. While it may be easier to believe that such signifying arrangements would add secondary meaning to the denotation in the form of connotation, if they add anything at all, they do participate very directly in the production of meaning.

Films are almost always composed of many series of shots that deliver only partial glimpses of the fictional referents they are assumed to represent.

The actual "Hôtel du Nord" of Marcel Carné's film of the same name (1938), would then be an outside facade, an establishing shot of the front lobby, a high-angle shot down the staircase, a shot inside one room, a medium close-up of a window shot from the outside, etc. It is by this sort of film articulation that denotation is constructed and organized. Such assemblage does not obey fixed rules but does respond to dominant uses of materials from film intelligibility. These conventional uses will vary according to the period and will even define historical modes of film découpage.

It should be noted that these principal signifying configurations were begun in the very early 1900s as filmmakers strove to develop

Shot 37   Shot 42
Shot 38   Shot 43
Shot 39   Shot 44
Shot 40   Shot 45
Shot 41   Shot 46

An example of editing alternating the character's glance (here Melanie Daniels in Alfred Hitchcock's *The Birds*, 1963) with the objects seen.

Shot 64

Shot 65

Shot 66

Shot 67

Shot 68

Shot 69

Shot 70

Shot 71

Shot 72

Shot 73

an increasingly narrative cinema, but they did not become stabilized for several decades.[34]

> "The pioneers of 'cinematographic language'—Méliès, Porter, Griffith . . . cared little about the symbolic, philosophical, or human 'message' of their films. Men of denotation rather than connotation, they wanted above all to tell a story; they were not content unless they could subject the continuous analogical material of photographic duplication to the *articulations*—however rudimentary—of narrative discourse."[35]

Thus, crosscutting was only gradually established in the years from Porter to Griffith until it could efficiently create the idea of simultaneity of two actions by the alternating succession of two series of images. The cinema's narrative ambitions had produced an intelligible schema of denotation as soon as the audience understood that from that point on an alternation of images on the screen could signify that the presented events were simultaneous within the literal, diegetic time of the fiction. This development had not yet been accomplished for Méliès's first spectators.

THE HETEROGENEITY OF FILM LANGUAGE

The pioneers of film aesthetics never ceased celebrating the cinema's originality or its complete autonomy as a means of expression. We have already emphasized the role of visual and audio analogy and also stressed the function of the language system in reading films. Yet the purely cinematic configurations involved in both processes never arise in isolation, and the image is no longer the entirety of film language. Ever since the advent of sound, we have not only had to account for the spoken word, but for sound effects and music as well.

The concept of material of expression, as defined by Louis Hjelmslev, allows us to be more precise concerning the composite character of film language—especially from the point of view of the signifier. The cinema, however, is not only heterogeneous in terms of its material, but it is also heterogeneous because of the co-presence within a film of elements specific to the cinema alongside elements that are not at all specific to the cinema.

The Materials of Expression

According to Hjelmslev, every language is characterized by either a single type of material of expression or some specific combination of materials of expression.

As the name suggests, the material of expression is the signifier's material nature, whether physical or sensory. More precisely, it may be considered the tissue within which the signifiers are set. (The term "signifier" is then reserved for the signifying *form*.)

Thus, there are languages constructed from a single material of expression and others that combine several materials. The former would be homogeneous languages according to this model, while the latter would be heterogeneous.

Music's material of expression, for example, is nonphonic sound, usually arising from instruments; however, opera's material is already less homogeneous since it adds phonic sounds in the form of singers' voices. The material of expression for painting is composed of visual signifiers and colors from quite diverse physical sources, creating a much more heterogeneous collection of signifiers.

The language of the sound film presents a particularly significant degree of heterogeneity because of its combination of five different materials. To begin with, the image track consists of two materials of expression. First, there are the multiple photographic images that are organized in a series and produce the illusion of movement. Second, film includes graphic written material that may be substituted for the analogical images, as in the case of intertitles, or may be included within the image as either subtitles or graphic figures within the shot itself.

Some silent films accord a very important status to written texts. For instance, *October* (Eisenstein, 1928) contains 270 intertitles out of the 3,225 total shots, while it also features a very high number of written statements within the images themselves in the form of banners, slogans on walls, picket signs, flags, close-ups of newspaper headlines, handbills, etc. Moreover, Carl Theodor Dreyer's *Passion of Joan of Arc* (1928) systematically alternates close-up shots of faces with intertitles featuring testimony from the ongoing trial. Similarly, there are a number of sound films that use written materials heavily: *Citizen Kane* (Welles, 1941) contains a great many inserts of headlines, election placards, and excerpts that Kane has either written or typed.

With the arrival of the sound track, cinema gained full control of three additional materials of expression: verbal language, music, and analogical sound effects. These three materials occur simultaneously with the image; it is this very simultaneity that integrates them into film language, because taken on their own these three would simply constitute another language, that of radio.

Only one of the five materials is specific to cinematic language and that, of course, is the moving image. It is because of the issue of specificity that theorists have often tried to define the essence of cinema in the image alone.

This definition of the cinema by way of physical-sensory criteria comes in response to a simple empirical approach adapted from a limited theory. Such a definition risks pushing us toward theorizing the cinema as the only system capable of accounting for all the significations located within films.

The cinema is also heterogeneous in another sense whose theoretical consequences are much more clearly decisive. There are some signifying configurations that intervene in film that require an appeal to film signifiers, but there are also other configurations within most films that are not specific to the cinema. These signifying configurations are precisely what Metz (following Hjelmslev, Greimas, and Barthes, among others) labels "codes." Because this term has indeed provoked innumerable arguments, it is essential here to clarify code before beginning discussion of the specificity within film messages.

The Concept of Code in Semiology

Throughout *Language and Cinema*, Metz calls upon an opposition between concrete ensembles (film messages) and systematic ensembles or abstract entities, which are codes. This opposition is borrowed from the work of Hjelmslev. The codes are not truly formal models, as they often are in logic, but rather units aspiring to formalization. Their homogeneity is not of a sensorial or material nature but is instead on the order of the logic of coherence, possessing an explanatory or enlightening potential. A code is understood in semiotics as a field of commutations. Within this field the variations of the signifier correspond to variations of the signified, and a certain number of units take their meaning only in relation to other member units.

In one of its original uses in information theory the word "code" (as in civil code or dress code) designates a system of either compliance or violation. In linguistics it designates the language system as a structure that is internal to language. In sociology or anthropology, "code" designates systems of behavior (as in codes of good manners) within collective representations. Moreover, within everyday language the word "code" always indicates a wide variety of systems accounting for a number of uses, such as the zip code or Morse code.

A code is therefore an associative field constructed by an analyst that reveals any logical or symbolic organization underlying a text. Hence, it is not at all necessary to see it as a *rule* or an obligatory principle.

The linguistic notion of code was extended to the study of narrative structures by Greimas and Barthes. In his textual analysis of Balzac's *Sarrasine*, Barthes isolates five codes within the text (cultural, hermeneutic, symbolic, action, and referential) while explaining that they should not be interpreted "in the rigorous scientific sense of the term since they designate associative fields and a supratextual organization of notations that impose a certain idea of structure; the instance of code is essentially cultural."[36]

A code is no longer a purely formal concept; instead it must be considered from a double perspective: first, in the sense of the analyst who constructs it and uses it in the process of structuration of a text; and second, from the perspective of the history of forms and representations, to the extent that a code is the instance by which signifying configurations previous to a given text or film are implied within it. Thus, these two different perspectives on the code are not concerned with the same "moment" of the code: one precedes the other. This abstract entity is also transformed by the work of the text and will be made implicit within an ulterior text where it will again need to be explained, and so on.

The Codes Specific to the Cinema

A substantial number of signifying configurations or codes are directly linked to a type of material of expression; in order for codes to operate, the host language must offer some material traits. For example, let us consider the code of rhythm, which would include all figures based on relations of duration. It should be obvious that such a code could only occur and function within a language that possessed a temporalized material of expression. Admittedly, one might comment upon the "rhythm" within a painting's visual composition, but this usage of the term would occur in a strictly metaphorical sense.

Thus, it follows that the number of signifying configurations that can only occur in the cinema is fairly small. These specific codes must, therefore, be linked to the cinema's particular material of expression, that is, the moving photographic image and certain forms for structuring that are unique to film. For example, "montage," in the most limited definition of the term, would be one such specific code.

Another traditional example of a specific code is camera movement. This code involves the totality of the film field of vision as it relates to the stasis of mobility that can occur within the cinematic shot. Obviously, at any moment the camera either may rest static or may follow some path of movement (vertical, horizontal, circular), or some combination of those paths. Every shot is constantly making its choices explicit by having eliminated all the figures of potential movement or stasis that are not present.

This code is specific to film because it requires the utilization of materials of cinematic technology. Unusually clear examples of the utilization of camera movement as codes specific to the cinema occur in the films of Hungarian director Miklos Jancso, especially *The Confrontation* (1969) and *Red Psalm* (1971), which are composed of very long shot sequences with lengthy traveling shots.

By contrast, the code of shot scale, which is often cited as one of the ABCs of filmmaking in manuals of cinematography, is not specific to the cinema since it also functions within the realm of still photography.

Establishing a clear opposition between specific and nonspecific codes, however, is not easy to justify. Instead, forming a hypothesis centered around the degrees of specificity is much more productive. Two poles are proposed here. First, there are the limited number of specific codes; second (as we will explain in the following section) are all the codes that are absolutely nonspecific to the cinema. Between these two poles we will outline a hierarchy of specificity based on the size of the zone of extension for each code considered.

The material of expression most characteristic of the cinema is the multiple, mechanically moving image and its placement in sequences. As we proceed toward more particular traits of this language, the degree of specificity of the code becomes proportionally pronounced.

The codes of visual analogy, for example, pertain to all figurative images; these codes, then, are only mildly specific to the cinema even though they play a central role.

"Photographic" codes linked to camera angles (framing angles), shot scale, and the clarity of focus concern all mechanical images obtained via physio-chemical technology; thus, these codes are more specific to film than broader codes of visual analogy. Furthermore, all codes involving the placement of images into sequences are still more clearly specific even though they are also valid for the *photo-roman* and the comic strip.

The only codes that are exclusively cinematic (and also televisual since the two languages are very similar) are tied to the movement of the image. Such codes would include camera movement and dynamic matches. Moreover, a figure such as the match on action is particular to the cinema and may be contrasted to other types of matches that can be approximated in comic strips.

It is also worth noting that many codes that are not at all specific to the cinema have nonetheless been extensively exploited by the cinema. For example, the opposition between a high-angle and a low-angle shot is often employed to accentuate various character traits.

There is another phenomenon that warrants our attention: the integration of a nonspecific code into a language. In such a case, the resulting consequences and the necessary transformations of that code are certainly of interest.

The code of colors, for instance, arises within every language wherein the signifier may be colored, as in fashion or photography. In any given film, this code must nevertheless submit to the sensitivity and particular values of the film stock used; for example, the characteristics of the three-strip Technicolor process in use until the early 1950s are very different from those of Eastmancolor stock in the 1960s.

Similarly, the voice of a film character may not at first appear to be very specific to the cinema (belonging as it does to the code of vocal quality), because the same voice could be heard in the theater, on the radio, or on tape, record, or compact disk. Yet one can normally distinguish between whether the voice is recorded or not recorded, and then one may also be capable of determining the recording technique by noticing whether the voice was recorded live or was postsynchronized. Finally, the simultaneity of voice and the projected images helps make the voice totally specific to film or television. It should not be surprising, therefore, that such specificity in the presentation process should produce codes such as particular voice qualities that are indeed unique to film.

However, the fact that one code is more specific to a language than some other code does not mean that the former is necessarily any more important than the latter. A specific code that helps characterize the language may nonetheless play a very modest role within it. Thus, pretending that one film is more cinematic than another simply because it employs a greater number of codes that are specific to the cinema is an indefensible position. A film exploiting a great many camera movements, rhythmic matches, and superimpositions is no more cinematic than a film composed of totally static shots whose narration is accomplished in voice-off, as in Marguerite Duras's *Woman of the Ganges* (1972), for example. All we can claim is that in the former instance the materiality of the cinematic signifiers is more conspicuously demonstrated than in the latter.

Nonspecific Codes

Film language belongs to the group of nonspecialized languages; there is no realm of meaning that is unique to film, and its material of content is undefinable. In a way, cinema can say anything, especially after the arrival of sound. By contrast, there exist other languages devoted to a much more narrow semantic range, as, for example, in the language of naval signals. The exclusive function of these signs is to give useful signals for navigation. Their material of expression has been adapted to this single, precise goal. (It is also worth underlying here that the naval signals may also be presented within a film such as *Das Boot* [Wolfgang Peterson, 1981], while the naval sign system can never hope to convey the film's material of content.)

However, as Hjelmslev has shown in his study of the language system, other languages have a material of content as wide as the total realm of their semantic surface. Their meaning becomes socially universal and they must in turn be composed of equally universal codes. Still other codes may have a multiple specificity, which is to say that they can intervene within all languages whose material of expression includes their particular pertinent trait. An example would be the code of rhythm cited earlier.

If the cinema is a nonspecific language capable of saying everything, the fact remains that by reason of the specificity of its material of expression (the codes that constitute it) it can still have a sort of privileged relationship with certain areas of meaning. Hence, all semantics linked to visuals or mobility may be deployed without limits. Within narrative films one may notice the abundance of themes linked to vision. For example, there are innumerable film melodramas involving blind characters or characters suddenly losing their sight.

Thus, the cinema is a meeting place for a great number of nonspecific codes as well as a smaller number of specific codes. In addition to visual analogy, and the photographic codes already mentioned, one might also cite narrative cinema's use of all codes proper to a narrative that operate on a level where they become independent of the narrative vehicles. This is the same for all codes of content. Studying a film means studying a very large number of signifying configurations that are not specifically cinematic. Such study of nonspecific codes therefore requires a vast undertaking calling upon a large number of disciplines or fields of knowledge. In fact, attaching a precise list of all the codes that are specific to the cinema is impossible here since their isolation is still not far enough advanced. However, making a list of all the nonspecific codes used by the cinema would be even more absurd—it would take the form of an encyclopedia.

THE TEXTUAL ANALYSIS OF FILM

When discussing the concept of code (pp. 160–161), we indicated that in *Language and Cinema* Christian Metz established two different or opposing entities. First, there were the material ensembles or film messages, which are the concrete "texts"; second, there were the systematic ensembles constructed by the analyst and labeled "codes." The term "text" soon gave rise to a whole new category of film study, namely, the textual analysis of film. Such analyses received a considerable degree of attention during the decade following *Language and Cinema's* publication in 1971. Roger Odin, who compiled a thorough bibliography of such studies in 1977, already found more than fifty examples of textual analyses.

However, the direct lineage between the theoretical work of *Language and Cinema* and these subsequent analyses is still not perfectly clear. Several studies, like Raymond Bellour's analysis of a sequence from *The Birds* (Hitchcock, 1963), actually preceded Metz's study. (Bellour's article was published in *Cahiers du Cinéma* in 1969.) Moreover, the number of these studies referring to Metz's definition of the text is actually fairly slim. Nonetheless, they all maintain a more or less insistent conceptual relationship with the semiotic project in the large sense of the term, while Metz's book constitutes the blueprint.

It is also necessary to point out that the general semiological environment (external to the cinema) also helped determine the genesis of these analyses. Publication of Roland Barthes's *S/Z*, Claude Lévi-Strauss's mythological studies, diverse narrative studies of literary texts, and, of course, various structuralist projects all contributed to the changing perspective being applied to film. In the end, there was a shift toward a greater attention to the *literal* aspect of signification.

Next we will detail the full sense of the word "text" as it is used in *Language and Cinema* so that we may investigate more fully its semiological origin and its meaning outside of film studies—particularly within literary analyses that echo some film analyses. Finally, we will characterize what seems to us to constitute the principal originality and interest of this realm by concentrating on specific problems all this poses for film studies. Specifically, how can we constitute a film as text?

The Concept of Film Text in Language and Cinema

The concept of text initially appeared in order to define the principle of pertinence by which semiology proposed beginning its study of film. Semiotics considered the film text a "signifying object" or "unit of discourse." Film (like the entire phenomenon "cinema" of which film is a subset) actually allows a number of critical approaches that all correspond to a different acceptation of the object; thus, it is vulnerable to different principles of pertinence. It may be considered from a technological point of view or as a physiochemical base (as in "This *film* is highly sensitive to light"). Moreover, film may be approached from an economic point of view, as a collection of prints ("This *film* has broken all attendance records"), as well as from a thematic perspective involving content analysis ("Besides prostitution or domestic labor, women performed no professional activities within French *films* of the 1930s"). It may even be studied as a document capable of revealing the sociology of its reception ("This Griffith *film* provoked race riots and condemnations from the NAACP").

Thus, speaking of a "film text" entails perceiving the film as a signifying discourse, analyzing its internal system(s), and studying all observable signifying configurations. Nevertheless, the semiological approach can cover two quite different practices.

The first procedure studies the film as a *message* of one or more cinematic codes. This sort of analysis may involve either the study of film language in general or one of its specific figures. For instance, one might study the fragmented editing within *Muriel* (Alain Resnais, 1963). Such a study must contrast the editing techniques of that single film with the editing in other similar or opposed films.

The second, clearly *textual* practice studies the system proper to a single film. For example, the role of fragmented editing in *Muriel* would no longer be studied simply as one figure of film language, but rather in relation to other signifying configurations within the same work. In the end, such a study will then propose the significations that all these figures create, such as "the impression of existential fracturing, the nearly phenomenological schizophrenia of daily life, and deep perceptual 'distraction.' "

Metz employs a Hjelmslevian definition of "text" to indicate that the term serves to name all signifying *progression*, or all process, whether the text concerns linguistic or nonlinguistic or mixed signification. Film obviously involves mixed texts. "Text," therefore, designates a series of images, a series of musical notes, a tableau on which spatial signifiers develop, etc. The term "film text" corresponds to the "filmophonic" level as defined by Etienne Souriau and Gilbert Cohen-Séat in their filmology glossary, which states that "film functions as an object perceived by spectators during the time of its projection."[37]

The film text is therefore opposed to the film system. A film's system includes its principle of coherence, its internal logic, and its intelligibility as constructed by the analyst. In further contrast, this system has no concrete existence, while the text, which is indeed a material event, preexists any intervention by the analyst.

Within every film there are two abstract instances dependent on the systematic dimension. First, there is the system proper to this particular film. Second, there are the codes (themselves highly systematic) that are constructed by the analyst, but are not singular or specific to the text. Some codes are general because they involve the entire collection of all films: editing would be one such code. Other codes are not specific because they may belong to a narrow category or group of films; for example, the films of the 1930s made unusually heavy use of certain marks of punctuation such as fades, dissolves, and wipes. Even if they are rather particular, these codes are never unique; instead they always concern more than one film. Only texts are singular.

Case Study: The Textual System of D. W. Griffith's Intolerance

Griffith's *Intolerance* (1916) is composed of four different tales that are initially presented separately, but are then shown one after the other in a continually more rapid alternation. The stories involve the fall of Babylon, the Passion of Christ in Palestine, the St. Bartholomew Day's Massacre in sixteenth-century France, and

a modern episode situated in the United States during the era contemporary with the film. Thus, *Intolerance* is structured in an
original manner that employs parallel editing to organize its entire
construction.

This parallel editing is a particular type of sequential construction
that belongs to a specifically cinematic code, that of editing in the
sense of the syntagmatic ordering of entire sequences. Obviously,
this sort of construction may also intervene within a literary or theatrical narrative, but here it is specifically cinematic to the extent
that it must mobilize the cinematic signifier of a dynamic succession of moving images in order to produce its specific and intense
visual and emotional effect. Parallel editing is only one of the editing
figures available in 1916, and it is distinguishable from other sorts
of sequential ordering. For example, other editing structures include
crosscutting, which creates the impression of simultaneity between
two series, as well as simple linear editing wherein sequences are
connected to one another according to a chronological progression.

> In his *Civilization across the Ages* (1908), Méliès was content to jux-
> tapose a series of tableaux shots according to a chronological axis. Cross-
> cutting, which was one of the editing figures refined by Griffith and his
> Biograph two-reelers, also occurs in *Intolerance*, though merely within
> individual episodes. For example, crosscutting is perhaps most noticeable
> during the final part of the modern tale as the automobile pursues the
> train. During this chase scene the crosscutting heightens suspense since
> the life of our innocent hero, unjustly condemned to be hanged, rests on
> the outcome of the pursuit.

Film language, understood here as the abstract relational system
consisting of all film production prior to *Intolerance*, thereby offered Griffith a signifying configuration—namely, parallel editing—which that film's textual system would use, rework, and transform. This editing device is extended over the entire film and then
accelerated as it passes from a parallelism between groups of sequences (the film's opening), to a parallelism between sequences
(the middle), until it finally results in a parallelism between sequence fragments. In the end, the parallels are made between shots
whose sequential unity has been completely pulverized, until the
film achieves a "meat grinder montage," to use Eisenstein's expression. The final acceleration is solely produced by the work of parallelism itself, a movement that totally transforms the initial configu-

ration of this sort of editing until it is destroyed. The film system is labor by the film upon the film language.

Such generalized parallel editing is inseparable from the thematics proper to the film, based on extracinematic signifying configurations. Here an ideological configuration radically opposes the historical examples of intolerance with the allegorical image of goodness and tolerance represented throughout by the figure of the mother rocking her child. The film's textual dynamics are based upon a separation that is clearly established at the beginning of each episode devoted to fanaticism. Nonetheless, the separation is repudiated and then transformed into a fusion charged with making the identity of intolerance visually concrete in spite of the diversity of its various faces.

The ideological thematics mobilized by *Intolerance* try to make connections with determinations exterior to the film. These thematics conform to the general phenomenon made concrete by the reconciliatory ideology that characterizes American society after the Civil War. However, the thematics also inform a specifically cinematic figure, parallel editing, which in turn gives material form to the thematics. As a result, the film system is profoundly mixed. The system becomes a dynamic meeting place for the cinematic and the extracinematic as well as for language and text. The conflicts of these encounters metamorphose the initial metabolism of each of the parties.

The Notion of Text in Literary Semiotics

The term "text" is also used within film studies with reference to a different, if not contradictory, conception of the word. This other definition comes originally from Hjelmslev, and usually remains very much implicit. However, it seems essential to us to clarify this other implicit use of the term, especially because of its frequency.

As we will explain further on, this particular meaning of the word "text" is connected to the theoretical interventions of Julia Kristeva, the collective work of the journal *Tel Quel*, and the subsequent critical current in the early 1970s. This theoretical strategy intended to promote simultaneously a new sort of reading and a new literary production. By beginning with a rereading of Lautréamont, Mallarmé, and Artaud (all in the wake of Georges Bataille and Maurice Blanchot), it involves provoking a favorable climate for "textual" productions. (Both theory and fiction are seen as textual to the extent that the thrust is to deny the boundary between the two.) Hence, both the theories and fictions written by or supported by members of *Tel Quel*, such as Philippe Sollers, Jean Ricardou, Jean Thibaudeau, and Pierre Guyotat, were enthusiastically encouraged.

We recount this episode of the Parisian literary chronicle here because it influenced certain film journals that were particularly permeable to the new theories, such as *Cahiers du Cinéma* from 1970 to 1973. Moreover, this theoretical trend even caused the birth of a new film journal, *Cinéthique*. Just as with the literary field, this theory advocated supporting certain "challenging" texts; in film studies this would include a film like *Méditerranée* (Jean Daniel Pollet, 1963). It even played a role in the creation of new films, especially experimental films such as those by the Dziga-Vertov Group (Jean-Luc Godard and Jean-Pierre Gorin) and *La Fin des Pyrénées* (J. P. Lajournade, 1971).

It is not easy to provide a synthetic summary of the concept of the text, especially since it can only be understood as a dissemination of meaning. Nonetheless, Roland Barthes succeeded in accomplishing this difficult task very concisely, without betraying its complexity. In several articles, most notably "From Work to Text" in *Image-Music-Text* and "Théorie du Texte" in *Encyclopaedia Universalis*, Barthes defined the notion of text. His work has strongly influenced much of the textual analysis of film and will serve as the core of our discussion of the text and semiotics.

In film studies, it was Raymond Bellour, in his "Le Texte introuvable," who clearly explained the origins of this other conception of the text.[38] He links it to the concept of the text elaborated by Barthes, who opposed "work" to "text." According to this interpretation, the work is defined as a material fragment or an object that can be touched (Barthes is obviously thinking of a literary work). Its surface is "phenomenal." Hence, it is a finite, computable object that occupies real space. While a work can be held in your hand, a text involves language; thus, it is a methodological realm, a production, and a passage.

It is therefore not possible to count texts; one can only claim that within this or that work there is textuality. A work may be defined in terms heterogeneous to language: we might speak of its physical materiality or the sociohistorical factors that led to its material production. By contrast, the text remains homogeneous to language through and through. It is nothing but language and can only exist via language. A text can only be revealed within a labor or production. Thus, we can see that this other notion of the text is largely equivalent to what Christian Metz labels the "textual system," while the work—the concrete object by which the text is elaborated—corresponds precisely with Metz's "text" since both are proven developments and manifest discourses.

This equivalence between text and textual system becomes particularly obvious when Metz defines the textual system as a displacement and underlines the antagonistic relationship established between the moment of the code and the textual instance. "Each film is built on the destruction of its own codes. . . . The proper task of the filmic system is to underplay actively each of these codes by asserting its own particular logic and *because* it asserts it, an assertion which is necessarily accomplished through the negation of that which is not itself, i.e. codes (which are, as such, no longer important and become but the 'building blocks' of another structure). In each filmic system, the (cinematic or extracinematic) codes are both present and absent: present because the system is built *upon* them (on the basis of them, with/against them), absent because the system is only a system to the extent that it is something other than the message of a code (or a series of these messages), i.e., because it begins to exist only when (and where) these codes begin to cease to exist in the form of codes, because it *is* this very movement of negation, of destruction-construction. In this regard, certain notions advanced by Julia Kristeva in another domain are applicable to the film."[39]

Thus, we will be very careful when using the term "text" so as to preserve both of its accepted meanings. The two conceptions "textual system" and "text," in the Kristeva-Barthes sense, are fairly synonymous. The cross-fire of terms arises from the fact that one member of the opposition—namely, "work,"—is practically never mentioned in Metz's *Language and Cinema.* For Metz, the notion of the film text is valid for all films. Thus, as opposed to the second accepted meaning of the term we have defined here, Metz's use of the word "text" is never restricted or limited.

The semiotic meaning of "text," therefore, is a concept at once both strategic (because polemical) and programmatic. It privileges certain works—namely, those where one finds "textuality"—and it also promotes a new practice of writing. It stands in opposition to the classical notion of a work and the ancient conception of a text as something to be derived from the work. Traditionally, the latter was the voucher of what was written, guaranteeing its permanence and preserving its stability. This ancient conception of the text closed off the work, chained it to its letter, and bound it to its signified. The text was tied to a metaphysical truth because it authenticated the written and its literariness, its origin, and its meaning. In other words, it established its "truth."

Semiotics substituted a new text, a product of signifying practice, for the ancient text. Thus, the classical theory made sure to stress the finite tissue of the text, because, as Barthes points out, the word "text" derives etymologically from tissue or texture. (Hence, the text was seen as a veil behind which one searched for the truth, the "real message," in brief, the "meaning.") However, the modern theory of a text "turns away from the text-veil and tries instead to perceive the tissue within the texture, in its interlacing of codes, formulae, and signifiers at the center of which the subject moves about and becomes defeated, like a spider who melts in its own web."[40]

It is certainly this "interlacing" of codes, cited by Barthes, that perfectly evokes certain textual analyses in film, especially studies by Bellour and Marie-Claire Ropars-Wuilleumier. As Bellour explains in "Le Blocage symbolique,"[41] an analysis of *North by Northwest* (Hitchcock, 1959), it is impossible to tie up in a single bundle the multiplicity of strands from this "spider's web" because the film system is based on "the reiterative progression of series, the differential regulation of alterations, and the similitude and diversity of disruptions." Hence, a textual analysis summary can offer nothing more than "a bare skeleton of a structure which, while certainly not worthless, will never achieve the multiplicity that is structured within, around, through, above, and below it."

This new theory of the text only involves the literary work, since a work merely needs to signify in order to be considered a text. Barthes explains, therefore, that all signifying practices (including pictorial, musical, and film activities) may engender textuality. Works are no longer considered simple messages, finished products, or even *énoncés*; rather, they are perpetual productions and thus enunciations through which the subject always continues to struggle. This subject is undoubtedly the author, but also the reader. The theory of texts leads to the promotion of a new practice—reading: the reader thereby becomes nothing less than the person *who wishes to write* by devoting himself or herself to the erotic practice of language.[42]

One of the primary consequences of this conception is certainly that it postulates an equivalence between writing and reading—the commentary becomes a text in its own right. The subject of analysis is no longer exterior to the language it describes since it too exists within language. There can no longer be a discourse "about" the work, but instead, by entering into "the undifferentiated proliferation of the intertext," such a discourse becomes a production of another text equal in status to the original text.[43]

Rather than entering into a protracted discussion of the theoretical foundations of these radical notions, we will underline several key difficulties they pose for the cinematographic realm. Textual production may only register within language. Furthermore, the permutation between reader and "producer" is simplified somewhat in literature by the similarity of the materials of expression between the object language and the critical language. However, this homology disappears with film since the cinema's specific visual and audio signifiers contrast with the writing of any commentary. Hence, obstacles exist that must obstruct textual analyses of film. It is precisely these obstacles that Bellour refers to when he explains that in a certain sense the film text is "unfindable" because it can never truly be cited. In film, not only is the text not quotable, but the work is unquotable as well.

Nevertheless, Bellour overturns this aporia dialectically by postulating that textual shifting [*mouvance*] is inversely proportional to the fixedness of the work.

Bellour compares musical textuality with that of film. In music, the score is fixed while the work changes because the performance changes. In a sense this shifting may be said to increase the work's textuality since the text, as Barthes states repeatedly, is the shifting itself. "Yet rather paradoxically, this shifting is not reducible to language which would like to seize it to make it rise once again by redoubling it. In this way, the musical text is less textual than the pictorial text, or especially than the literary text, whose shifting is in some ways inversely proportional to the fixedness of the work. The possibility of keeping to the letter of the text is in fact its condition of possibility. . . .

"In effect, the film presents the particularity, remarkable in a spectacle, of being a fixed work. . . . The performance in a film cancels itself out in the same way for the profit of the work's immutability. As we have seen, this immutability is a paradoxical condition of the conversion of work into text to the extent that it favors (if only by the abutment it constitutes) the possibility of a route for language which detours the multiple operations by which the work becomes a text and then returns them to the path. However, this movement, which draws a film closer to a painting or a book, is at the same time contradictory: the film text never really stops escaping the very language that is being used to constitute it.

"Thus, film analysis never ceases to mimic, evoke, or describe. It cannot, with its sort of desperate principle, help but attempt a frantic com-

petition with the object it struggles to understand. Because of this attempt to seize and retake the object, film analysis ends up being the locus
of a perpetual dispossession. Film analysis never stops filling in a film
that never stops receding; it is the jar of the Danaïdes *par excellence.*"[44]

The Originality and Consequence of Textual Analysis

As we mentioned at the beginning of this chapter, very novel film
analyses proliferated throughout the 1970s. It becomes quite difficult to label them all "semiotic" since their degree of proximity to
that discipline was quite varied. How then do we characterize this
new breed of analysis? Moreover, in what ways do these analyses
differ from earlier in-depth film studies, which, though rare, nonetheless existed?

ESSENTIAL CHARACTERISTICS OF TEXTUAL ANALYSIS. We can pose
the hypothesis that textual analysis has two basic characteristics:
it provides precise attention to "form" or signifying elements; and
it involves a constant interrogation of the methodology being used
and thus imposes a theoretical autoreflection upon every stage of
analysis.

The Attention to "Pertinent Detail." Even though film analyses
prior to 1970 were rich, deep, and careful, it was nonetheless rare to
see the author refer to this or that mise-en-scène detail or point to
specific shot compositions or transitions between shots.

Admittedly, such references to detail were sometimes made by André
Bazin. In fact, the depth of field between the glass in the foreground and
door in the background in the shot of Susan's suicide from *Citizen Kane*
(Welles, 1941) as well as the pan within the interior courtyard of the
building in Jean Renoir's *The Crime of M. Lange* (1935) have both become
canonical examples from Bazin's work. However, the use of such examples by Bazin was always integrated within a more general argument dedicated to realism in the cinema. Similarly, Eisenstein systematically illustrated his theoretical arguments with extremely accurate reference to
specific shots. It is precisely because of these traits that we may consider
both Bazin and Eisenstein precursors of textual analysis.

Hence the limited number of stylistic or formal analyses and, inversely, the abundance of thematic studies within extensive analyses. For example, we may cite the studies by Michel Delahaye devoted to the films of Marcel Pagnol and Jacques Demy and those by
Jean Douchet on Alfred Hitchcock, Vincente Minnelli, and Kenji
Mizoguchi. While these studies may differ in their overall strategies,

each is built around dominant thematic networks within the oeuvre of a filmmaker. Owing as they do to the famous "auteur theory" arising from *Cahiers du Cinéma* in the 1950s and 1960s, they are undoubtedly among the richest of this style of criticism.

Textual analysis considerably limits such ambitions yet substitutes other goals in their place. It generally abandons the entire oeuvre of a single director to attack instead a fragment of a particular film. Textual analysis deliberately cultivates a sort of myopic reading on the level of the image.

This careful attention to formal structures of a film (for which we have pointed out many precursors since the 1920s) was strongly reactivated in the work of Noël Burch. Burch's articles, first published in *Cahiers du Cinéma* in 1967, were collected as *Theory of Film Practice* (originally published in 1969) and may be said to predate actual textual analysis.

From his first analysis, devoted to *Nana* (Renoir, 1926), Burch reveals both a theoretical ambition and a great talent for concrete observation of stylistic figures of film, a talent that will be found once again in the best subsequent analyses. However, Burch's rigor suffers because of his dependence upon his memory of shots and sequences. The first true textual analyses will stumble over the same hurdle until they overcome it thanks to analytic projectors, editing tables, and videotape recorders that allow the researcher to stop the image.

By setting out to return to the primacy of the signifier, textual analysis reveals its concern not to leap immediately to an interpretive reading. Instead, it often stops at the moment of "meaning," and thus it regularly runs the risk of falling into paraphrase or purely formal description. Its wager rests on the ever problematic articulation between interpretive hypotheses and detailed commentary about isolatable elements of the film.

The Privileging of Methodology. In opposition to traditional studies (especially those not founded upon empiricism and the author's intuition), which almost never risk making their theoretical references explicit, textual analysis is characterized by an interrogation of its methodological options that is as constant as it is passionate. It searches unceasingly to drive out false evidence while going over the epistemological reflections of even its most humble concepts with a fine-toothed comb. Furthermore, it systematically and repeatedly questions the pertinence of its tools of analysis. This interrogation of the entire process goes hand in hand with a keen awareness of the arbitrariness of any demarcation of the object of study. Thus, because most textual analyses wish to remain cautiously thorough, they limit themselves to fragments, which in turn leads them to confront the problem of segmentation.

Textual analysis is not the concrete application of a general theory such as the semiological study of film language. Instead, there is a constant back and forth movement between its two steps: the first tries everything, while the second is an activity of knowledge. It is "an essential moment" of semiological study, as Dominique Chateau has written.[45]

Finally, textual systems elaborated by such analyses are always seen as potential and multiple. Hence, textual analysis is also characterized by a fear of reduction to a unique system or a "final signified." Bellour employs a geometric metaphor to specify this relation between the reality of the work and the potentiality of the text: "The procedure of analysis circumscribes that which it treats as the effect of projection of a reality whose effects it can only indicate as a vanishing point, in the sense that it always encloses the effects of a volume that is still developing. Therefore, it is always essential that the analysis be *true* in the sense that it develop its own virtuality as not completed in the text. Moreover, it should quite rightly always realize there is a relation between the spectator and the film, rather than any sort of reduction."[46]

CONCRETE PROBLEMS OF TEXTUAL ANALYSIS. Besides its theoretical problems,[47] textual analysis also runs up against very concrete obstacles above and beyond the actual process of analysis. In order to constitute a film as text, one must first get a handle on the work, yet this action is much more difficult to accomplish for film than for literature. Studying a film with even a minimal degree of precision always poses the problem of memorization, which is a fundamental condition of the perception of films, since their rate of delivery, at least during normal projection, is never dependent upon the spectator. Two complementary strategies have been devised to overcome this difficulty: the creation of a detailed description (découpage) and frame-by-frame analysis.

Preliminary Stages of Analysis. A film analysis then assumes two conditions: first, the establishment of an intermediate state between the work and its analysis; and second, fairly radical modification of the conditions for viewing the film. In "Le Texte introuvable," Bellour underlines the paradox that film analysis can only occur via the destruction of the object's specificity.

> [The moving image] is fairly uncitable because written language cannot restore what the projector can offer, namely, a movement whose illusion guarantees reality. This is why any

static reproduction, even one employing many frame enlargements, can do nothing more than reveal a sort of radical impotence in presenting the film's textuality. Nonetheless, such reproductions are essential. In effect, they represent an equivalent
that is always organized by the needs of the reading of the still
frames seen at an editing table. These still frames have the contradictory function of opening up the film's textuality at the very
moment when they are interrupting the film's unfolding. In a
sense, this is what occurs when one stops upon a sentence in a
book in order to reread and reflect upon it. However, it is not the
same sort of movement that is being stopped. With a book, the
continuity is suspended and meaning is fragmented, yet no attack is being made on the very existence of the material specificity of a means of expression.

Frame-by-frame analysis and the frame enlargement that reproduces it are simulacra; obviously, they never cease letting the
film escape, yet, paradoxically, they also permit it to flee as a
text.[48]

It is not only the film text, however, that is "unfindable." The
film text, as we saw above, is by definition unlocatable since it has
no existence except by way of its virtuality, as a system to be eter-
nally constructed. Yet the work is also unfindable on several levels.
The film work is first of all prosaically difficult to locate. The film
has to be booked in a theater and regularly projected. Such initial
access to the work shows the degree to which the analyst is dependent upon the institution of cinema (commercial distribution of feature films and programming by film clubs, archives, or universities).
For example, in their book *Nosferatu*, Michel Bouvier and Jean-
Louis Leutrat illustrate the problems that can arise for a researcher
in trying to determine the status of specific copies of a film and the
difficulty in selecting the most accurate copy. Availability and quality of videotape copies is obviously a larger though related issue; yet
even here access to copies generally depends upon commercial and
noncommercial distributors and retail outlets.

It does not suffice to have simply seen the film; instead one must
see it repeatedly. However, one should also be able to manipulate
the film to select fragments, compare shots and scenes that are not
actually sequential, contrast the opening and closing sequences, etc.
All of these operations assume direct access to both the film and a
means of projection. They also assume the availability of a specific
sort of projector/viewer that allows going both forward and back-
ward, slowing and speeding up the film, or even pausing on a single

frame. In brief, one must have access to an editing table or analytical projector.

It is perhaps unnecessary to underline the physical and legal quasi-impossibility of access to the film itself. Because of copyrights and distributors' exclusive contracts for a given period, a researcher's rights can usually only be exercised after the commercial or even noncommercial projections, with personal use often remaining illegal. (The problem is further complicated by the usual necessary wait for a film to be made available in 16 mm and/or for its rental costs to drop before most academics are able to gain full access.) All of these nearly insurmountable obstacles help explain the delay between the initially privileged critical accounts of a film and the systematic textual analysis of the same film.

Obviously, the technological revolutions of videocassettes and laser disks have greatly modified the means of access of films in general; however, they must be analyzed from different physical media and upon a television monitor, both of which greatly alter the film work itself.

These collective material conditions only displace the problem by a step. Film analysis, if only because it is so precise, implies concrete references to the object, and these references themselves imply a visual and audio transcription supplied by the projection. Yet the transcription is hardly automatic; it is a veritable transcoding from one medium to another and thereby engages the subjectivity of a transcriber. Furthermore, there is always a certain range of visual and auditory perception, namely, that which is most specific, which escapes the description and transposition of writing. This is the very phenomenon emphasized by Barthes in his study "The Third Meaning," where he writes: "The filmic is that in the film which cannot be described, the representation which cannot be represented. The filmic begins only where language and metalanguage end."[49]

Nevertheless, more or less novelistic or detailed descriptions of films have existed since the origin of publications devoted to the cinema. The tradition of retold films takes off in the 1910s, the great epoch of serials and the era of novelizations in the popular press. The tradition has seen many decades of prosperity. Today such collections have been replaced by published découpages of films, as seen for instance in L'Avant-Scéne Cinéma (since 1961). These découpages do not all offer the same degree of rigor, but they are unquestionably more precise than published novelizations that are based on the film's scenario.

Use of the Method in Didactic Situations. If the film work is absent when one reads a textual analysis, it is by contrast present in a didactic situation. It is likewise present in the practice of the film club, but in the form of an immediate memory that can only be verified by projecting the discussed sequence again. The didactic practice prolongs and systematizes this process. It depends on the concrete analysis of units of discernible signification at the time of the perception of the film, which it then submits to its own rhythm by decomposing each phase.

The goal of such didactic situations is to illustrate the functioning of the film's signifiers and to give a concrete face to the figures of film language by generalizing the many diverse routes for reading. After all, to a certain degree, nothing is more abstract than the *idea* of cutting on the axis, yet nothing is more concrete or visible than the identification of one of these instances during projection.

Otherwise, the didactic practice is mostly verbal; it is based on verbalization and spoken exchanges. Thus, educational situations allow one to avoid the fixed nature of written interpretations and the risk of reduction; by contrast, didactic exchanges are perfectly able to restore the dynamics of textual functioning by circulating the networks of meaning without making them static.

Difficulties in Laying Out the Analysis and Problems of Citation. While the use of verbal dialogue has revealed itself as particularly productive in the practice of film analysis, the advancement of textual analysis nevertheless demands a return to the written. The findings of the research must be displayed via methods that have proven themselves in other fields, in spite of the specifics of film. The critical approaches taken by postwar cinephiles in France (a period of great expansion for film clubs) were particularly valuable. For instance, it was during this era of film-club screenings and commentary that Bazin's rich critical writings developed much of their force and freshness.

Textual analysis assumes, therefore, quite obviously, the publication of texts. Yet these texts are particularly delicate to write because they shape the reading and the reader's degree of attention and, consequently, determine whether the analysis is interesting. Because of the difficulties in transcribing film that we have discussed, textual analysis finds itself constantly obliged to mobilize a great number of examples, which then bog down the process. Inversely, a simplistic allusion increases the opacity of the presentation. Bellour describes these same findings in "Le Texte introuvable":

This is why film analyses, once they become the least bit precise and even while they remain . . . strangely partial, are always so long in relation to what they discuss—even if, as we know, all analysis is interminable. This is why they are so difficult, or more accurately, awkward to read, repetitive, and complicated; I will certainly not say they are useless, but rather these conditions are the necessary price one pays for their strange perversity. This is why they always seem a little fictive. They play with an absent object and, because they involve making that object more present, they are never able to give themselves the means of fiction without having to borrow those means at the same time.[50]

As a result, the strategy of film analysis for writing must strive to achieve a difficult balance between specifically critical commentary and the always deceptive equivalents of film citations, such as segmentations, frame enlargements, reproductions, etc. To accomplish all this, analysis must, with the greatest possible degree of competence, employ all possible resources for composing the page and for the complementary arrangement of text and photographic illustration.

We can cite here several of the most successful unions between textual analysis and citations from the absent film corpus. First, there is Thierry Kuntzel's study of The Most Dangerous Game (Ernest B. Schoedsack, 1932) entitled "The Film-Work 2";[51] second, the two volumes of film analysis edited by Bellour, Le Cinéma américain; and, finally, the double film issue of Enclitic (Fall 1981/Spring 1982). These studies call upon a very plentiful iconography that structures the general arrangement of the text by way of sequence descriptions and segmentations.

The Cinémathèque Universitaire in Paris also sponsored a series of frame reproductions from October (Eisenstein, 1928) that includes 3,225 frames from the film—one per shot. This series of frame reproductions offers an indispensable complement to the analysis of that film.[52]

Each of these approaches tries to circumscribe the materiality of the film object. There does exist, however, a more radical manner of overcoming the heterogeneity of the critical language and the object language of analysis (the film). It consists of using film itself as support for the analysis of cinema. Didactic films have no problem citing excerpts of other films—they can simply reproduce them as a critical analyst would cite a literary text. This sort of cinema has its classics (besides things like the Blackhawk educational films) such as *Naissance du cinématographe* (Roger Leenhardt, 1946), *Ecrire en images* (Jean Mitry, 1957), and more recently *Before the Nickel-odeon* (Charles Musser, 1982). There will certainly be others in both film and video formats.

5 | FILM AND ITS SPECTATOR

THE FILM SPECTATOR

There are a number of ways to consider the film spectator. You may be interested in spectators insofar as they constitute the public, the film audience, or the audience of certain films. In other words, the spectator may be considered as part of a "population" (in the sociological sense of the word) that indulges in a defined social activity: going to the movies. This audience (or population) may be analyzed statistically, economically, and sociologically. This sort of approach toward studying the film spectator, however, is actually much more of an approach for studying film spectators as groups, and we will not really address concerns about that sort of film public in this book since such approaches, for the most part, spring from theoretical foundations and goals that do not fully belong within our more aesthetic focus. Assuredly, there is some interaction between the evolution of the film audience and the general aesthetic evolution of films. Recent investigations have combined historical interest in audiences with reception studies in a number of directions. Many feminist theorists and historians are expanding new inquiries into women and spectatorship (as in *Home Is Where the Heart Is*, edited by Christine Gledhill). Similarly, studies in the early cinema continue to uncover new information about the first film spectators, as witnessed by *Iris* issue 11, "Early Cinema Audiences" (Summer 1990), edited by Donald Crafton.

What we will essentially be most occupied with in this chapter is the relation of the spectator to film in terms of an individual, psychological, and aesthetic experience, or what we would call a subjective experience. In other words, we are interested in the subject-spectator rather than the statistical spectator. The question of the subject-spectator has been widely debated over the past decade, especially from a psychoanalytic perspective, and we will begin to confront that approach shortly. At the moment, however, we must rapidly outline the various issues and approaches with which the question of film spectatorship has been historically associated.

The Conditions of the Representative Illusion

At the same time that the end of the nineteenth century witnessed the invention of the cinema, it saw a new discipline appear: experimental psychology (whose first laboratory was founded in 1879 by Wilhelm Wundt). In its first 110 years this discipline has expanded greatly. However, one might say that the advent of the silent cinema and then its evolution toward an autonomous and increasingly elaborate art form—in other words, the period of the 1910s and 1920s—coincided with the development of important theories of perception, most notably visual perception. It is in relation to the most famous of these theories, gestalt theory, that we must situate two researchers who, one in 1916 and the other at the beginning of the 1930s, explored the phenomenon of the representative illusion of the cinema and the psychological conditions that presupposed this illusion in the spectator: we are, of course, speaking of Hugo Münsterberg and Rudolf Arnheim.

Hugo Münsterberg was without a doubt the first true theoretician of the cinema, even though his educational background made him a philosopher and psychologist (he was a student of Wundt), and the essence of his work was devoted to books on applied psychology. In his book *The Film: A Psychological Study*, which is brief yet extremely dense, he is initially interested in the spectator's reception of film. More specifically, he is interested in the relations between the nature of film means and, on the one hand, the structure of films and, on the other, the large categories of the human mind (taken within a philosophical perspective clearly marked by German idealism, and Immanuel Kant in particular).

One of Münsterberg's greatest merits is having demonstrated in particular that the phenomenon of the production of apparent movement (a phenomenon essential to the cinema) may be explained by a characteristic of the brain (the phi-phenomenon) rather than by the so-called retinal persistence of vision. Münsterberg thereby established the basis—which is admittedly often forgotten—for all modern theorization concerning the effect of perceived movement. Next, building on this explanation of the movement effect as a prop-

erty of the human mind, Münsterberg then developed a conception
of the entire cinema as a mental process or an art of the mind. Thus,
for him, the cinema was an art deriving from several key mental
activities:

—attention: film is a recording that is organized according to the
same processes by which the mind gives meaning to reality; (this is
how Münsterberg interprets the close-up, for instance, or the emphasis of various camera angles);

—memory and imagination: these two activities together permit
the understanding of the compression or dilution of time, the concept of rhythm, the possibility of flashbacks, the representation of
dreams, and, more generally, the invention of editing itself;

—emotion: finally, emotion, the ultimate stage of psychology,
which is translated within the narrative itself, is considered by
Münsterberg to be the most complex cinematic unit; it may be analyzed in terms of the most simple units and yet responds to the degree of complexity of the human emotions.

Thus, from the simple illusion of movement to the full and complex gamut of emotions, and passing via psychological phenomena
such as attention and memory, the entire cinema is created to address the human mind by mimicking the mind's own mechanisms.
Psychologically speaking, a film does not exist on film stock or on
the screen, but only within the mind, which provides its reality.
Münsterberg's central thesis is formulated as follows: "The photo-
play tells us the human story by overcoming the forms of the outer
world, namely, space, time, and causality, and by adjusting the
events to the forms of the inner mind, namely, attention, memory,
imagination, and emotion."[1] This claim expresses more a conception of the cinema than a psychology of the spectator, but it nonetheless assigns the spectator a very precise place; the spectator is
the person for whom the film (at least the aesthetic film) ideally
functions. From the most elementary level of the reproduction of
movement to the most carefully elaborated level of the emotions
and the fiction, everything is created to reproduce and represent the
functioning of the spectator's mind. The spectator's role, therefore,
is to *actualize* an ideal, abstract film that only exists for, and because of, the spectator.

Rudolf Arnheim is primarily known as an art critic and perceptual
psychologist. In accordance with the lessons of the gestalt school to
which he was connected, Arnheim insists upon the fact that our
vision is not simply a question of the stimulation of the retina,
rather it is a mental phenomenon, involving a whole field of percep-

tions, associations, and memorizations. In some ways then, we could be said to see more than what our eyes alone show us. For example, if objects decrease in apparent size as they move away from us, our mind compensates for this diminution, or more precisely, it *translates* it in terms of distance.

For Arnheim, the central problems of the cinema are therefore linked to the phenomenon of the mechanical (photographic) reproduction of the world. Film can automatically reproduce sensations analogous to those affecting our sense organs (our eyes, for instance), yet it accomplishes this feat without the correctives of our mental processes. Film is concerned with what is *materially visible*, but not what is truly within the human sphere of the *visual*.

One can see how Arnheim attaches himself to the gestalt movement. He rests on the assumption that in the perception of the real the human mind is that which not only gives reality its meaning, but also gives it its physical properties. Thus, the color, form, size, contrast, luminosity, etc., of objects in the world are in some ways the product of the mind's operations by way of our perceptions. Vision is thereby "a creative activity of the human mind."[2]

Arnheim's position is nevertheless a bit more moderate than the extreme "mentalism" of Münsterberg. Admittedly, Arnheim sees both perception and art as founded upon the organizing capacities of the mind, but he considers the world (which causes the perceptions) as susceptible to certain forms of organization. Even if the senses and the human brain fashion the world (especially in artistic material), Arnheim considers that the structures imposed upon the world by the brain are, finally, a reflection of the structures found in nature. These would be general schemata like rising and falling, domination and submission, harmony and discord, etc.

In spite of the evolution of psychology since the 1920s, these theories (which have been only briefly summarized here) are far from obsolete today. Moreover, to a certain extent, they have even been reengaged and brought up to date in the work of Jean Mitry and some of the earliest texts of Christian Metz. The glaring limitations of these theories are especially obvious in the narrowness of the aesthetic choices they allow. Münsterberg, with his graded scale of psychological phenomena that a film must treat, already privileged the commercial fiction film and excluded from his field of study all documentary, educational, and propaganda films. Still more narrowly, Arnheim proclaimed value judgments that were very severe, and even sectarian. In particular, Arnheim's system led him to valorize exclusively the silent cinema, rejecting *en masse* the sound cinema, which he considered to be a degeneration or a pernicious growth that would produce, according to gestalt theory and within the entire organism, the diminution of external constraints.

Insofar as the aesthetic or critical choices are concerned, these preferential claims are certainly worthy of discussion. On the other hand, they can only weaken the general validity of a theory of the psychological mechanisms of illusion—mechanisms that the arrival of sound certainly did not end, even if it did transform them profoundly. Furthermore, in spite of their keen intellectual interest, these approaches are generally received today as particularly appropriate for the "artistic image" period of the cinema, and they typically find themselves reactivated and used in relation to the experimental cinema.

The "Working" of the Spectator

We can see then that the first film psychologists became almost naturally interested in an art that had many characteristics that were relatively close to actual properties of the human mind. This stage of exploration, which had sprung up in a somewhat naive wonderment at this seeming equivalence between film and mind, was quickly succeeded by an approach that was both more pragmatic and more useful. This new approach may be simplified as follows: since the intimate mechanisms of film representation resemble those of essential psychological phenomena, why not consider this similarity from the opposite angle? In other words, how, by way of film representation, might one *induce* emotions; how can film *influence* the spectator?

We have already encountered this preoccupation earlier, particularly in our discussion of Eisenstein, where we saw that influencing the spectator was a central trait of his theoretical system (see chapter 2). More generally, we might say that this concern, more or less implicitly and more or less consciously, appeared rather early in the cinema and was present in the work of all the great filmmakers.

Even though there was never the least theorization about it in his writings, one can surmise, for example, that D. W. Griffith was extremely sensitive to the influence exerted by his films. It is clear that the climax of *The Birth of a Nation* (1915), with its "last minute rescue" (which actually occupies an enormous portion of the narrative), plays quite deliberately on the anxiety provoked in the spectator by the alternating montage construction with the admitted intention of forcing sympathy for the Ku Klux Klan "saviors."

However, if American directors were undeniably the first to play so well upon the emotions of the spectator, it was nonetheless in Europe that the theoretical lessons of their effectiveness were truly formulated. Although Hollywood produced a large number of solidly propagandist films (besides *Birth of a Nation*, we can include here all the films made to justify and ideologically support the U.S. entry into World War I in 1917), this propaganda was never really analyzed as such by the Americans. Even in Europe, the concern with affecting the spectator took very diverse forms, and it is hardly more than by way of a pun that one occasionally attaches labels such as the French impressionist (filmmakers of the "first avant-garde" such as Louis Delluc, Jean Epstein, Abel Gance, and Marcel L'Herbier) or German expressionist schools.

One could certainly find, among such French and German directors and critics, a consciousness that is occasionally quite perceptive concerning the psychological means of action in the cinema. It is, however, among the Soviet directors that reflection on this theme, at least during the 1920s, takes its most systematic form. Two circumstances, moreover, that were closely related to each other explain this development. The first is the very institutionalization of Soviet cinema as a means of expression, communication, and also of education and propaganda, which was more and more narrowly controlled by branches of the state (this is the full meaning of the famous formula attributed to Lenin that "of all the arts, the cinema is the most important one for us").[3] Second, there is the fact that the first experiments regarding the cinematic material, by Lev Kuleshov and his studio, strongly influenced the possibilities of montage as a means of imposing a single meaning onto sequences of images.[4]

> The celebrated experiment consisted of following the same close-up of an inexpressive actor with various shots (a table well stocked with food, a corpse, a naked woman, etc.). The finding was that the close-up of the actor, as a function of its proximity to the other shots in the sequence, took on various inflections. This experiment has become known as the "Kuleshov effect." The experiment is often interpreted exclusively as a demonstration of the linguistic and syntagmatic potential of the cinema, but it was also the first occasion of becoming fully aware of the possibility of *controlling* the spectator's reactions by an appropriate manipulation of the film material.

Within these critical and theoretical texts of the 1920s, Kuleshov never envisioned, at least not directly, the full consequences his conception of montage would have on film and its spectator. It was one of his students, Vsevolod Pudovkin, who first and most clearly isolated the consequences.

> In a small treatise written by Pudovkin in 1926 on film technique, he wrote the following:
> "There is a law in psychology that lays it down that if an emotion gives birth to a certain movement, by imitation of this movement the corresponding emotion can be called forth. . . . One must learn to understand that editing is in actual fact a compulsory and deliberate guidance of the thoughts and associations of the spectator. If the editing be merely an uncontrolled combination of the various pieces, the spectator will understand (apprehend) nothing from it; but if it be coordinated according to a definitely selected course of events or conceptual line, either agitated or calm, it will either excite or soothe the spectator."[5]

Pudovkin's conception of the power of editing is certainly naive, postulating in a fairly simplistic manner an equivalence, or even similarity, between film events and basic emotions. Stated thus, at least tendentiously, it proposes the possibility for a sort of analytical calculus of spectator reactions that is rather comparable to the rigid lessons drawn by the young Eisenstein from the teachings of reflexology that we described earlier (see chapter 2).

The most essential point remains the affirmation of the very idea of an influence being exerted by a film on the spectator. This general but strong idea was taken up, under slightly varied forms, by all the important Soviet directors of the 1920s.

> Here are two examples. Dziga Vertov, 1925: "The choice of facts recorded will suggest the necessary decision to the worker or peasant. . . . The facts culled by the kinok-observers or cinema worker-correspondents . . . are organized by film editors according to party instructions. . . . We bring to the workers' consciousness facts (large and small), carefully selected, recorded, and organized from both the life of the workers themselves and from that of their class enemies."[6] Eisenstein, 1925: The artistic product . . . is above all a tractor that works the spectator's psyche according to a given class orientation."

Naturally, this idea, convincing as it is, nonetheless comes up shy of a real calculation of the action exerted upon the spectator, which is to say, it falls short of any true and calculated mastery of the film form. The many attempts at this sort of mastery all revolve more or less around the implementation of the idea, raised in regard to Pudovkin and Eisenstein, of a sort of catalogue of elementary stimuli possessing predictable effects. The film would then simply have to combine them judiciously. It was upon this conceptual base, among others, that all the elaborate editing charts were established during this period by Eisenstein, Pudovkin, and others. It is also upon this same idea that Kuleshov implicitly based a good part of his teaching in the form of rules for the actor's craft, which prescribed that the actor deconstruct each gesture into a series of elementary movements so that they might be more easily mastered. Similarly, Kuleshov's rules for mise-en-scène called upon the director, for example, to try whenever possible to make movements within the frame coincide with the parallel movements at the frame's edges, so they would be easier for the spectator to perceive.

These "rules," which were occasionally presented more as recipes, are certainly minimal and today they appear rather debatable. Therefore, the best Soviet filmmakers continually transformed them and improved their practice (if not necessarily their theory) in the direction of greater efficiency of form. Since this is not the place to analyze their work in detail, we will simply call attention once again to all of Eisenstein's work in the 1930s and 1940s surrounding the concept of the organic whole. There is also the importance that Pudovkin, more pragmatically, granted throughout his career to working on time, rhythm, and tension, always in the direction of a maximum emotional hold on the spectator (see, for instance, the final sequences of *Mother* [1926] and *Storm over Asia* [1929]).

This stage of the reflection upon the film spectator was certainly never brought to completion, primarily because of the mechanical nature of the adjacent psychological theories, which led to obvious impasses. Nevertheless, it remains an important step, essentially, because of its desire for *rationality*, and it will never be equaled, except perhaps by the psychoanalytically inspired approach that we will consider below.

All of the efforts regarding spectator control depended upon the notion of influence derived from the parameters of the image, and their demise was hastened by the advent of the sound cinema, a film form in which, at least at its inception, the essence of meaning and therefore of potential influence was accomplished via dialogue. Eventually, the question of the cinema's influence, and the conditioning of the spectator, was occasionally revived from a wide variety of critical perspectives, but reflection upon this influence proceeded more and more via the paths of sociology and/or theories of ideology over the next several decades, and much less (indeed, not at all) via any theory of subject-spectator as the center of affective reactions to film stimuli.

Filmology's Spectator

It was after World War II, beginning in 1947 within the Institute of Filmology, that there arose a renewed interest in the film spectator. During the 1930s and the recent global conflict, practical applications of the cinema had revealed the emotional impact of film images, particularly in the realm of propaganda. According to Marc Soriano, secretary editor of the institute's review, "Before filmology, one was restricted to verifying a basic truth, that the projection of a film affected the audience. As far as how and why, that was another question. It was thus this 'how and why' that the nascent filmology tackled."[7]

> Created in 1947 by Gilbert Cohen-Séat, who had published his *Essai sur les principes d'une philosophie du cinéma* the previous year, the Institute of Filmology strived to gather together academics and members of the film community, including directors, writers, and critics, under the prestigious presidency of Mario Roques (professor of the College of France).
>
> The institute published the *Revue Internationale de Filmologie*, beginning in the summer of 1947; and its twenty issues, which stretch to the end of the 1950s, collectively laid the foundation for subsequent film theory. The nascent semiology would, in fact, return to a central problem for filmology, which was precisely the issue of the impression of reality. Edgar Morin's book *Le Cinéma ou l'homme imaginaire*, which we will discuss shortly, was published in 1956 and serves as a sort of bridge between these two schools. Beginning with the first issue of the *Revue de Filmologie*, a number of articles were dedicated to the issue of spectatorship. Examples include Henri Wallon's "Some Psychophysiological Problems Posed by the Cinema" and Jean Deprun's "Cinema and Identification," which explicitly refers to Freudian theories of identification.
>
> This issue was fundamentally treated in the anthology directed by Etienne Souriau entitled *L'Univers filmique*. The second chapter, written by Jean-Jacques Rinieri, is entitled "The Impression of Reality in the Cinema: The Phenomena of Belief" and is broadly commented upon by Metz in his first article, which is devoted to the same topic.

The filmological studies are interested from the start in the psycho-physiological conditions of the perception of film images. They apply methods of experimental psychology and increase the tests that permit the observation of spectator reactions under given conditions. For instance, in his 1948 study "The Visual Perception of

Cinema, Television, and Radar Images," Dr. R. C. Oldfield proposes clearing up the psychological problems of perception of film images, which he classifies within the sequence of artificial images, by comparing them with the evolution of radar technology. He considers the issue of "faithful resemblance," assumes the existence of a scale of resemblance, and reminds us that the film image is purely physical, composed as it is of a definite spatial distribution of luminescent intensities upon the screen's surface. Oldfield sets the limits of the image's photographic fidelity according to the texture of dots and the alternation of the relation between contrast and direction. He clearly establishes that the screen image is the result of a psychic process that may be measured and quantitatively processed and that precise and objective criteria of fidelity exist.

These observations lead him to conclude that visual perception is not simply a passive registering of an external stimuli; rather, it consists of an activity of a perceiving subject. This spectatorial activity includes regulatory processes whose goal is to maintain a balanced perception. These mechanisms of constancy implement, for example, the maintenance of the apparent size of the screen and of the figures on the screen, no matter how far the screen may be from the spectator.

A second aspect of filmology's research involving film perception is characterized by the study of differential perceptions according to audience types. Numerous studies thus confront perception by children, "primitive" peoples, and maladjusted youths, just to cite several typical examples featured in Edgar Morin's book. Such studies often refer to electro-encephalography and analyze the readings obtained following projected film sequences.

We find such studies, for instance, in the following articles: Henri Gastaut, "Psychological, Somatic, and Electroencephalographic Effects of a Rhythmic Intermittent Luminous Stimulus," *Revue Internationale de Filmologie* 7/8:213–229; Ellen Sierstad, "Young Children's Reaction to the Cinema," *Revue Internationale de Filmologie* 7–8:241–245; Gilbert Cohen-Séat, H. Gastaut, and J. Bert, "Modifications in the E.E.G. during Cinematic Projection," *Revue Internationale de Filmologie* 16 (January–March 1954): 7–25; G. Heuyer, S. Lebovici, et al., "Notes on the E.E.G. of Maladjusted Children during Cinematic Projection," *Revue Internationale de Filmologie* 16 (January–March 1954): 57–64; and G. Heuyer, S. Lebovici, and L. Bertagna, "Experimental Studies of Nervous Activity during Film Projection," *Revue Internationale de Filmologie* 9 (January–March 1952): 71–79.

This side of the filmologists' study of the spectator leads us straight into medical "semiology." However, the perspective taken by the philosopher Etienne Souriau within the Institute of Filmology is much closer to the perspectives of an aesthetics of film and the spectator, at least in relation to the way they would later develop. In his classic study on "the structure of the film universe and the vocabulary of filmology," he devotes himself to defining the various levels that, according to him, are involved in the structure of the film universe. Among these levels, he distinguishes the one that concerns the "spectatorial facts."

The spectatorial realm is, for Souriau, the place where the specific mental act of understanding the film universe (the diegesis) materializes according to the screen's data delivery. He labels "spectatorial" all subjective elements that initiate the spectator's psychic personality. For example, the perception of film time is objective and measurable in regard to a film's actual projection, while it is subjective on the spectatorial level. The latter level is operating when the spectator judges that the film "drags" or "moves too quickly." Moreover, a phenomenon of disengagement may arise between the two temporal levels. If, for instance, the screen's events experience a very rapid acceleration, it is possible that certain spectators will not follow the accelerated rhythm and will disengage. In this situation they fail to realize what is taking place and are left with only an impression of confusion and disorder. Just such a disjunction is observable with the use of special effects whose arbitrary or contrived nature may threaten their credibility. This is the case in *Les Visiteurs du soir* (Marcel Carné, 1943) when the music slows to mark the stopping of time.

Etienne Souriau also explains that the spectatorial elements may continue well beyond the film's projection. They integrate most obviously the spectator's impressions upon leaving the theater with all the elements involving the profound influence exercised by the film, whether it be memory or a sort of productive impregnation of the models of behavior. This also pertains to the state of expectation created by the film's posters, which thereby constitute, for example, a prefilm spectatorial element (see *Revue Internationale de Filmologie* 7–8).

The Film Spectator as Imaginary Person

In 1956 Edgar Morin published his *Le Cinéma ou l'homme imaginaire*, which was then termed sociological anthropology. In the preface to the most recent edition, Morin proposes that "this book was a meteorite." In fact, the importance and originality of his study was grossly underestimated during the three decades following its publication. Moreover, due to its profoundly novel character, once published, it was not easily situated in any of the standard classifications for classroom texts because "it speaks of the cinema but not of art or the film industry . . . [and] it does not immediately pertain to any predetermined category of readers."[8]

Several pages from *Le Cinéma ou l'homme imaginaire* had previously been published in *Revue Internationale de Filmologie* in 1955. In other words, there is a direct connection between the filmologically inspired texts and Morin's book. The latter is also enriched by references to classical film theory (such as Jean Epstein, Ricciotto Canudo, and Béla Balázs) and is systematically grounded in the filmological studies by Michotte van den Berck and Gilbert Cohen-Séat. However, his anthropological perspective is new since Morin considers the cinema in light of anthropology as much as he considers anthropology in light of the cinema. As a result, he suggests that the imaginary reality of the cinema reveals certain anthropological phenomena with particular keenness.

"All of perceived reality, therefore, goes through the image's form. Next, it is reborn as memory, which is to say, an image of an image. Thus, the cinema, like all figuration (painting, drawing) is an image of an image; however, like the photograph, it is an image of the perceptive image, and even better than the photograph, it is an animated image, or a living image. It is in its capacity of a representation of a living representation that the cinema invites us to reflect upon reality's imaginary and the imaginary's reality."[9]

Morin begins with the transformation, which he finds quite startling, of the "cinematograph," an invention with a scientific finality, into the cinema, which becomes a machine to produce imaginary situations. He studies the inventors' writings and contrasts them with declarations by the earliest filmmakers and critics, who all expanded upon Guillaume Apollinaire's phrase that considered the cinema "a creator of surreal life."[10] Furthermore, Morin takes into account Etienne Souriau's observation that "there is a sort of marvelous and nearly congenital atmosphere to the film universe."[11] However, Morin next clarifies the imaginary status of film perception by discussing it via the relation between the image and the "double."

Reviving Jean-Paul Sartre's writings that considered the image as

The fantastic in two films by Jean Cocteau: *Beauty and the Beast* (1946).

Orphée (Jean Cocteau, 1950).

a "presence-absence" of the object, wherein the object is defined as an authentic presence and a real absence, Morin refers to the perception of the world by archaic and infantile mentalities. These forms of thought share the traits first, of not being immediately conscious of the absence of the object, and second, of believing in the reality of their dreams as much as in waking reality. The film spectator occupies an identical position when s/he gives a "soul" to things perceived on the screen. Close-ups animate the object, and, as Morin writes, "the drop of milk in Eisenstein's *The General Line* (1926–29) finds itself endowed with a sense of refusal and adhesion, as well as a sovereign life."[12]

According to Morin, film perception offers all the aspects of magical perception. Such perception is common in "primitives," infants, and neurotic individuals. It is founded upon a common system that is determined "by the belief in the double, metamorphosis and ubiquity, 'universal fluidity,' reciprocal analogy between microcosm and macrocosm, and anthropo-cosmomorphism."[13] Significantly, all these traits correspond precisely with the constituent aspects of the film universe. If, for Morin, the relations between the structures of magic and those of the cinema had only, before him, been sensed intuitively, by contrast, the kinship between film's universe and that of dream had been perceived frequently. Thus, film rediscovers "a dreamed, weakened, rebaptized, enlarged, closer, deformed, and obsessive image of the secret world where we withdraw in our waking hours as well as our sleep from this life that is larger than the life where sleep the crimes and the heroics that we will never accomplish, and where our deceptions drown and our craziest dreams germinate."[14]

In his subsequent chapters, Morin analyzes the mechanisms common to dreams and film by tackling projection-identification by which the subjects, rather than simply projecting themselves into the world, also absorb the world into themselves. He deepens the study of cinematographic participation by establishing that the impression of life and reality proper to film images is inseparable from a first burst of participation. He relates the latter to the absence or atrophy of motor, practical, or active participation and stipulates that this passivity places spectators in a regressive situation, returning them to an infantilelike state as if under the effect of artificial neuroses. He draws the conclusion that film techniques offer provocations, accelerations, and intensifications of projection-identification.

In expanding his argument, Morin takes care to distinguish identification with a character on the screen (which is the most banal and most mentioned phenomenon of projection-identification and is only one aspect of the process) from "polymorphous projection-identifications" that go far beyond the level of character and converge to plunge the spectator into the film's milieu as well as its action. The polymorphous nature of identification casts light upon a primary sociological fact that is nonetheless often forgotten: there is a great diversity of films and a parallel eclecticism of taste among the same movie-going public. "Thus, the identification with a look-alike as well as the identification with a stranger are both stimulated by film, *and it is the second aspect that clearly contrasts with the participations of real life.*"[15]

In the section labeled "Technique for Affective Satisfaction," within chapter 4, "The Soul of the Cinema," Morin summarizes his research hypothesis as follows:

"In developing the latent magic of the image, the cinematograph became filled with participations before being metamorphosized into the cinema. The starting point was the photographic duplication, which was then animated and projected onto the screen; this stage then directly began a chain of genetic processes of stimulation. The charm of the image and the image of the world within reach made up the exhibition; the exhibition stimulated the formation of new structures internal to a film; the *cinema* is the product of this process. The cinematograph aroused participation. The cinema stimulated it, and the projection-identifications open into and become exalted within anthropo-cosmomorphism. . . . Above all, we must consider the magical phenomena as the hieroglyphs of an affective language."[16]

Subsequent developments elaborated upon filmology's considerations of the impression of reality and the problem of cinematic objectivity by maintaining that the camera mimics our visual perception process. René Zazzo, for example, writes that "the camera has empirically found a mobility that is the same as for psychological vision."[17] Filmology also confronted what Morin calls "the dream reality complex" because the film universe blends the attributes of dream with the precision of the real by offering the spectators a materiality external to themselves, even if it is simply an impression left upon the film stock.

It would be difficult not to be struck today by the pertinence and timeliness of Morin's ideas, which simultaneously prefigure the semio-psychoanalytic work of Christian Metz in *The Imaginary Sig-*

nifier (1977) as well as more recent approaches, such as Jean-Louis
Schéfer's *L'Homme ordinaire du cinéma* (1980), which we will discuss in this chapter's final section.

A New Approach to the Film Spectator

This problem of the film spectator, which we have just begun to
address, was already at the center of the filmology movement's debates during the 1950s. However, in the 1970s, after the development of semiology, the question of the spectator underwent a sud-
den spurt that seems today to have substantially slowed down.

> Once semiotics began to constitute itself as a pilot theory in the field
> of cinema, it essentially devoted itself to a linguistic model for the im-
> manent analysis of cinematographic language and its codes. Such a con-
> cern, when applied with methodological rigor, excludes any considera-
> tion of the subject-spectator. This was the epoch, for instance, of Metz's
> "Grand Syntagmatic."[18]
> Next, following the work of Roland Barthes, the interest of semiology
> swiftly shifted from the study of codes to that of texts (see the previous
> chapter). With this change in perspective would come the rediscovery of
> the "deep" presence of a reader's place within the text itself, even if that
> discovery only led initially to a place for a reader who articulated codes
> in order to accomplish the labor. This step, inaugurated by the publica-
> tion of Barthes's *S/Z*, saw the rapid multiplication of textual analyses of
> film in which the place and work of the film spectator were beginning to
> be drawn, in filigree.
> This evolution of theoretical research could not fail to arouse a meta-
> psychological perspective within studies dealing specifically and directly
> with the question of the film spectator, as, for instance, in the work of
> Jean-Louis Baudry and Metz.

From this same slant toward the approach of a theory of the spectator, the research has several angles of attack at its disposal. We
will cite four principal angles that have been employed by the theoretical works we mention in this chapter.

1. *What is it that the film spectator desires?* What is the nature of
the desire that pushes us to shut ourselves up for two hours in a
darkened room where transitory moving images flicker on a screen?
What is it we are seeking there? What is it precisely that we exchange our admission price for? The answer is certainly to be found
in the direction of a state of abandonment, of solitude, and of lack.

The film spectator is always more or less a refugee in need of restoring some irreparable loss via the cost of a short-lived regression that is socially fixed and lasts only during the time of projection.

2. *Which subject-spectator is tempted by the cinematic apparatus* with its dark room, the suspension of motor function, and the overinvestment in visual and auditory functions? Undoubtedly, the subject-spectators who are caught up in the cinematic apparatus find some of the same circumstances and conditions they have experienced in their imaginary or their primal scene. There is the same sensation of exclusion in front of this scene cut off by the cinema's screen as if by the shape of a keyhole, the same sentiment of identification with characters who bustle about in a place from which the spectator is excluded, the same voyeurist drives, and the same impotence of motor functions while the eye and ear take over dominance.

3. *What is the metapsychological condition for the subject-spectator during the projection of a film?* How do we situate the film state in relation to the adjacent realms of dream, fantasy, hallucination, and hypnosis?

4. *What is the actual place of the spectator during the film screening?* How does the film constitute its spectator within the dynamics of its unfolding? During projection, and afterward in memory, can one speak of a spectatorial "film work" in the same way as of Freud's dream work?

These theoretical advances, which are relatively recent and brief in relation to the entire body of film theory, were made by a successive series of thrusts within a certain disorder. As such, they were actually made in a rather uneven and uncoordinated manner in relation to their principal directions. As a result, some paths, taken in the heat of debate, found themselves to have been overdeveloped, while others, for purely conjectural reasons, were left aside and uncultivated.

Rather than offering yet another fastidious and necessarily splintered account of these different theoretical approaches (which the absence of critical distance makes difficult to evaluate), we have chosen a more systematic (and more original) path toward exploring what is generally called identification in the film spectator. First, however, we will take a brief but indispensable detour by describing the concept of psychoanalysis. In effect we have decided it would be more productive to articulate in coherent fashion *one* of the possible approaches to the question, by fully unfurling its theoretical implications, rather than running out of breath trying to describe all the embryonic and even anarchic approaches to this question, which is so important for the future of film theory: the issue of the spectator.

THE FILM SPECTATOR AND IDENTIFICATION IN FILM

The Role of Identification in the Formation of the Ego

A series of analogies has allowed film theory to bring the film spectator closer to the psychoanalytic subject via several postures and psychic mechanisms. Nevertheless, it is fitting initially to consider what psychoanalytic theory itself means by identification. This clarification is especially useful here given that this psychoanalytic concept, along with many others, has experienced particularly wild or free use in the field of film theory and criticism and has thereby led to much confusion.

Within psychoanalytic theory, the concept of identification has occupied a very central position ever since Sigmund Freud's 1923 elaboration of the second theory of the psychic apparatus (known as the second topology) where he established the concepts id, ego, and superego. Far from existing simply as one psychological mechanism among many, identification is simultaneously the basic mechanism in the imaginary constitution of the self (the fundamental function) and the nucleus—the prototype of a number of instances and ulterior psychological processes by which the self, once constituted, will continue to differentiate itself (the assessment function).

PRIMARY IDENTIFICATION.   The meaning of the expression "primary identification" has varied considerably within psychoanalytic theory's vocabulary, and it has shifted across time as well as from one theorist to another. We will employ it here in Freud's sense, as "the direct and immediate identification situated prior to any investment by the object." For Freud, the human subject would, from the earliest time of its existence (within the phase preceding the Oedipal complex), rest in a relatively undifferentiated state where the object and subject or the ego and the id would not yet know how to pose themselves as independent.

Primary identification, marked by the process of oral incorporation, would be "the most original form of affective bond with an object." Moreover, this first relation to the object, in juncture with the mother, would be characterized by a certain confusion or indifferentiation between the ego and the id. During the primitive oral phase of the subject's evolution, characterized by the process of incorporation, one would not be capable of distinguishing between investment in the object (which poses the object as an autonomous and desirable other) and identification with the object. This identification with the object is inseparable from what is known as the mirror phase.

THE MIRROR PHASE.   It is during the mirror phase that the possibility of a dual relationship between ego and id is established. Jacques Lacan, who elaborated this mirror stage, situates it between six and eighteen months. At this moment in the child's development, the small child still has relatively weak motor skills. The child has problems coordinating movements; thus, it is by the child's *look*, in discovering his or her own image and the image of the counterpart [*semblable*]—such as the image of the mother who holds the child, for instance—that the child will constitute in imagination a true corporeal unity. The child will thereby identify with himself or herself as a unity, by perceiving the counterpart as an other.

This moment when the child perceives his or her own image in a mirror is fundamental for ego formation. Lacan insists on the fact that this initial prefiguring of the ego and first differentiation of the subject is constituted on the basis of *identification with an image* in an immediate dual relationship belonging to the imaginary. This entry into the imaginary precedes access to the symbolic.

The child begins to construct his or her ego by identifying with the image of the counterpart, or other, as a corporeal unity. The mirror experience, which founds a primordial form of "I," involves an identification where the ego begins, as entry into the game, to be roughed out as an imaginary formation. This identification with the image of the counterpart via the mode of the imaginary constitutes the matrix of all future identifications, labeled secondary, by which the subject's personality will then structure and differentiate itself.

For Lacan, the mirror phase corresponds with the advent of primary narcissism by bringing an end to the fantasy of a fragmented body that preceded it. Thus, narcissism is initially bound up with identification. To begin with, narcissism would be the loving captation of the subject by this first image in the mirror where the child constitutes his or her corporeal unity according to the image of the other. Consequently, the mirror phase will be the prototype for all narcissistic identification with the object. This narcissistic identification with the object then leads us straight into the problem of the film spectator.

It was Jean-Louis Baudry who underlined precisely the double analogy between the situations of the "child in the mirror" and the film spectator. His first analogy is between the mirror and the screen. Both instances obviously involve a framed, limited, and circumscribed surface. This property in both is undoubtedly what fundamentally allows them to isolate an object from the world and, at the same time, to constitute it as a total object.

We know how the film frame resists being perceived in its function as a border cutting off the image, and also how the most partial object or the most fragmented body functions, as far as the spectator's perception is concerned, as a total object or a retotalized object, by the centripetal force of the frame. So it seems that few filmmakers took on the task, which is ideologically disturbing for the spectator, of exploiting the frame's fragmenting function. In modern cinema, we may cite Jean-Marie Straub, whose films bear witness in every shot to this alternative conception of the frame.

For Metz, if the screen is in a sense equivalent to a primordial mirror, a fundamental difference nonetheless exists between them since the image on the screen, unlike the mirror, never reflects the actual body of the spectator. This same point recalls Barthes's account of the image: "Here then, at last, is the definition of the image, any image: that from which I am excluded. . . . I am not in the scene: the image is without a riddle."[19]

Baudry's second analogy is between the state of a child's undeveloped motor skills and the position of the film spectator implied by the cinematic apparatus. Lacan placed emphasis on a double condition linked to the biological prematuration of the child [petit d'homme], which determines the imaginary constitution of the ego at the time of the mirror phase. The double condition is the immaturity of the child's motor skills (lack of coordination), which leads the child to anticipate his or her corporeal unity, and, the inverse, the precocious maturity of his or her visual organization. With an inhibition of motor skills and a preponderant role of the visual function, we rediscover two characteristics specific to the film spectator's situation. Everything therefore operates as if the apparatus established by the cinematic institution (including a screen that sends us back images of other bodies, our immobile seated position, and the overinvestment of our visual activity centered necessarily on the screen because of the darkened room) mimics or partially reproduces the conditions that, during early childhood, presided over the imaginary constitution of the ego at the time of the mirror phase.

The fascination filmmakers have had since the cinema's birth for mirrors and reflections of all sorts has often been mentioned and even analyzed. Some directors have even made a sort of specialty of mirror shots in their films. Joseph Losey's *The Servant* (1963) and *Secret Ceremony* (1968) are good examples. The cinema's fondness for mirrors obviously owes to other determinations; however, it would not be out of line to see in it, beyond all the purely aesthetic and thematic motivations, the reflection of this analogy between the screen and the primordial mirror.

The other stage of identification, that of secondary identification, generally involves the Oedipal complex.

SECONDARY IDENTIFICATION AND THE OEDIPAL COMPLEX. It is well known that the Oedipal complex occupies a fundamental place in psychoanalytic theory and that Freud bestowed a central role upon this crisis and its position and resolution for the structuring of the personality. Similarly, Lacan writes that the Oedipal complex marks a radical transformation of the human being; it is the passage from the dual relation proper to the imaginary (which characterized the mirror phase) to the symbolic register—a passage allowing the individual to become constituted as subject while establishing his or her singularity.

The Oedipal crisis, which Freud situates between the ages of three and five, springs from the path of secondary identifications that will follow and replace relations with the father and mother within the triangular Oedipal structure. Thus, it is necessary to return briefly to Freud's description of the Oedipal complex, because of, or rather in spite of, the somewhat simplified vulgarizations of this Freudian concept that continue to circulate.

Briefly, the Oedipal crisis is characterized by a collection of investments in the parents and by an ensemble of desires. Included would be the child's love and sexual desire for the parent of the opposite sex and jealous hatred and desire for the death of the parental figure of the same sex, who is perceived as a rival and prohibitive authority. If we remain for the moment with this simple, so-called positive form of the Oedipal complex, we can already discern a fundamental ambivalence. The small boy, for instance, who has begun to direct his libidinal desires toward the mother, experiences a feeling of hostility toward his father. However, at the same time, because of this same *lack* in his unsatisfied desire for the mother as forbidden object, he will identify with the father, who is perceived as an aggressor, as rival in the triangular Oedipal situation, and who opposes the desire. The young boy finds himself in a position of desiring his mother, thereby hating his father; yet by way of identification the boy enjoys in his imagination the father's sexual prerogatives with the mother. In the same way that the primal scene is excluded, experienced by the boy as aggression, the young child regresses into an identification with the aggressor in the form of the father.

In the cinema, where scenes of physical and psychological aggression are quite frequent, there is a basic dramatic elasticity, and, predisposing a strong identification, the spectators will often find themselves in the ambivalent position of simultaneously identifying with the assailant and the assailed, the executioner and the victim. Ambivalence, whose ambiguous nature is inherent in the spectator's pleasure in this type of sequence, regardless of the director's intentions, is basic to the fascination exerted by horror and suspense films. The success of films like *Psycho* (Hitchcock, 1960), *Alien* (Ridley Scott, 1979), or *The Terminator* (James Cameron, 1984) relies upon just such an ambivalence.

Furthermore, contrary to any simplification of the Oedipal complex, Freud always insisted on the fundamental ambivalence of the investments in the parents at the time of the Oedipal crisis, an ambivalence tied to the child's bisexuality. By the interplay of homosexual components, the Oedipal complex always simultaneously presents itself under what is called a "negative" form: presence of love and desire related to the parent of the same sex, and jealousy and hatred toward the parent of the opposite sex.

"Moreover, identification is ambivalent from the beginning," writes Freud. "It may be directed as much toward the expression of tenderness as it is toward that of the desire for suppression. . . . This difference between identification with the father and attachment to the father as a sexual object may easily be expressed in a formula: In the first case the father is what one wishes TO BE; in the second, he is that which one wishes TO HAVE." Oedipal relations are therefore always complex and ambivalent, and each model of the father and mother may serve simultaneously according to the "to be" or the "to have," and as subject as much as object of desire, via the mode of identification (of desiring the being) or of libidinal attachment (desiring the having).

Because of the combined action of eyelines and continuity editing in the classical film, the characters find themselves caught up in a similar oscillation: now they are the subject of the look (they are the ones who see the set and others), now the object watched by an other (another character or the spectator). By employing this play of eyelines, mediated by the position of the camera, the classical film scene's continuity editing proposes to the spectator, in a fairly banal manner that is inscribed in its

Terror within the silent cinema:
Nosferatu (F. W. Murnau, 1922).

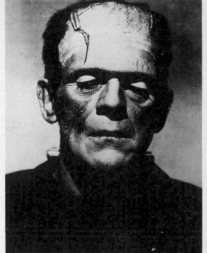

Terror in the sound
cinema: top, *Dracula* (Tod
Browning, 1931); middle,
Frankenstein (James
Whale, 1931); bottom,
Horror of Dracula (Terence
Fisher, 1958).

codes, this statutory ambivalence of the spectator in relation to the glance, or desire for the other, of the spectator. This process has been clearly illustrated by Raymond Bellour in his analyses of *The Birds* (Alfred Hitchcock, 1963) and *The Big Sleep* (Howard Hawks, 1946), and by Nick Browne's analysis of *Stagecoach* (John Ford, 1939).[20]

The end of the Oedipal period, or the outcome of the crisis, will be achieved by the process of identification (though the degree of success in overcoming the crisis will depend on the subject). The child's investments in the parents are abandoned, as such, and then transform themselves into a series of what are called secondary identifications, by which the different instances of ego, superego, and the ego ideal will establish themselves. The superego, to use the example most often developed by Freud, thereby derives directly from the Oedipal relation to the father as a forbidding instance or as an obstacle to the realization of desires.

SECONDARY IDENTIFICATION AND THE EGO.   The secondary identifications, by which the subject will, in a more or less successful manner, escape the Oedipal crisis, thus structurally follow and take the place of Oedipal investments and will constitute the ego or subject's personality. These identifications are the matrix for all the subject's future identifications, by which his or her ego will gradually differentiate itself. Obviously, the secondary identifications, whose prototype remains the relations within the Oedipal triangle (the complexity of which has been shown), are, even by this Oedipal origin, dedicated to ambivalence. Feminist theorists are analyzing the "negative" of the Oedipal struggles in order to account more actively for female subjectivity.[21]

Within this evolution forming the "I," and the entrance into the imaginary before access to the symbolic, identification is the basic principle of the imaginary constitution of the ego. We are indebted to Lacan for having insisted on this imaginary function of the ego: the ego defines itself by identification with the image of the other, "for an other and by an other." The ego is not the subject's center or place of synthesis, rather it is constituted by, in Lacan's words, "a bric-a-brac of identifications," by a non-coherent, often conflictual contingent ensemble, and by a veritable patchwork of incongruous images. Far from being the locus of a synthesis of the subject's self-understanding, the ego will instead define itself according to its function of misunderstanding: by way of the permanent play of identification, the ego is, from its origin, dedicated to the imaginary and to allure. Via successive identifications, the ego constructs itself as an imaginary instance in which the subject tends to alienate himself or herself, and this instance is nevertheless the condition *sine qua non* of the subject's self-synchronization, of his or her entry into language and access to the symbolic.

Cultural experiences will obviously participate in these ulterior secondary identifications throughout the subject's life. As cultural experiences based on strong identification, the novel, theater, and the cinema—with their production of an other as similar figure—will play privileged roles in these secondary cultural identifications. The ego ideal, for example, will continue to develop and evolve via identification with very diverse models, even partially contradictory ones, encountered by the subject, whether in his or her lived experience or in cultural life. The ensemble of these identifications with heterogeneous origins does not form a coherent relational system but will instead resemble a juxtaposition of diverse ideals that are more or less compatible among themselves.

Identification as Narcissistic Regression

Another important characteristic of film spectatorship is that it involves a subject in a state of lack.

THE REGRESSIVE NATURE OF IDENTIFICATION.   Identification, according to Freud, represents the most primitive form of affective attachment; it often occurs that the choice of the libidinal object yields its place to identification. Each time that Freud is led to describe this transformation of the choice of object (on the order of having it) to identification with the object (the order of being it), he underlines its regressive nature. This passage to identification involves, for an already constituted subject, a regression to a stage anterior to the relation to the object; this is a more primitive and more undifferentiated stage than the libidinal attachment to the object.

Most often, this regression founds itself on a *state of lack* whether it involves a reaction to the object (as in mourning, for instance) or a more permanent state of solitude, which is to say, a loss involving others. Freud writes, "When one has lost the object or is forced to renounce it, typically one compensates by identifying with the object by establishing it once again within the ego in such a way that the 'objectal' choice regresses toward identification."

This regressive feature of identification, linked as it is to the state of a lack, already merits several comments in relation to the film spectator. First of all, it should be clear that the cinema is a cultural experience that is consented to and is relatively conscious. Furthermore, the film spectator knows quite well, like the reader of a novel, that this experience excludes *a priori* all objectal choice for the obvious reason that the object appearing on the screen is already an absent object, an effigy, or, as Metz writes, an "imaginary signifier." It nonetheless remains that the choice to enter a movie theater always more or less brings on a consented regression, a bracketing off of this world that precisely gives rise to the action, and the choice of object and its risks, for the benefit of the fiction's imaginary universe. In addition, this desire for regression (even when socially ritualized, as in the legitimate and nearly inconsequential cultural activity of going to the movies) indicates that the film spectator always remains, well within cultural legitimations, a subject in the state of lack, prey to mourning and solitude. It is not at all the same for television viewers since they are less often in a "retiring" or solitary state, and, moreover, much less inclined toward strong identification.

THE NARCISSISTIC NATURE OF IDENTIFICATION. Identification is a narcissistic sort of regression to the extent that it permits the ego's restoring of the absent or lost object and the denial, by this narcissistic restoration, of the absence or loss. It is this process that leads Guy Rosolato to claim that identification "offers the subject the opportunity to satisfy himself without recourse to the external object. Identification allows the reduction (in neurotics) or suppression (in absolute narcissism) of relations with others."[22] If identification with the other consists of establishing it in the ego, this narcissistic relationship, under cover of the real, may strain to substitute, with obvious benefit for the subject, for the risks of the choice of the object. The process resembles the "falling back" of the fetishist onto the fetish, willfully manipulatable and permanently available on the order of things disengaged from all real relations with others and the ensuing risks.

Narcissistic identification would then have a tendency to valorize solitude and phantasmal relations at the expense of relations to the object. Moreover, it may present itself as a solution involving withdrawal into the self, far from the object. According to Gilles Deleuze, it is even incorrect to present identification commonly as a reaction to the loss of an object, to the state of loss, or as a restoration after the fact. Instead, identification may also be first and "determine this loss, carry it out, and even will it."

This narcissistic component of identification and penchant for solitude and for withdrawing from the world (if only for ninety minutes) enters very clearly into play with our desire to go to the cinema and our pleasure as spectators. We might also say that the cinema, and especially the narrative cinema as institutionally constituted to function with identification, always implies (in spite of all the cultural or ideological denials) a spectator in a state of narcissistic regression, which is to say, secluded from the world as a spectator.

It is in this latter sense of the term that we may interpret Frantz Fanon's statement that Fernando E. Solanas inscribes in an address to the audience in *The Hour of the Furnaces* (1967): "Every spectator is either a coward or a traitor." When applied to the cinema, this phrase broadly echoes Bertolt Brecht's theories for the theater, according to which, at the limit, all identification is dangerous to the extent that it suspends judgment and the critical mind. This state of the film spectator's identification (which is an effect of narcissistic regression, withdrawal, immobilization, and aphasia) has been an unavoidable problem throughout the cinema's history. Identification has been a stumbling block for any directors (particularly militant or documentary directors) who have had the desire or will to make films that influence the course of events or that motivate the spectators to become more conscious or active in their social lives.

Among the most commonly employed strategies for combating this regressive trait of identification are the three large categories that follow. First, filmmakers may consider fiction or the classical narrative as a suspect form and therefore reject its conventions (as in the films of Dziga Vertov); second, they may call for a "cinema of the real" (as in the case of cinema direct or *cinéma vérité*); and third, they may forge a mixed form that simultaneously accepts and deconstructs a fiction. This final strategy had become quite widespread, particularly in Europe, during the late 1960s and early 1970s, as may be witnessed by the output of a number of filmmakers, especially Philippe Garrel (*Marie for Memory* [1967], *The Inner Scar* [1970]), Marcel Hanoun (*The Authentic Trial of Carl-Emmanuel Jung* [1967], *Winter* [1970], *Spring* [1971]), Marguerite Duras (*Destroy, She Said* [1969], *Yellow the Sun* [1971]), Jean-Marie Straub and Danièle Huillet (*History Lessons* [1972]), and Robert Kramer (*Ice* [1968]), among others.

We should finally point out that propagandist films, for their part, have often fully appreciated and exploited this state of the viewer's narcissistic regression for their own benefit, by constructing fictions capable of forging strong identifications.

A REACTIVATION OF THE ORAL STAGE.   This regressive state of identification reactivates in the subject a relation to the object that characterizes the oral stage. For Freud, identification acts as a product of the first phase, the oral phase of the libido's organization, during which one incorporates the desired and appreciated object by eating it, which is to say, by suppressing it. We must add to this account of general identification that in the case of the cinema in particular the very conditions of projection (dark theater, inhibited motor activity for the spectators, and their passivity before moving images) reinforce almost artificially this regression to the oral stage.

This oral structure of identification, which, according to Jean-Louis Baudry, is largely determined in cinema by the film apparatus itself, is essentially characterized by ambivalence and the failure to distinguish between internal/external, active/passive, influencing/submitting, and eating/being eaten. In this indistinguishing state, one rediscovers the model for relations the infant enters into with the breast, as well as that for the dreamer and the "dream screen." In this oral incorporation characterizing the relations between spectator and film, "the visual orifice has replaced the buccal orifice: the absorption of images is at the same time the absorption of the subject in the image, prepared, predigested by his entering in the darkened theater."[23]

We should note in passing that many strong fictions in the cinema redouble this absorption of the subject in the image on the levels of both the script and thematics. This loss of consciousness of the image's limitations is accomplished by offering a character for the spectator to identify with who is himself or herself absorbed or inhaled in an unsettling place (like Nosferatu's castle), within a labyrinth (as in a Fritz Lang film), or, more typically, within some adventure where the character will lose footing in his or her own consciousness. In Hitchcock's films, for example, the lead male character often sets out to restore his bearings, and he accomplishes his goal, at a profit, by the end of the film.

IDENTIFICATION AND SUBLIMATION.   Psychoanalysis lacks a fully articulated theory of sublimation, which is a concept that has barely been reworked since Freud first sketched its outlines. It is nonetheless clear (particularly in *The Ego and the Id*) that Freud designates the origin of all sublimation in the very mechanism of identification. Once the ego is induced, for whatever reason (mourning, loss, or neurosis), to renounce its choice of the libidinal object and/or once it struggles to restore or reconstruct the lost sexual object in itself, by identification, it simultaneously renounces directly sexual goals via a process Freud describes as the prototype of all sublimation.

For Melanie Klein, sublimation, which is closely linked with the narcissistic dimension of the ego, would be a tendency that would push the subject to repair and restore the "good" object. We will find this very strong inclination in the film spectator to restore the good object. Moreover, this inclination is perhaps fundamental to the *spectator's constitution of the film* out of the puzzle of discontinuous sounds and images that constitute the film signifier. However, as we will see, this constitution of the film into a good object also generates theoretical difficulties to the extent that it always tends to construct the allure of an object more homogeneous, more monolithic, and more global than what is certainly the reality of the projected film.

During the 1970s, some films, labeled "deconstructive," pretended to break the filmic good object and the transparency of narration and at the same time pretended to transform the relation of identification into a more critical relation toward the image and sounds. These films often clashed with the spectator's supple ability (linked as it is to sublimation and the narcissism of the viewer's state) to reconstitute even the most deconstructive films into good objects, even if only as good objects of discussion and theorization.

DOUBLE IDENTIFICATION IN THE CINEMA

Following this succinct yet indispensable detour through psychoanalysis's general theory of identification, we may now confront more specifically the question of identification in the cinema. For a long time in writings on the cinema there was not so much a theory of identification as a use of the term in its most general, widest-held, and somewhat vague sense. This meaning, which springs from its everyday use, basically designates the subjective relations that the spectator may maintain with some film character. This word "identification" thus vaguely incorporates a psychological concept and allows critics to account for this experience wherein the spectator, during a screening, shares the hopes, desires, anxieties, in short the emotions, of one character or another. The spectator puts himself or herself into the character's place or momentarily thinks s/he is the protagonist; the viewer thereby loves or suffers with the character, as if by proxy, and this experience is at the base of the spectator's enjoyment and governs it to a large extent.

Even today it is not rare after a screening for discussion to turn to considering which character each spectator more or less identified with. Similarly, critics often refer to this sort of identification with a character when they review a film. This current use of the concept of identification—which admittedly involves a certain truth about the process of identification in the cinema, even if it does so in a simplistic manner—essentially designates an identification with the character, that is, with the figure of the other, the counterpart represented on the screen.

Baudry's theoretical research in relation to what he has labeled "the basic cinematographic apparatus," for which the camera is a metaphor, led theorists for the first time in film studies to isolate the operation of double identification. This concept refers to the Freudian model's distinction between primary and secondary identification in ego formation. Within this double identification in the cinema, primary identification (still not fully theorized) refers to identification with the subject of vision or the representing instance. This primary stage serves as a base for and conditions the secondary identification, which is the identification with the character or the represented. This second stage, then, was the only sort of identification referred to by earlier theoretical applications. As Baudry writes, "Thus the spectator identifies less with what is represented, the spectacle itself, than with what stages the spectacle, makes it seen, obliging him to see what it sees; this is exactly the function taken over by the camera as a sort of relay."[24]

This intervention in 1970 concerning the "basic apparatus" was one of the components of an important and rather lively theoretical debate between French theorists and critics, such as Baudry, Marcelin Pleynet, Jean-Patrick Lebel, and Jean-Louis Comolli, among others. Moreover, this debate was also played out in a number of film journals, namely, Cinéthique, Change, Cahiers du Cinéma, Tel Quel, and La Nouvelle Critique. In particular, the debate surrounded the basic apparatus and its relations with representation and ideology, and ultimately the issues escalated to include a more general political debate concerning the very function of the cinema. It must be noted that this debate did not remain limited to theorists alone, but instead, as time passed, it often carried over to the practice of certain filmmakers. For example, we need simply cite the films from this period directed by Jean-Luc Godard and the Dziga Vertov Group.

Primary Identification in the Cinema

Primary identification in the cinema must be carefully distinguished from primary identification in psychoanalysis (see the previous section). It goes without saying that all identification in the cinema (including that defined by Baudry as primary identification) is the result of an already constituted subject who has passed through the primitive indifferentiation of early infancy and thereby reached the symbolic and is thus based on psychoanalytic theory's secondary identification. In order to avoid any confusion, Metz proposes reserving the expression "primary identification" for the pre-Oedipal phase of the subject's history and labeling the spectator's identification with his or her own glance "primary cinematographic identification."

In the cinema, what allows the possibility for diegetic secondary identification, or identification with the represented (such as identifying with a character in a fiction film), is initially the spectator's ability to identify with the subject of vision, with the camera's eye, which saw before the spectator did. Without this capacity for identification, a film would be nothing more than a succession of shadows, forms, and colors on the screen that would be literally unidentifiable.

The spectator, seated in a chair, immobilized in the darkness, sees animated images move across the screen (though, as we mentioned earlier, there is only the illusion of continuity and movement, made possible by the phi-phenomenon and the appropriate rate of flashing still images that are in turn illuminated during the projector's stop-start motion). These two-dimensional images offer the viewers a simulacrum of their perception of the real universe. The traits of this simulacrum, whose familiarity may even make them appear natural, are determined by the basic apparatus or, to simplify, the camera. The camera was constructed precisely in order to produce certain effects and a certain type of subject-spectator and is based on the model of the camera obscura as elaborated by the Italian Renaissance as a function of a conception that is historically and ideologically dated from the perspective and subject of vision (see chapter 1).

Primary identification for the cinema is the means by which spectators identify with their own glance and also prove to themselves that they are the locus of the representation by being the privileged, central, and transcendental subject of the vision. The individual spectator sees the landscape from his or her unique point of view, and one can also say that this landscape is entirely organized for one pinpointed and unique place, which is precisely that of the spectator's eye. It is the spectator who, in a traveling shot, accompanies (without even moving his or her head) a cowboy galloping across the prairie, and it is this spectator's glance that constitutes the precise center of a scene's circular sweeping movement in a panning shot. This privileged place, which is always unique and always central (and obtained in advance without any motor effort), is the place of God, or the all-perceiving subject, gifted with ubiquity. This positioning constitutes the subject-spectator according to idealism's ideological and philosophical model of the centered subject.

The spectator certainly realizes—for at another level s/he always knows—that is not s/he who assists the scene with no mediation. It is commonly understood that a camera previously recorded it for the viewer and placed it in that spot and that this flat image and these colors are not real but are a two-dimensional simulacrum chemically inscribed onto a film strip and projected on a screen. Primary identification nevertheless ensures that the audience identifies with the subject of vision—the unique camera "eye" that saw this scene before the spectators and organized the representation for them in this manner and from this privileged point of view. While certainly absent from the film image, which never reflects his or her own body (in contrast to the primordial mirror), the spectator is nonetheless overpresent, in another fashion, as the locus of all vision; without his or her vision, to a certain extent, there would be no film. The spectator is also present as all-perceiving subject and, by the manipulation of classical continuity editing, is "omnivoyant," being present as a transcendental subject of vision.

However, while classical continuity editing does strive to provide the best point of view for understanding the story, the spectator is still never truly all-seeing since the editing, framing, and mise-en-scène participate in withholding and controlling the flow of story information. Suspense and even spectator interest in following the story, therefore, are created by the film's narration, not simply by the audience's all-knowing glance. In fact, the narration's guidance of the spectator's view point plays a role that is at once a primordial and dramatic element of film vision.

Only this primary identification can explain the fact that, finally, it is not necessary that the image of the other or semblance be visible in a film for the spectator to be able nonetheless to find his or her place. Even in a film without characters or a fiction in the classical sense (such as Michael Snow's La Région centrale [1970], where the camera sweeps about in front of a Canadian landscape for three hours from a fixed location) there is always the fiction of a glance with which to identify.

We should recall once again here Robert Montgomery's Lady in the Lake (1946), which was a radical attempt in film history to make the character's vision coincide with the spectator's vision throughout an entire film. Furthermore, we might say that it flattens secondary identification onto primary identification in such a way that the whole film is seen, more or less, through the eyes of the main character, who only appears on the screen when he comes across a mirror and can "see" his own image. Michael Powell's *Peeping Tom* (1960) also plays with varying degree of coincidence between glance of the spectator, the camera, and a character (especially to create horror effects).

Baudry's analysis of this primary identification aims to bring to light the connection, which until then had been left unexamined, between the cinema's basic apparatus (the philosophical, ideological, and historical presuppositions behind the laws of Renaissance perspective that still serve as the cinema's model), and the "phantasmal" reinforcement of the idealized subject by the cinematographic apparatus as a whole. As Baudry writes, "Ultimately, the forms of narrative adopted, the 'contents' of the image are of little importance so long as an identification remains possible. What emerges here (in outline) is the specific function fulfilled by the cinema as support and instrument of ideology. It constitutes the 'subject' by the illusory delimitation of a central location—whether this be that of a god or of any other substitute. It is an apparatus destined to obtain a precise ideological effect, necessary to the dominant ideology: creating a phantasmatization of the subject, it collaborates with a marked efficacy in the maintenance of idealism."[25]

This reversal of perspectives concerning identification may have allowed a strong theoretical thrust by fueling the debate mentioned above, yet it also had the curious effect of blocking somewhat the reflection on secondary identification in the cinema. Practically ever since, secondary identification has remained in a vague and rather undefined state such as it did before Baudry's uncovering of double identification in the cinema. Since his intervention, film theorists seem to consider diegetic identification as driven by itself and, literally now, rather secondary. Nevertheless, while it may initially seem difficult and perhaps not very productive to push further the analysis and description of primary identification elaborated by Baudry and expanded by Metz, secondary identification remains a rather unexplored terrain that is doubtless rich in theoretical potential. Hence, we will now linger briefly over secondary identification.

Secondary Identification in the Cinema

PRIMORDIAL IDENTIFICATION WITH THE NARRATIVE. "Whether a little more or a little less, every person becomes suspended from *narratives*, from *novels*, which reveal to him or her the multiple truth of life. Only these narratives, at times read in trances, situate a person before destiny," writes Georges Bataille.

Initially, the film spectator, like the reader of a novel, is perhaps such a person suspended from narratives. Beyond the particularities of the various narrative modes of expression, there is undoubtedly a fundamental desire to enter into a narrative when we go to the movies or begin a novel. In the same way that we have described primary cinematographic identification as the basis of all secondary diegetic identification, we might speak of a primordial identification with the narrative act itself that is independent of whatever form and material of expression a particular narrative might employ. When someone nearby tells a story (even a story not directed at us) or when a television set in a bar shows part of a film, we are immediately hooked by these story fragments, even when we will never know their beginning or end. This capturing of the subject by a narrative, any narrative, reveals some primordial condition of identification by which every story told is, to some slight degree, our story. We may cite here Meir Sternberg's conception of the text as a dynamic system of gaps that the reader confronts with hypotheses. The reading process thereby becomes the text's posing of both temporary and permanent gaps that the reader must confront and test, with a varying degree of conclusiveness.[26]

There exists within this attraction for the narrative act itself, whose fascination may even be observed in infants, a powerful motor for all more finely differentiated secondary identifications, previous to more selective or elaborate cultural preferences. This identification with the narrative in its own right undoubtedly holds, to a large degree, with the analogy that is often raised between fundamental narrative structures and the Oedipal structure. We could say that every narrative, to a certain degree, replays the Oedipal scene, which is the confrontation between desire and the law.

Every classical narrative inaugurates the captivation of its spectator by carving out an initial crevice between a desiring subject and his or her object of desire. The entire art of narration then consists of regulating the constant pursuit of this object of desire—a desire whose accomplishment is always postponed, blocked, menaced, and delayed until the narrative's end. The narrative circuit, therefore, occurs between two instances of equilibrium, or nontension, which mark the beginning and the end. The initial state of equilibrium is quickly marked by a flaw or a gap that the narrative must endlessly try to fill in or bridge via a series of obstacles, false trails, twists of fate, or spiteful human acts. However, the narrative function is to maintain the threat of this gap as well as the desire of the spectator finally to see the resolution that marks the end of the narrative, the return to a state free of tension. This resolution may be accomplished by bridging all the gaps between the subject and the object of desire, or the opposite, which is resolution with the definitive triumph of the law and its permanent prohibition of any successful union.

> In *Structural Semantics*, A. J. Greimas builds on Vladimir Propp's *Morphology of the Russian Folktale* and Etienne Souriau's *20,000 Dramatic Situations* to forge what he calls an "actantial model," which is to say, a simple structure of dramatic functions that allows Greimas to account for the base structure of most narratives. It is easy to see how this structure is put into place in relation to the confrontation between desire and the law (of interdiction) that is the initial motor of every narrative: the first pair of actants put in place are the subject and the object, according to the axis of desire; second, there are the sender and receiver of the object of desire, according to the axis of the law; and finally, third, are the opponent and helper in satisfying the desire. The actantial structure evidently is a structure homologous to the Oedipal structure (see chapter 3, on narrative codes).

We have already mentioned that identification, as regression, most often establishes itself as a state of lack. As Guy Rosolato writes, "Identification attaches itself to a lack. If a demand is made, the lack may be the other's refusal to fulfill the demand. Satisfaction is delayed, but an opposing will is also refused, and identification is launched."[27] Within this description of the process of "launching" identification we find once again all the elements of the basic structure of narrative wherein desire arrives to articulate a lack and delay the satisfaction that launches the subject of desire (and the spectator) in active pursuit of an impossible satisfaction that is always delayed or even permanently launched again onto new objects.

At this deep structural level, where all stories resemble one another, the initial captivation of the spectator undoubtedly occurs via the simple fact that there is "some" narrative. This primordial diegetic identification is a deep reactivation, which remains relatively undifferentiated, of identifications with the Oedipal structure. The spectator, as well as the listener or reader, certainly senses that there operates within this narrative, from which the spectator is usually personally absent, something that deeply concerns him or her. Moreover, this unsettling element resembles the viewer's own unpleasant dealings with desire and the law so much that the spectator relates it to his or her self and origin. In this sense, every narrative, whether it takes the form of a quest or an inquest, is fundamentally a search for a truth in desire within its articulation to both lack and the law. In other words, spectators search for their own truth, or, as Bataille writes, they search for "the multiple truth of life."

This search involves the most archaic level of the subject-spectator's relation to the film narrative, but barely touches upon the matter of cultural values that allow differentiating or hierarchizing narratives according to their quality and complexity. On this level, the least polished film, as well as the most elaborate, is capable of hooking us. For instance, everyone has had the experience, sitting in front of the television, of becoming caught up in and identifying with the story of a film that we would otherwise judge unworthy (intellectually, ideologically, or artistically) of our interest as easily as a film that we recognized as a classic.

Undoubtedly, this primordial identification with the narrative act itself serves as an essential base for a diegetic identification that is more differentiated by one film narrative or another. We might ask whether this primordial identification with the narrative (like the primary identification with the subject of vision) is not a necessary condition for the film to be elaborated by the spectator as a coherent fiction from the discontinuous mosaic of images and sounds that constitute the signifier.

IDENTIFICATION AND PSYCHOLOGY.   The film theorist should keep continuously aware of the fact that usually, when one speaks of a film, one speaks of a memory of the film. Moreover, this memory is already re-elaborated since it is a reconstruction accomplished after the fact, and it thereby lends the film a homogeneity and coherence that it did not really have during the actual projection. This distortion particularly holds true in relation to film characters, who readily seem to us, in our memory, to be endowed with relatively stable and homogeneous psychological profiles that we can refer to as we speak or write about the film, rather as if the characters were real persons.

We will see that this distortion is deceiving and that a character, as a creation of film stock, is usually constructed in a much more discontinuous and contradictory fashion during projection than it is in our memory. After the screening, however, spectators tend to believe (as they are invited to do by film reviewers and casual conversation about films) that they identified via sympathy with one character or another because of the character's personality, dominant psychological traits, and general behavior. This process is not unlike the way we experience a sort of global sympathy for someone in daily life because, we believe, of their personality.

If it is true that secondary identification in the cinema is fundamentally an identification with a character as a figure of our likeness or as a fellow human being, or as a locus for affective investments by the spectator, we would nonetheless be wrong to consider identification as an effect of the sympathy we might feel for a certain character. Rather, the opposite seems to hold true, and not simply for the cinema: Freud has clearly found that we do not identify with other people through sympathy; "instead sympathy is born out of identification." Thus sympathy is the effect and not the cause of identification.

There is one fairly widespread and banal form of identification that is particularly illuminating: partial identification. Partial identification is "strictly limited," according to Freud, and "restricts itself to borrowing a single trait from the object." This identification via a single trait frequently arises among individuals experiencing no sympathy or libidinal attraction for the object, and it typically functions on a collective level, as in the case of Hitler's mustache or Bogart's gestures.

Having established that identification is the cause of sympathy, we are left with the question of amorality and the basic malleability of the film viewer. Within a well-made film narrative the spectator may be led to identify with and, due to the resulting effects of this identification, sympathize with a character with whom, on the levels of personality, type, and ideology, the spectator would never sympathize in real life. Moreover, were that character encountered in real life, the spectator might even be disgusted by him or her. The film audience's relaxed vigilance allows it to identify with almost any character if the narrative structure leads it to do so. Hitchcock provides famous examples in both *Psycho* (1960) and *Shadow of a Doubt* (1943), wherein his spectators are led to identify with principal characters who are *a priori* unsympathetic: Melanie the thief, Norman the murderer, and Uncle Charlie the murderer of rich widows.

The fact of identification causing sympathy also becomes obvious in the naive failure of constructed films that assume that the traits and actions of the "good" character should suffice to produce the spectator's undivided sympathy and identification.

The most compact form generally taken by film in our memory, in relation to the experience of its progressive production by the spectator during projection, allows us to point out a second illusion. This illusion consists of attributing a much greater stability and permanence to the secondary identification than it possesses in reality. We too often believe that the spectator totally identifies with one or occasionally two characters throughout the film and that this identification occurs for psychological reasons and operates in a relatively stable and monolithic manner. Identification would thereby attach itself to characters in a long-lasting fashion for the film's duration, and it would be relatively static.

We do not deny that a great number of films—and, to simplify matters here, particularly the most formulaic and stereotypical films (or even contemporary television series)—function largely according to a rather monolithic identification that is regulated by a phenomenon of recognition and by a stereotyped typology of characters: the good, the evil, the protagonist, the traitor, the victim, etc. We may say that in this case the identification with a character proceeds because of an identification of (and with) the character as *type*. There can be no doubt about the efficacy of this form of identification—after all, its perennial and quasi-universal nature stands as proof. However, this sort of typing effectively reactivates, in a tried and true manner that operates on a level that is both worn and deep, affects directly springing from identifications with the roles of the Oedipal condition. There is, for instance, identification with the character faced with thwarted desire, admiration for the hero who represents the ego ideal, and fear before the paternal figure, etc.

Within this stereotypical manner, which is typically repetitive and lazy and thus all the more manifest and directly readable, something operates that is nonetheless essential to the anchoring of the spectator to the film character. This process is at work, to a certain extent, in all fiction films, and it undoubtedly plays an essential role in all identification with a character in a film: identification has a typological role.

Nonetheless, without some outrageous simplification, this archaic substratum of all character identification cannot account for the complex mechanisms of diegetic identification with the cinema, and, in particular, for the two more specific traits of this identification. First, there is the fact that identification is an effect of the structure—a question of place more than of psychology. Second, identification with a character is never that total or monolithic, but, on the contrary, remains extremely fluid, ambivalent, and permutable during the film's projection, which is to say, while it is being constituted by the spectator.

Identification and Structure

THE SITUATION.   If it is not sympathy that engenders identification with the character, but rather the opposite, the cause and mechanism of secondary identification in the cinema remain open to question. It certainly appears that identification is an effect of the structure of the situation, rather than an effect of the psychological relation to the characters.

Hitchcock explains this very process to Truffaut: "Let's take an example. A curious person goes into somebody else's room and begins to search through the drawers. Now, you show the person who lives in that room coming up the stairs. Then you go back to the person who is searching, and the public feels like warning him, 'Be careful, watch out. Someone's coming up the stairs.' Therefore, even if the snooper is not a likeable character, the audience will still feel anxiety for him. Of course, when the character is attractive, as for instance Grace Kelly in *Rear Window*, the public's emotion is greatly intensified."[28] This empirical "law" of Hitchcock's, which was also masterfully illustrated in his *Marnie* (1964), is valuable because it clearly explains an essential point: it is the situation (here someone is in danger of being surprised) and the manner in which it is presented to the spectator (the enunciation) that will, in a quasi-structural manner, determine the spectator's identification with one character or another at a given moment in the film.

We might also find an equally empirical confirmation of this structural mechanism of identification in the experience (made particularly commonplace by television viewing) of watching an extract, scene, or sometimes only several shots from a film you have never seen. This rarely involves a film's beginning. Instead the spectator is rather abruptly confronted with unknown characters whose film pasts are also unknown and who are involved in the middle of a fiction that is barely known. And yet, even in these artificial conditions of film reception, the spectator will quickly, almost instantaneously, enter into a sequence whose thematic ins and outs are unclear; moreover, the spectator will immediately find his or her place and thus become interested in the fiction.

If the audience becomes hooked so quickly by an isolated sequence from the middle of a film, and if it finds its place, it is because there is some identification that operates without a necessary psychological understanding of the characters, their precise role in the narrative, their motives—in a word, all the things that would have required a fairly long period of progressive familiarization with the characters and their story. In fact, for the audience to find its place, it only needs the space of one sequence or scene (and this is particularly noticeable with child spectators, who quickly become interested in a film, fragment by fragment, without fully understanding the overall plot or psychological motives). All the audience requires to become inscribed within a scene is a structured network of relations, *a situation*. Consequently, it is unimportant whether the spectators know the characters yet: within this rational structure mimicking any intersubjective relationship, the audience will readily organize a certain number of places, arranged in a certain order and fashion, all of which is the necessary and sufficient condition of identification.

> "Identification," Barthes writes, "is not a psychological process; it is a pure structural operation: I am the one who has the same place I have. I devour every amorous system with my gaze and in it discern the place which would be mine if I were a part of that system. I perceive not analogies but homologies. . . . The structure has nothing to do with persons; hence (like a bureaucracy) it is terrible. It cannot be implored—I cannot say to it: 'Look how much better I am than H.' Inexorable, the structure replies: 'You are in the same place; hence you are H.' No one can *plead* against the structure."[29]

Hence, identification is a question of place, an effect of structural position. It follows that the situation is important as the base structure for identification in a classical narrative: every situation that arises during a film redistributes the places and distributes a new network, or a new positioning of the intersubjective relations at the heart of the fiction. Moreover, we know in psychoanalysis that one subject's identification with another is rarely global; instead it more frequently refers to the intersubjective relation via some aspect of the relation to him or her. It is no different in the cinema, where identification passes through this network of intersubjective relations that we commonly call a situation, where the subject finds his or her bearings.

> This identification with a certain number of places at the heart of an intersubjective relation is also the condition for the most everyday language where the alternation "I" and "you" is the very prototype of identifications that make language possible. These two words designate nothing other than the respective places of two interlocutors in discourse, and they necessitate a reciprocal and reversible identification without which every subject would remain trapped in his or her own discourse with no chance of understanding others or entering into discourse. "If we rapidly

take our place within the interplay of intersubjectivities," Lacan writes, "it is because we occupy our own place anywhere. The world of language is only possible insofar as we occupy our own place anywhere."

The Oedipal origins and structural operations of all identification, as well as the specific characteristics of a film narrative (particularly classical editing), are sufficient in determining the fluid, reversible, and ambivalent nature of the cinema's identification process. To the extent that identification is not a psychological sort of relation with some character, but rather depends upon a play of places with a situation, we can not consider it a monolithic, stable, or permanent phenomenon throughout the entire length of the film. On the contrary, during the real process of viewing a film it seems that each sequence or each new sequence (to the extent that it modifies this play of places or relational network) suffices to start identification once again, redistribute the roles, and redesign the spectator's place. Identification is almost always much more fluid and unstable while the spectator constitutes the film during projection than it will seem retrospectively during the memory of the film.

All of this is certainly true for the film during its unfolding, during its diachrony, but even on the level of each scene, each situation, it seems that identification conserves more of its ambivalence and its initial reversibility than one would think. Within this play of places and this relational network established by each new situation, the spectator may be said to be in place anywhere, to paraphrase Lacan. During a violent scene, for example, the spectator will identify at the same time with the aggressor (with a sadistic pleasure) and with the victim (with anguish). During a very emotional scene, the spectator will simultaneously identify with the character in the desiring position (feeling a lack or anguish because that character's desire is stifled) and with the character who receives the pleas (thus experiencing narcissistic pleasure). Again and again, even in the most stereotypical situations, we almost always find this fundamental mutability of identification, this reversible affect, and these ambivalent positions that make film pleasure into a mixed pleasure that is often more ambiguous and more vague than the spectator really wants to admit or remember after a legitimating and simplifying secondary elaboration; however, such pleasure may be a feature of every imaginary relationship.

It certainly seems that the classical novel, which also nevertheless proceeds by successive situations, engages its reader in a relatively more stable identification than does film. This distinction undoubtedly results from the differences between novelistic enunciation and film enunciation. The surface text of a novel generally offers a fairly stable point of view clearly centered on a character. Typically, a novel begins with a first or third person mode of narration that will be maintained throughout its enunciation. By contrast, within the classical narrative cinema, the variability of points of view is, as we will see, actually inscribed within the code itself. Obviously, however, this is only a very general observation on a statistical level, and many exceptions, in the specific cases of both films and novels, could certainly be found.

THE MECHANISMS OF IDENTIFICATION ON THE FILM'S SURFACE LEVEL. It remains to point out, on the level of the surface text's smallest units, the microcircuits where the film narrative and spectator identification will both be produced. This time, however, we will concentrate on the shot-to-shot development in each sequence. What is most remarkable, and seems to be specific to film narrative—even if the nature of this code seems quite natural and invisible since we are so accustomed to it—is that extraordinary suppleness of classical narrative editing. The most banal scene in the cinema is constructed by constantly changing point of view, focalization, and framing. It stirs up a permanent displacement of the spectator's point of view in relation to the represented scene—a displacement that does not fail to inflect the process of spectator identification via microvariations.

Once again we must be very careful in revealing the similarity between what we wrote above regarding the characteristics of identification (apparently characterized by reversibility, the play of permutations, and changing roles) and the permanent point of view variations inscribed within the code of classical editing. If, effectively, it appears as if film's surface text mimics precisely the lability of the identification process via its subtle mechanisms, nothing justifies our seeing any sort of determinism wherein one of the mechanisms serves in any way as the model for the other.

The homology nevertheless becomes quite impressive when we begin to go beyond our cultural familiarity and measure the point at which classical cinema's editing (established as a very pregnant code) is violently arbitrary. There is nothing more apparently contradictory to our perception of a real-life scene than this permanent changing of point of view, distance, and focalization, unless it is precisely the permanent play of identification (within language and the most ordinary daily events) whose importance Freud and Lacan demonstrated within the very possibility of all intersubjective reasoning, dialogue, and social life.

One thing that can be proposed in regard to this homology is that the surface text's positioning of these microcircuits probably inflects the spectator's relation to the scene and characters by small permanent jolts and minuscule shifts in successive directions. This can only be accomplished by designating places and privileged routes and by marking certain postures and certain points of view rather than others. It would take too much space here to describe in detail the elements of the surface text that inflect this play of identification (all the more so since *all* the elements, plausibly, contribute to the play in their own fashion). We will limit ourselves, then, to pointing out those that participate in the process in the largest and most direct manner.

The multiplicity of points of view, which founds the classical editing of the film scene, is undoubtedly the fundamental base of these microcircuits of identification in the surface text. This is the element that makes the play of all other elements possible. In the cinema, the classical scene constructs itself (in the code) upon multiple points of view: each new shot's appearance corresponds to a change of point of view in relation to the represented scene (which is nevertheless felt to unfold in a continuous manner and within a homogeneous space). It is fairly rare, however, for each shot change to correspond to the establishment of a new and as yet unseen point of view in relation to the scene. Typically, classical découpage functions around the return to a certain number of points of view, and these return shots to the same points of view may be quite numerous (especially, for example, in the case of a shot/reverse shot).

The evolution of the cinema from primitive to transitional to classical depends partly, according to Kristin Thompson, on the shift to multiple camera positions and the systematic staging of multiple spaces. "The various continuity rules—establishing and re-establishing shots, cut-ins, screen direction, eyelines, Shot/Reverse Shots, crosscutting—served two overall purposes. On the one hand, they permitted the narrative to proceed in a clearly defined space. On the other, they created an omnipresent narration which shifted the audience's vantage point on the action frequently to follow those parts of the scene most salient to the plot."[30]

Each of these points of view, whether or not it also occupies a character's point of view, necessarily inscribes a certain hierarchy of the various figures in the scene. The shots confer varying degrees of importance on intersubjective relationships, privilege certain characters' points of view, and underline particular lines of tension and division. The articulation of these different points of view, the more

The multiplicity of point of view in classical editing: the first scene in *Hôtel du Nord* (Carné, 1938) presents a dozen characters dining at a First Communion celebration.

Hôtel du Nord (Marcel Carné, 1938).

frequent return to certain of the shots, and their combination—all of these elements are inscribed in the code and permit us to trace, as though woven into the diegetic situation itself, places and micro-circuits that are privileged for the spectator. These elements also permit the development of the code's identification.

In the classical narrative cinema, these multiple points of view usually accompany a play of variations in shot scale.

> It is hardly by chance that the labels for various shot scales—close-up, medium shot, medium-long shot, long shot—were established in reference to the actor's body within the frame. As we know, the very idea of editing a scene in different shot scales was born from the desire to make the spectator grasp the actors' facial expressions, underline their gestures, and mark their dramatic function, all by the inclusion of a close-up.

Undoubtedly, within this variation in the size of the actors on the screen and the varying proximity of the camera's eye to each character, there is an element determining the degree of attention, shared emotion, and identification with one character or another.

> We should be sufficiently convinced of all this by listening to several of Hitchcock's statements on the subject. According to him, the shot scale is perhaps the single most important element within a director's arsenal for manipulating the audience's identification with a character. He offers a number of examples from his own films. He explains, for instance, that in one scene from *The Birds* it was essential (in spite of all the technical difficulties) to follow Tippi Hedren's face as she rose from her chair and began to move about; otherwise, by simply cutting to a wider shot of her rising from the chair he might have broken the audience's identification with her and her terror.

This manipulation of shot scales, associated with the play of multiple points of view, authorizes within the classical découpage of the scene a very subtle combination, an alternation of proximity and distance, and the disengaging and recentering on characters. It also allows a unique inscription of each character into the relational network of the situation thus presented. For example, it permits the presentation of a character as one figure among many, or as a simple element of decor, or, by contrast, in another scene it may present characters as the virtual focus of our identification by isolating them through a series of close-ups. Using close-ups creates an intense *tête à tête* with the spectator, whose interest is thereby focalized upon the character, even when s/he may play a role that is completely effaced in the actual diegetic situation. For example, the shot scale may cue us to identify with a character ignored by the other characters. All of this, of course, provides only extreme and somewhat simplistic examples that should not obscure the complex subtlety permitted by the variation of shot scales inscribed in the code.

Within the cinema's microcircuits of identification, eyelines or glances have always been a prominently privileged vector. The interplay of eyelines regulates a number of editing figures, on the smallest level of articulations, which are simultaneously among the most frequent and most coded figures, as in eyeline matches and shot/reverse shots, for instance. This is not at all surprising since, as we have seen, secondary identification is centered on the relations between characters. Moreover, the cinema understood early on that eyelines constituted a governing principle that was specific to the means of expression within the art of implicating the spectator within the film's relations.

> The long era of silent cinema, during which the essential codes of classical editing were established, favored the consideration of the privileged role of eyelines all the more in light of the relative absence of expressivity, intonation, and nuance within the dialogue of intertitles.

The articulation from the glance to desire and enticement (theorized by Lacan in "Du regard comme objet petit a") predestined, as it were, that eyelines should play such a central role within an art form marked by the dual traits of being a narrative art (hence the avatars of desire) and at the same time being a visual art (hence an art of glances).

> Thus, within many theoretical texts the eyeline match has become an emblematic figure of secondary identification in the cinema. It is often with this figure that a "subjective" shot (supposedly seen by a character) directly follows a shot of the character looking (and the shot/reverse shot may then be considered, to a certain extent, a special sort of eyeline match). Within this empowerment of the glance between the spectator and the character theorists have wanted to see the figure *par excellence* of identification with the character.

In spite of its apparent clarity, however, this example has surely helped warp the question of identification in the cinema by an excessive simplification. Analyzing the process of developing identification by the microcircuits of eyeline (and their articulation by editing) within a narrative film undoubtedly springs from a much more detailed theorization wherein the eyeline match (even if it designates a limit point or a short circuit

The central role of the glance within the shot: top, *Le jour se lève* (Marcel Carné, 1939); middle, *Notorious* (Alfred Hitchcock, 1946); bottom, *Psycho* (Alfred Hitchcock, 1960).

Three shots
from the same
scene in *Muriel*
(Alain Resnais,
1963).

between primary and secondary identification) finally does not play any more than a specific role that is too specialized to prove exemplary.

Identification and Enunciation

We need only recall Hitchcock's account, cited earlier, of building suspense in *Marnie* ("*You show* the person . . . then *you go back* to the person who is searching . . . ") in order to witness that, in creating a scene that builds strong identification, the labor of the instance that shows or narrates is just as determining as the actual structure of what is shown or narrated. Moreover, this principle is fully understood by any storyteller who is not afraid to interrupt the "natural" flow of narrated story events. Rather, such filmmakers are willing to delay and modulate events, to create surprise and even false trails; their artistry consists precisely in mastering a definite enunciation (and its rhetoric), the effects of which determine the audience's reactions more than does the actual content of the enounced.

In our example from Hitchcock, it is obvious that a spectator can only "be apprehensive" on behalf of the intruder if the narrative instance has previously revealed the person mounting the stairs outside. If, however, the scene proceeds very differently and instead surprises the spectator with the person's arrival, it will function with much less identification for the character. All this serves to show that within the process of identification the labor of narration (demonstration and enunciation) plays a clearly determining role. It contributes broadly in informing the spectator's relation to the diegesis and characters. It is narration, on the level of large narrative articulations, that will continuously modulate the spectator's knowledge of diegetic events; it will constantly control the information at his or her disposal as required during the film; it will hide certain narrative elements or, by contrast, anticipate others. Finally, narration will also regulate the progress and delay of the spectator's knowledge and the character's supposed knowledge, thereby continuously shaping the spectator's identification with diegetic figures and situations.

In all likelihood, there exists at some more global and rougher level of identification with the narrative a more massive and less subtle diegetic identification that is relatively indifferent to the specific labor of enunciation within every means of expression and in every individual text. This more inert stratum of identification may be said to arise more from the enounced and diegesis (in their structural outlines) than from the enunciation itself, and it may be understood to reveal a more regressive or Oedipal nature.

On the level of each scene, the labor of enunciation consists, as we have seen, of shaping the spectator's relationship with the diegetic situation, tracing its privileged microcircuits, and organizing the production and structuring of the identification process shot by shot. This labor by the enunciation is accordingly more invisible with the classical narrative cinema, where it is controlled by the code. Undoubtedly, it is there, at the level of small articulations on the text's surface, that the code is the most pregnant, the most stable, the most automatic, and therefore the most invisible.

Editing a scene according to several points of view, the return to an establishing shot, the shot/reverse shot, the eyeline glance, as well as the use of arbitrary codified elements, helps the spectator participate directly in the labor of enunciation. Nonetheless, the audience, by force of cultural habit, perceives it all as enunciation's "degree zero," or as the most natural method by which a story can be told in the cinema. Certainly classical editing rules, and particularly rules for matching, aim precisely to efface the marks of this enunciative labor and to render it invisible. Its mission is to see to it that the situations present themselves to the spectator as if by themselves and that the code appears sufficiently banal and worn to seem to function quasi-automatically while giving the illusion that the enunciative instant is absent or vacant.

This editing strategy is obviously one of the strengths of the classical narrative and especially classical Hollywood cinema, and one reason behind the extraordinary dominance of this mode of film narratives. The detailed and invisible control of enunciation maintains the audience members' impression that they actually enter the narrative, that they identify with one character or another via sympathy, and that they react to given situations rather as they would in real life. All of this reinforces the illusion for each spectator that s/he is simultaneously the center, the source, and the unique subject of the emotions produced by the film. Yet it also leads the spectator to deny that this identification is also the effect of a manipulation and the labor of enunciation.

Since the 1960s and its valorization of auteur theory (particularly in Europe), we have seen more and more filmmakers asserting themselves by a personal enunciation and also signing, as it were, their films with some more or less flamboyant and arbitrary marks of their own characteristic enunciation. This is certainly the case for famous directors like Ingmar Bergman (*The Silence* [1963], *Persona*

[1966]), Michelangelo Antonioni (*Eclipse* [1962], *The Red Desert* [1964]), Jean-Luc Godard (*Contempt* [1963], *Two or Three Things I Know about Her* [1966]), and Federico Fellini (*La Dolce Vita* [1960], *8½* [1963]).

At the beginning of the 1970s, a large theoretical debate surrounded ideology as conveyed by the classical cinema and, in particular, its transparency and effacement of the marks of enunciation. Several filmmakers, in keeping with their political or ideological concerns, believed it best to inscribe the work of enunciation (which is to say the production process) clearly within their films. For example, we may cite *Octobre à Madrid* (1965) by Marcel Hanoun, and *Tout va bien* (1972) by Godard and Jean-Pierre Gorin, as well as all the films produced by the Dziga Vertov Group.

It would appear, in the two cases, that a more noticeable and foregrounded presence for the enunciating instance should at least partially block the identification process, if only in making more difficult the spectator's illusion of being the locus and unique origin of all identification because the film reveals the presence of the normally hidden figure of the master of enunciation. However, this assumption would underestimate the spectator's capacity for restoring the film to a "good object." For more intellectual spectators and/or cinephiles, this figure of the master of enunciation has in turn often become a figure with whom to identify. Ultimately, such identification is fairly classic from the structural point of view; the master of enunciation (the auteur, even if s/he contests the role) is also, in his or her way, the one whose will opposes the spectator's desire or delays it (launching identification) with the prestige in addition of a figure incarnating some ego ideal for the cinephile.

The Film Spectator and the Psychoanalytic Subject

Everything that has preceded in this chapter springs from psychoanalysis's classic conception of identification as narcissistic regression and assumes the following as a completely arbitrary postulate: one may test the film spectator's state or activity with theoretical instruments established by psychoanalysis to understand the subject. This assumes *a priori* (and therein lies a sort of wager) that the film spectator is perfectly homological with and reducible to the psychoanalytic subject, or at least its theoretical model. This conception of the spectator is beginning to be questioned more and more. For example, Jean-Louis Schéfer writes that there is a cinematic enigma irreducible to the fiction of the psychoanalytic subject as centered around the ego. Instead, the cinema should be described for its effects of amazement and terror, and for its production of a displaced subject, "a sort of mutant subject or a less understood person."[31]

The path taken until now in film theory would not allow cinema to be understood as a new process that must be studied outside of the reassuring homology between the subject and the cinematographic apparatus. For Schéfer, however, the cinema is not made to allow the spectator to rediscover himself or herself (as in the theory of narcissistic regression), but also, and more importantly, it was created to surprise and amaze: "You go to the cinema—everyone does—for more or less terrifying simulations, and not for a bit of dreaming. Searching for a bit of terror and a bit of the unknown . . . when I am at the movies I am a simulated being . . . and that is the paradox of the spectator which must be addressed."

Feminist Theory and the Spectator

Feminists too have challenged (and been challenged by) the standard notions of identification. One feminist goal for investigating the film subject and identification involves rereading Saussure, Althusser, Freud, and Lacan in order to confront notions of language, gender, identification, and pleasure. By investigating the cinematic apparatus and its discursive code systems, as well as the diegetic realm a film depicts, feminists have begun a productive interrogation of the cinema's modes of address and ideological implications. That inquiry actively spans a wide spectrum of research, but we will simply point here to three facets of feminist study that relate to our preceding discussions.

First, feminist theorists have expanded and attacked notions of visual pleasure and subjectivity. Certainly one of the most often cited and reprinted texts is Laura Mulvey's exemplary "Visual Pleasure and Narrative Cinema," first published in *Screen* in 1975. One of the powerful but also problematic conclusions Mulvey makes is that classical cinema constructs pleasure for a male viewer alone; and thus, feminist cinema must break away from the conventions and codes of that traditional, pleasurable cinema.

Accounting for, defining, and defending sexual difference led to a number of evolving theoretical models during the 1970s and 1980s. Among the many histories of feminist film theory and criticism, *Re-Vision: Essays in Feminist Film Criticism* (edited by Mary Ann Doane, Patricia Mellencamp, and Linda Williams) offers a rich introduction to many of the shifts in strategies and assumptions. One initial concern was whether one must attack all film texts produced under a patriarchal system or whether certain films could be re-couped as representing the failures of traditional film discourse. The division produced two distinct schools. On the one hand were theorist-filmmakers calling for the production and analysis of an al-ternative cinema; these feminists "were convinced that women's 'truth' demanded radically new forms of representation if it was to emerge at all."[32]

On the other hand were feminists dedicated to "reading against the grain," which allowed them to analyze a wider range of film texts. Work by Raymond Bellour, Luce Irigary, and Julia Kristeva helped guide this rereading process to reveal how males are tradi-tionally represented in Western literary and film discourse while the female is systematically absent. As Janet Bergstrom and Mary Ann Doane explain in their introduction to Camera Obscura's special issue on "The Spectatrix," "Reading against the grain as a feminist, one could salvage texts previously thought to be entirely compli-cit. . . . It is perceived by many as a way to reappropriate texts and pleasures renounced by a more pessimistic analysis of patriarchy's success."[33] According to Elaine Marks and Isabelle de Courtivron, one goal of such "rereading" involved making concrete connections between the representation of women and larger aspects of culture and ideology.[34] Feminist theorists such as Kaja Silverman, Annette Kuhn, Gaylyn Studlar, the Camera Obscura collective, and many others helped establish the direction for the analysis of subjectivity, pleasure, and film discourse. The study of popular culture, particu-larly television, springs directly from these concerns with cultural discourse, patriarchal formations, and methods of feminist textual analysis.

The second aspect of feminist film theory that deserves mention here was the shift to rereading film history. One initial trap for femi-nism was, and is, the ahistorical analysis of texts; thus, by the 1980s there was a more concerted effort to reexamine large historical con-structs and to connect psychoanalysis and semiotics with econom-ics, technology, and aesthetics.

As Bergstrom and Doane write, "Psychoanalysis seemed to mandate and perpetuate a treatment of spectatorship that was ahistorical. The urge to move beyond generalities, or to test them against particular instances, manifested itself both in a renewed search for historical specificity in modes of spectatorship (in the work of critics such as Haralovich, Spigel, Jacobs, Hansen, Petro) and in approaches inspired by work in British cul-tural studies."[35] The body of feminist critics currently combining theoretical with historical research is obviously a very large and active group that includes the Camera Obscura collective as well as scholars such as Gaylyn Studlar, Maureen Turim, and Diane Waldman.

The third important aspect of feminist film studies concerns the shift toward genre (which is reflected above in Bergstrom and Doane's comments about "salvaging" texts). The work on classic genres, such as E. Ann Kaplan's book on film noir, and on "women's pictures" and melodramas (less rigorous film groupings) has provided another avenue of study and specialization. However, one often unstated claim is that feminist analysis, in whatever form, is somehow more appropriate for those genres (and nongenres) than other forms of analysis. Just as some feminists reduce the entire apparatus of television to a gendered entity, claiming TV is somehow more "feminine" than the motion picture (although just how economic, technological, historical, and aesthetic aspects of a medium can be personified and reduced to a sexual entity is never convincingly argued), some theorists also treat certain areas of genre as the privileged realm of feminist analysis. This notion, along with the persistence of some theorists in arguing that male spectators have "unproblematic" access to the symbolic while the female belongs more to the side of the imaginary, must be challenged by the continuing evolution of the study of spectatorship.

The fields of feminist film theory, history, and criticism are vast and far from homogeneous, as the wealth of texts over the past two decades reveals. We cannot attempt here to list all of them since the discipline is so dynamic as to be evolving daily. However, we would like to point out that feminist projects not only grow out of the long history of film and literary theory; they have also changed it permanently by testing and expanding the notions of subject/object relations, discourse, and pleasure. More work is finally being done on historical aspects of film—not simply in writing histories of women in the industry or outlining dominant "images of women" throughout various points in film history—but in accounting for the relations between spectatorship (reception, fetishism, pleasure), industrial practice (marketing, production, and acting modes), and aesthetics.

CONCLUSION

At the end of this exploration of today's most important questions for a theory of film, the reader will have noticed the breadth, the complexity, and, we hope, the profound interest of these reflections on the art of moving images. We would like to attach, in closing, a brief summary of the theories (whether they actually are or are not constituted as doctrines per se) to which we have alluded in passing.

The first trait that stands out concerning the theories of cinema and their succession is their longevity. Actually, there is perhaps no human output that is not immediately accompanied by a formal, theoretical reflection, or at least—and this is the etymology of the word "theory"—an observation, a thorough contemplation of this output. One might certainly remark that intellectual speculation kept pace with the cinema's invention, which continued throughout the nineteenth century. It is no less striking to note that the appearance of the cinema as spectacle, then as art and means of expression, was almost totally contemporaneous with its theorization. Moreover, all the film movements, schools, and important genres recorded by historians were accompanied by, or closely preceded or followed by, some more or less important theoretical activity. Film history is not short on these theoretical revolutions, and many famous examples mark the cinema's hundred-year life span.

Therefore, the second trait that distinguishes theories of the cinema is, in retrospect, their profound historicity, or more exactly, the coherence of the link that unites them with cinematic production in each era. This is evident when one considers great figures like André Bazin and Sergei Mikhailovich Eisenstein: Italian neorealism nourished Bazin's "ontological" and "cosmophanic" theories, just as the experimentalism of the 1920s (even beyond the strict limits of the Soviet montage school) inspired Eisenstein's love of montage, manipulation, and conflict. However, on a larger scale, the history of theories demonstrates at a glance the emergence of a small number of "continents" (or "archipelagos," if one prizes metaphorical precision), which a chronology marked by major accidents (the two world wars or the advent of sound, to cite incommensurable phenomena) allows us to pinpoint with ease.

Let us recall the great names. There was first of all—giving priority to chronology will avoid both aesthetic and ideological selection—the epoch of progressive constitution, then the almost exclusive reign of the formalist tradition. It was a rhetoric that developed fully after World War I and during the era of incessant upheavals in film art in the 1920s and then found its classic form by the early 1930s (while dominant practice had changed, and, in a completely different sense of the word, the cinema itself had become classic). Since 1916, in the second part of his famous essay, Hugo Münsterberg affirmed, from a neo-Kantian perspective, that the requirement for film's aesthetic validity rested with the process of transforming reality into an imaginary object submitting to a particular poetics (playing, for the directors, upon the three basic categories of reality: time, space, and causality).

That same year Griffith's *Intolerance* appeared; it involved incredible manipulation that must have fulfilled Münsterberg's ideal. Several years later, and upon quite different philosophical grounds, the same attitude was again taking shape. During the course of this study we have already discussed the approaches of Eisenstein and Yuri Tynianov; we certainly need to add to their two names several of their contemporaries and compatriots. We begin with Lev Kuleshov, whose *Kuleshov on Film* (1929) is perhaps the most impudent, and thus the most dangerous, advance on the path toward a comparison of film organization and the functioning of a language system. The excesses of such an approach have often been criticized, and rightly so, but what concerns us here is above all the constancy with which Kuleshov and his students accompanied all of their studies with a series of experiments and of films whose systematic nature, without precedent, would never be rivaled.

In Germany at nearly the same time, Rudolf Arnheim, in his brief but categorical essay, was establishing the extreme limits that the formalist current of thought would attain. For him, film could be an art only insofar as the cinema distances itself from the perfect reproduction of reality, and, in a way, thanks to the very defects of the cinematic apparatus. This famous and unequaled thesis has assured Arnheim's reputation, but at the same time it has actually marked

the end of one type of approach that had become completely inca-
pable of considering the profound modifications affecting the art of
cinema, let us say, between 1928 and 1932.

However, this is not to say that this approach is completely dead;
many theorists, and not simply less important ones, have revived
and championed its cause. In this way Béla Balázs twice proposed,
in 1930 and 1950, brilliant syntheses of all that the formalist current had brought in return to a history of the cinema. More recently
yet, essays by Barthélémy Amengual and Ivor Montagu, which appeared during the 1960s, refer to without really renewing this great
tradition.

Incontestably, however, the postwar period has been primarily distinguished by another pole, previously overshadowed by the formalist tendency, which one might designate, for want of a better term,
a "realist" approach to the cinema. This approach, as we just mentioned, did not fall from the sky: its premises are found in the work
of Louis Feuillade, for example (in an admittedly unelaborated form)
or, more clearly, in all the critical reflections with which John Grierson accompanied the flowering of the documentary movement during the 1930s and 1940s. Of course, this current is definitely marked
by the figure of André Bazin. There again, what we find most important is less the existence of a Bazin school (which was at first strictly
limited to France, with the *Cahiers du Cinéma* of the 1950s and
1960s and the New Wave) than that Bazin's reflections were contemporaneous with other approaches completely independent of his
own, but which moved in roughly the same aesthetic direction. We
may cite the work of Etienne Souriau, for example, or especially the
summa published by Siegfried Kracauer in 1960, significantly sub-
titled *The Redemption of Physical Reality*, which its author presents as a "material aesthetics." This aesthetics was founded on the
primacy of content, and it opens onto a conception of cinema as a
sort of scientific instrument created in order to explore certain types
or particular aspects of reality.

It cannot be said that we are completely out of this latter period;
however, it survives almost exclusively under the weakened form of
"film criticism," which is based on its assumptions without truly
seeking to examine them and still less to justify them.

Finally, a third period (which is ours) is not marked by a synthesis
of the two preceding eras but rather is typified by a flowering of film
theories that, in spite of their differences, share a common trait of
appealing to much more advanced and systematic techniques of formalization. Nonetheless, this period opened with an explicitly synthetic endeavor, namely, the impressive *Esthétique et psychologie*

du cinéma by Jean Mitry. Quite deliberately, Mitry left no stone unturned, not only putting to work his extensive knowledge of film history, but also taking advantage of all the authors who had preceded him. Despite the difficulties inherent in this type of enterprise, and the false steps that followed, Mitry marks a prime stage in film theory by requiring, for all essential problems, the greatest scientific rigor. Moreover, he did not hesitate, in order to address some specific point in a film, to call upon phenomenology, gestalt theory, psychology, and the physiology of perception; indeed, he even set himself up for a time as an epistemologist. Although it did not establish a school, although it belongs to no school, Mitry's book serves as a landmark: Christian Metz was well aware of this, for he devoted two long critical articles to Mitry's two volumes when they were first published. These two articles may be found today in the second volume of *Essais sur la signification au cinéma*.

The history of film theory since Mitry is distinguished by the ever more extensive importation of concepts, indeed of entire conceptual systems, stemming from the so-called human sciences—linguistics and psychoanalysis at the forefront, but also involving sociology and history. At the same time, theoretical activity became more and more academic and stopped trying to double as critical activity (or polemic/normative reviewing), and it stopped trying to refer to some contemporary body of films in a privileged manner. While it is still true that some theorization depends, whether consciously or not, on a genre, a type, or a school of films (such as Alain Robbe-Grillet for Jost and Chateau's book, or Jean-Luc Godard and Jean-Marie Straub for Bonitzer), the more generally accepted notion is now that any theorization should strive for universality. At the same time, the spread of film courses has also spurred renewed interest in the analysis of older films on a much larger scale than ever before.

Thus, the last twenty years have been doubly marked: on the one hand, by an abundance of works inspired by semiology (in its large sense) and narratology, while, on the other hand, they are distinguished by the blossoming of film analyses (whether or not they are expressly modeled after textual analysis). However, the preceding chapters have attempted to account for this entire period, so we do not need to expand on it here.

It is obviously more difficult to summarize current directions in research (and more difficult yet to forecast the upcoming decade). Without being able to claim absolutely that the semiological vein has been completely exhausted, we may point out a double tendency that demonstrates what has been described as a "death of semiology" (Metz). On the one hand, there is the desire, as witnessed most notably by a number of recent books (and it is most striking in certain collections and accounts of colloquia and conferences), to take stock of and summarize the movement. On the other hand, there are equally numerous and dispersed attempts to escape this relative impasse; examples include appeals to generative semantics and "Textlinguistik," among others. Obviously, this so-called death of semiotics is nothing of the kind (at least not the kind of death that leads to reincarnation), and it remains important today to pursue semiotics by a general formalization, just as it is important (even if just pedagogically) to practice filmological analysis in all its forms.

It seems to us, however, that the last few years have been marked by a diversification of research directions. Hence, there has been a return to a strong interest in film history (admittedly primarily by Americans of late), which many researchers have methodically and systematically undertaken and which is usually far superior to the methods of the pioneers of the discipline (although the "history of science" has generally made few advances in the last twenty years). In addition, we have seen a good half-dozen books devoted largely to economic issues in the cinema—not unrelated certainly to the transformation of the means of expression itself (development of television and small-format video, concentration of production and distribution, etc.). Finally, rare approaches have been illustrated by several high-quality texts, approaches such as sociology of cinema or, in another domain, what one might call its iconology.

It is still too early to judge the place or overall value of all these attempts. We will thus modestly conclude this rapid overview of film theories by noting how much this current diversification attests once again to the anthropological and social dimension of cinema studies, as well as the interconnections between cinema and the social sciences.

NOTES

1. Film as Audiovisual Representation

1. In French there is a word for the individual film frame on the celluloid, *photogramme*, which is quite separate from the word for the border or frame of the image, *cadre*. To avoid confusion the term "frame" is used to designate the "photogram" or material "film frame," while the double term "image border" is used to label the *cadre* [translator's note].

2. Rudolf Arnheim, *Film as Art*, 12.

3. André Bazin, *Jean Renoir*, 87.

4. Noël Burch, *Theory of Film Practice*, 17–30, esp. 21.

5. For more on sound's role in unifying disparate shots, see Mary Ann Doane, "The Voice in the Cinema: The Articulation of Body and Space," *Yale French Studies* (ed. Rick Altman) 60 (1980): 33–50.

6. Pascal Bonitzer, *Le Regard et la voix*.

7. E. H. Gombrich, *Art and Illusion*; Arnheim, *Film as Art*, 8–34.

8. Focal length is a parameter that is dependent upon the lens construction alone. The amount of light entering the camera depends on the f-stop setting and the amount of light emitted by the filmed object. A third parameter for depth of field is the distance between the object and the lens.

9. Jean-Luc Godard, *Godard on Godard*, 236.

10. Jean-Louis Comolli, "Technique and Ideology: Camera, Perspective, Depth of Field," in *Movies and Methods*, ed. Bill Nichols, vol. 2, 40–57.

11. Today the standard speed is 24 frames per second; yet, as we know, this was not always the case. Silent films had a slower projection speed (16 to 18 fps), which was also less strictly determined, and the speed actually fluctuated quite a bit. During the late 1920s, for instance, which was a period of transition from silent to sound, the speed kept accelerating.

12. We should point out that the filming of silents was very often accompanied by a musical background, usually played by a violinist present on the set, trying to suggest the mood sought by the director.

13. See Donald Kirihara, "A Reconsideration of the Institution of the Benshi," *Film Reader* 6 (1985): 41–53; Joseph L. Anderson and Donald Ritchie, *The Japanese Film*, 23–26; Noël Burch, *To the Distant Observer*, 76–84.

14. See, for instance, Robert C. Allen and Douglas Gomery, *Film History: Theory and Practice*, 115–128.

15. Bazin, *What Is Cinema?* vol. 1, 24.

16. In French the term used for silent cinema is *muet*, which is also the word for mute or speechless [translator's note].

17. Barthélémy Amengual, *René Clair*.

18. Alexander Walker, *The Shattered Silents*, 132.

2. Montage

1. In French the word *montage* refers to the technical process of editing in the material sense, yet it also denotes the larger notion of "assembly" or the arrangement of shots, as well as the interaction of those shots. In English "montage" refers to the juxtaposition of two or more shots in a rapid sequence. "Editing" is used here to express *montage* in its most narrow and material sense, "montage sequence" for the juxtaposition of brief shots in a rapid sequence, and "montage" for the more abstract sense of the term [translator's note].

2. Marcel Martin, *Le Langage cinématographique*.

3. "Syntagma" is a linguistic term for the units of meaning linked in actual relations within chains of sequential units. Such syntagmatic chains may, in the cinema, be made of scenes on a large level or, more typically, series of shots.

4. Examples would include *Benjamin* (Michel Deville, 1968) cited in *Une femme douce* (Robert Bresson, 1969), *Casablanca* (Michael Curtiz, 1942) in *Play It Again, Sam* (Woody Allen, 1972), or *The Lusty Men* (Nicholas Ray, 1952) in *Nick's Movie* (Wim Wenders, 1980), among others.

5. Examples would include *Intolerance* (D. W. Griffith, 1916), *One Plus One* (Jean-Luc Godard, 1968), and *Pigsty* (Pier Paolo Pasolini, 1969) among others.

6. Christian Metz, "Montage et discours," in *Essais sur la signification au cinéma*, vol. 2, 95.

7. Ibid., 90–91.

8. Martin, *Le Langage cinématographique*, 131.

9. Béla Balázs, *Theory of the Film*, 123.

10. Jean Mitry, *Esthétique et psychologie du cinéma*, vol. 1, 287–410.

11. Balázs, *Theory of the Film*, 118–138.

12. Vsevolod Pudovkin, "On Editing," in *Film Theory and Criticism*, ed. Gerald Mast and Marshall Cohen, 82–84.

13. Sergei M. Eisenstein, "Methods of Montage," in *Film Form*, 72–83.

14. Literally, "king montage" [translator's note].

15. André Bazin, *What Is Cinema?* vol. 1, 46.

16. Ibid., 48.

17. Ibid., 50.

18. André Bazin, *Orson Welles*, trans. Jonathan Rosenbaum, 77.

19. Burch, *Theory of Film Practice*, 3–16.

20. Bazin, *Orson Welles*, 80.

21. Bazin, *What Is Cinema?* vol. 1, 166.

22. Roland Barthes, "The Third Meaning," in *Image-Music-Text*, 56.

23. Eisenstein, *Film Form*, 49, 54.

24. See in particular "Word and Image," in *Film Sense*, 3–68.

25. Bazin, *What Is Cinema?* vol. 1, 24.

3. Cinema and Narration

1. Christian Metz, *Langage et cinéma*, 5–44.

2. Burch, *Theory of Film Practice*, 18–22.

3. Christian Metz, "Problems of Denotation in the Fiction Film," in *Film Language*, 108–146.

4. Editors of *Cahiers du Cinéma*, "John Ford's *Young Mr. Lincoln*," in *Movies and Methods*, ed. Bill Nichols, vol. 1, 493–529; also in *Screen Reader* 1 (1977): 113–152.

5. See Metz, *Film Language*, 16–29.

6. André Bazin, *What Is Cinema?* vol. 1, 154–163.

7. Ibid., 161.

8. See, for example, David Bordwell, "Jump Cuts and Blind Spots," *Wide Angle* 6/1 (1984): 4–11, or "La Saute et l'ellipse," *Revue Belge du Cinéma* 16 (Summer 1986): 85–90.

9. François Truffaut, *Hitchcock*, 207, 211.

10. Claude Lévi-Strauss, *Structural Anthropology*, vol. 2, 142–144, 145–197.

11. Georges Sadoul, *Dictionary of Films*, 332.

12. Gérard Genette, *Narrative Discourse: An Essay in Method*.

13. Mitry, *Esthétique et psychologie du cinéma*, vol. 1, 184.

14. Genette, *Narrative Discourse*, 212–262.

15. Emile Benveniste, *Problèmes de linguistique générale*, vol. 1, 238–245.

16. Barthes, *Image-Music-Text*, 119.

17. Thierry Kuntzel, "The Film-Work," *Enclitic* 2/1 (1973): 38–61; "The Film-Work 2," *Camera Obscura* 5 (1980): 7–68.

18. Roland Barthes, *S/Z* (English ed.), 84–85; *S/Z* (French ed.), 92.

19. See A. J. Greimas and J. Courtés, "Programme narratif," in *Sémiotique: Dictionnaire raisonné de la théorie du langage*, vol. 2, 177–181.

20. For more on suspense and fetishism, see Roland Barthes, *The Pleasure of the Text*.

21. Vladimir Propp, *Morphology of the Folktale*; Claude Lévi-Strauss, *Structural Study of Myth and Totemism*, and *Structural Anthropology*, vols. 1 and 2.

22. Propp, *Morphology of the Folktale*, 21.

23. See Greimas and Courtés, "Acteur," in *Sémiotique*, vol. 1, 7–8.

24. In France the practice of writing *ciné-romans* based on popular or prestigious films is much more common than in the United States. These novelizations are often accompanied by production stills or frame enlargements from the films themselves, supplying a photographic referent to the characters [translator's note].

25. Lee Marvin plays the part of Vince Stone, while Gloria Grahame is Debby Marsh.

26. Edgar Morin, *Les Stars.*

27. Bazin, *What Is Cinema?* vol. 2, 60.

28. Ibid., 27.

29. For more on notions of the *vraisemblable* or plausible, see Christian Metz, "The Saying and the Said: Toward the Decline of a Plausibility in the Cinema?" in *Film Language*, 235–252.

30. Gérard Genette, *Figures II*, 73–75.

31. See especially Bazin, "The Ontology of the Photographic Image" and "The Myth of Total Cinema," in *What Is Cinema?* vol. 1, 9–22; and Amedée Ayfre, *Dieu au cinéma: Problèmes esthétiques du film religieux*, and "The Universe of Robert Bresson," in *The Films of Robert Bresson*, ed. Ian Cameron, 6–24.

32. See, for instance, Jean-Louis Baudry, "Ideological Effects of the Basic Cinematographic Apparatus," in *Movies and Methods*, vol. 2, 531–542.

4. Cinema and Language

1. Abel Gance, "La Musique de la lumière," in *L'Art cinématographique* (n.p.: 1927); cited in Pierre Lherminier, *L'Art du cinéma*, 60–61.

2. Ricciotto Canudo, *L'Usine aux images* (Paris: Chiron, 1927); cited in Lherminier, *L'Art du cinéma*, 34–35.

3. Jean Epstein, *Bonjour, cinéma*; cited in Marcel L'Herbier, *Intelligence du cinématographe*, 261.

4. Hugo Münsterberg, *The Film: A Psychological Study*, 82.

5. Ibid., 100.

6. Balázs, *Theory of the Film*, 30–31.

7. V. I. Pudovkin, *Film Technique and Film Acting*, trans. Ivor Montagu, 87.

8. Juri Tynianov, "Fundamentals of the Cinema," *Cahiers du Cinéma* 220–221 (May–June 1970): 58–68.

9. Boris Eichenbaum, "Problems of Cine-Stylistics," *Cahiers du Cinéma* 220–221 (May–June 1970): 70–78.

10. Raymond Spottiswoode, *A Grammar of the Film*, 29.

11. Roger Odin, "Modèle grammatical, modèles linguistiques et étude du langage cinématographique," in *Cahiers du 20e siècle: Cinéma et littérature*, 9–30.

12. Metz, *Film Language*, 82–83.

13. Martin, *Le Langage cinématographique*, 278.

14. Ibid.

15. Ibid., 279.

16. Mitry, *Esthétique et psychologie du cinéma*, vol. 1, 47–48.

17. Ibid., 53–54.

18. Metz, *Film Language*, 31–91.

19. Ferdinand de Saussure, *Course in General Linguistics*, 16.

20. Louis Marin, *Essais sémiologiques, écritures, peintures*; Jean-Jacques Nattiez, *Densité 21.5 de Varèse: Essai d'analyse sémiologique*.

21. Saussure, *Course in General Linguistics*, 9, 14.

22. Christian Metz, *The Imaginary Signifier*, trans. Celia Britton, Annwyl Williams, Ben Brewster, and Alfred Guzzetti, 43–44.

23. Martin, *Le Langage cinématographique*, 279.

24. Metz, *Film Language*, 115.

25. Ibid., 62.

26. Umberto Eco, *A Theory of Semiotics*, 233–234.

27. Ibid.

28. Metz, *Film Language*, 105.

29. Metz, *Essais sur la signification au cinéma*, vol. 2, 18.

30. Pierre Francastel, *Art et technique*.

31. Eco, *A Theory of Semiotics*, 206.

32. Metz, *Language and Cinema*, 199–200.

33. Christian Metz, "Le Perçu et le nommé," in *Essais sémiotiques*, 138.

34. See David Bordwell, Janet Staiger, and Kristin Thompson, *The Classical Hollywood Cinema*, 1–240, esp. "Formulation of the Classical Style, 1909–28," 155–240.

35. Metz, *Film Language*, 95.

36. Roland Barthes, "Analyse textuelle d'un conte d'Edgar Poe," in *Sémiotique narrative et textuelle*.

37. Etienne Souriau, *L'Univers filmique*, 8.

38. Raymond Bellour, "Le Texte introuvable," in *L'Analyse du film*, 35–41.

39. Metz, *Language and Cinema*, 102.

40. Roland Barthes, "Théorie du texte," in *Encyclopaedia Universalis*, vol. 15, 1015.

41. Bellour, *L'Analyse du film*, 131–246.

42. Barthes, "Théorie du texte," 1016.

43. Ibid., 1017.

44. Bellour, "Le Texte introuvable," 38–41.

45. Dominique Chateau, "Le Rôle de l'analyse textuelle dans la théorie," in *Théorie du film*, ed. Jacques Aumont and Jean-Louis Leutrat, 66–72.

46. Raymond Bellour, "A batons rompus," in *Théorie du film*, ed. Aumont and Leutrat, 24–25.

47. For more on theoretical problems, especially the potential lack of historical perspective in textual analysis, see David Bordwell, "Textual Analysis, Etc.," *Enclitic* 5/2–6/1 (Fall 1981/Spring 1982): 125–136.

48. Bellour, "Le Texte introuvable," 40.

49. Barthes, "The Third Meaning," in *Image-Music-Text*, 64.

50. Bellour, "Le Texte introuvable," 40–41.

51. Kuntzel, "The Film-Work 2," 7–68.

52. See Marie-Claire Ropars, Michèle Lagny, and Pierre Sorlin, *Octobre,* and *La Révolution figurée.*

5. Film and Its Spectator

1. Münsterberg, *The Film: A Psychological Study,* 74.
2. Rudolf Arnheim, *Art and Visual Perception,* 46.
3. According to Vance Kepley, it has never been proven that Lenin actually made this statement; see "Lenin and the Soviet Cinema: The Nationalization Decree Reconsidered," *Journal of Film and Video* 42/2 (Summer 1990): 3–14.
4. See special issue 6 of *Iris,* "The Kuleshov Effect" (1986), edited by Jacques Aumont.
5. Vsevolod Pudovkin, "From *Film Technique,*" in *Film Theory and Criticism,* ed. Mast and Cohen, 81.
6. Dziga Vertov, *Kino-Eye,* trans. Kevin O'Brien, ed. Annette Michelson, 49–50.
7. Marc Soriano, "Lire, assister," *Revue Internationale de Filmologie* 3–4 (October 1948): 299–304.
8. Edgar Morin, *Le Cinéma ou l'homme imaginaire,* vii.
9. Ibid., x–xi.
10. Ibid., 15.
11. Ibid., 16; he quotes Etienne Souriau, "Filmologie et esthétique comparées," *Revue Internationale de Filmologie* 10 (April–June 1952): 149.
12. Ibid., 188.
13. Ibid., 82.
14. Ibid., 85; he cites Jacques Poisson, "Cinéma et psychanalyse," *Cahiers du Mois* 16–17: 176.
15. Ibid., 110.
16. Ibid., 118.
17. René Zazzo, "Niveau mental et compréhension du cinéma," *Revue Internationale de Filmologie* 5 (n.d.): 33.
18. Metz, *Film Language,* 119–133.
19. Roland Barthes, *A Lover's Discourse,* trans. Richard Howard, 132.
20. Raymond Bellour, "Système d'un fragment," in *L'Analyse du film,* 81–122, and "The Obvious and the Code," in *Narrative, Apparatus, Ideology,* ed. Philip Rosen, 93–101; and Nick Browne, "The Spectator-in-the-Text," in *Narrative, Apparatus, Ideology,* 102–119.
21. See Kaja Silverman, *The Acoustic Mirror.*
22. Guy Rosolato, *Essais sur le symbolique.*
23. Jean-Louis Baudry, "The Apparatus: Metapsychological Approaches to the Impression of Reality in the Cinema," trans. Jean Andrews and Bertrand Augst, in *Narrative, Apparatus, Ideology,* 317–318.
24. Baudry, "Ideological Effects of the Basic Cinematographic Apparatus," trans. Alan Williams, in *Narrative, Apparatus, Ideology,* 295.
25. Ibid.

26. Meir Sternberg, *Expositional Modes and Temporal Ordering in Fiction*, 50–51.

27. Rosolato, *Essais*, 245.

28. Truffaut, *Hitchcock*, 51.

29. Barthes, *A Lover's Discourse*, 129–130.

30. Kristin Thompson, *The Classical Hollywood Cinema*, 213.

31. Jean-Louis Schéfer, *L'Homme ordinaire du cinéma*.

32. *Re-Vision: Essays in Feminist Film Criticism*, ed. Mary Ann Doane, Patricia Mellencamp, and Linda Williams, 8.

33. Janet Bergstrom and Mary Ann Doane, "The Female Spectator: Contexts and Directions," *Camera Obscura* 20–21 (1990): 20.

34. Elaine Marks and Isabelle de Courtivron, eds., *New French Feminisms*, xii.

35. Bergstrom and Doane, "The Female Spectator," 8.

BIBLIOGRAPHY

Allen, Robert C., and Douglas Gomery. *Film History: Theory and Practice*. New York: Knopf, 1985.

Altman, Rick, ed. *Genre: The Musical*. London: Routledge & Kegan Paul, 1981.

Amengual, Barthélémy. *Clefs pour le cinéma*. Paris: Seghers, 1971.

———. *René Clair*. Paris: Seghers, 1963.

Anderson, Joseph L., and Donald Ritchie. *The Japanese Film*. Princeton: Princeton University Press, 1982.

Andrew, Dudley. *The Major Film Theories*. New York: Oxford University Press, 1976.

Aristarco, Guido. *Storia delle teoriche del film*. Turin: Einaudi, 1951.

Arnheim, Rudolf. *Art and Visual Perception*. Berkeley: University of California Press, 1974.

———. *Film as Art*. Berkeley: University of California Press, 1957.

Aumont, Jacques. *Montage Eisenstein*. Bloomington: Indiana University Press, 1986.

Aumont, Jacques, and Jean-Louis Leutrat, eds. *Théorie du film*. Paris: Albatros, 1980.

Aumont, Jacques, and Michel Marie. *L'Analyse du film*. Paris: Nathan, 1986.

Ayfre, Amedée. *Dieu au cinéma: Problèmes esthétiques du film religieux*. Paris: PUF, 1953.

Baileblé, Claude, Michel Marie, and Marie-Claire Ropars. *Muriel*. Paris: Galilée, 1974.

Balázs, Béla. *L'Esprit du cinéma*. Paris: Editions Payot, reprinted 1977.

———. *Theory of the Film*. New York: Dover, 1970.

Balio, Tino. *The American Film Industry*. Madison: University of Wisconsin Press, 1976.

Barthes, Roland. "Analyse textuelle d'un conte d'Edgar Poe." In *Sémiotique narrative et textuelle*. Paris: Larousse, 1973.

———. *Image-Music-Text*. New York: Hill and Wang, 1977.

———. *A Lover's Discourse*. Trans. Richard Howard. New York: Noonday, 1990.

———. *The Pleasure of the Text*. New York: Hill and Wang, 1975.

———. *S/Z*. Paris: Editions du Seuil, 1970.

———. *S/Z*. New York: Hill and Wang, 1974.

———. "Théorie du texte." In *Encyclopaedia Universalis*, vol. 15. Paris: Encyclopaedia Universalis France, 1973.

Bataille, Robert. *Grammaire cinématographique*. Paris: Lefort, 1947.

Baudry, Jean-Louis. "The Apparatus: Metapsychological Approaches to the Impression of Reality in the Cinema." Trans. Jean Andrews and Bertrand Augst. In *Narrative, Apparatus, Ideology*, ed. Philip Rosen. New York: Columbia University Press, 1986.

———. "Ideological Effects of the Basic Cinematographic Apparatus." Trans. Alan Williams. In *Narrative, Apparatus, Ideology*, ed. Philip Rosen. New York: Columbia University Press, 1986.

Bazin, André. *Jean Renoir*. New York: Delta, 1973.

———. *Orson Welles*. Paris: Editions du Cerf, 1972.

———. *Orson Welles*. Trans. Jonathan Rosenbaum. New York: Harper & Row, 1978.

———. *What Is Cinema?* 2 vols. Berkeley: University of California Press, 1967.

Bellour, Raymond. *L'Analyse du film*. Paris: Albatros, 1979.

———. *Le Cinéma américain*. 2 vols. Paris: Flammarion, 1980–1981.

Benveniste, Emile. *Problèmes de linguistique générale*. 2 vols. Paris: Gallimard, 1966.

Bergala, Alain. *Initiation à la sémiologie du récit en images*. Paris: Cahiers de l'Audiovisuel, 1978.

Bergstrom, Janet, and Mary Ann Doane. "The Female Spectator: Contexts and Directions." *Camera Obscura* 20–21 (1990).

Berthomieu, André. *Essai de grammaire cinématographique*. Paris: La Nouvelle Edition, 1946.

Bonitzer, Pascal. *Le Regard et la voix*. Paris: Coll. "10/18," Union Générale d'Editions, 1976.

Bonnell, René. *Le cinéma exploité*. Paris: Editions du Seuil, 1978.

Bordwell, David. "Jump Cuts and Blind Spots." *Wide Angle* 6/1 (1984): 4–11.

———. *Narration in the Fiction Film*. Madison: University of Wisconsin Press, 1985.

———. "La Saute et l'ellipse." *Revue Belge du Cinéma* 16 (Summer 1986): 85–90.

———. "Textual Analysis, Etc." *Enclitic* 5/2–6/1 (Fall 1981/Spring 1982): 125–136.

Bordwell, David, Janet Staiger, and Kristin Thompson. *The Classical Hollywood Cinema*. New York: Columbia University Press, 1985.

Bouvier, Michel, and Jean-Louis Leutrat. *Nosferatu*. Paris: Gallimard, 1981.

Bresson, Robert. *Notes sur le cinématographe*. Paris: Editions Gallimard, 1975.

Brownlow, Kevin. *The Parade's Gone By.* Berkeley: University of California Press, 1968.

Burch, Noël. *Theory of Film Practice.* Trans. Helen R. Lane. Princeton: Princeton University Press, 1981.

———. *To the Distant Observer.* Berkeley: University of California Press, 1979.

Cameron, Ian, ed. *The Films of Robert Bresson.* New York: Praeger, 1970.

Chabrol, Claude, and Eric Rohmer. *Hitchcock.* Paris: Editions d'Aujour-d'hui, 1976.

Clair, René. *Cinéma d'hier, cinéma d'aujourd'hui.* Paris: NRF, 1970.

Cohen-Séat, Gilbert. *Essais sur les principes d'une philosophie du cinéma.* Paris: PUF, 1958.

Collet, Jean, Michel Marie, Daniel Percheron, Jean-Paul Simon, and Marc Vernet. *Lectures du film.* Paris: Albatros, 1980.

Comolli, Jean-Louis. "Technique and Ideology: Camera, Perspective, Depth of Field." In *Movies and Methods,* ed. Bill Nichols, vol. 2. Berkeley: University of California Press, 1985.

Cook, David. *A History of Narrative Film.* New York: Norton, 1990.

Delluc, Louis. *Cinéma et Cie.* Paris: Grasset, 1919.

Deslandes, Jacques, and Jacques Richard. *Histoire comparée du cinéma.* 2 vols. Tounai: Casterman, 1966, 1968.

Doane, Mary Ann. "The Voice in the Cinema: The Articulation of Body and Space." *Yale French Studies* (ed. Rick Altman) 60 (1980): 33–50.

Doane, Mary Ann, Patricia Mellencamp, and Linda Williams, eds. *Re-Vision: Essays in Feminist Film Criticism.* Los Angeles: American Film Institute, 1984.

Eco, Umberto. *A Theory of Semiotics.* Bloomington: Indiana University Press, 1979.

Eibel, Alfred. *Fritz Lang.* Paris: Editions Présence du Cinéma, 1964.

Eisenstein, Sergei M. *Film Form* and *Film Sense.* Trans. Jay Leyda. New York: Harcourt Brace Jovanovich, 1969.

———. *Notes of a Film Director.* New York: Dover, 1970.

Eisner, Lotte. *The Haunted Screen.* Berkeley: University of California Press, 1969.

———. *Murnau.* Paris: Editions Le Terrain Vague, 1964.

Epstein, Jean. *Bonjour, cinéma.* Paris: Editions de la Sirène, 1921.

———. *Ecrits sur le cinéma.* 2 vols. Paris: Seghers, 1974.

Faure, Elie. *Fonction du cinéma.* Paris: Denoël Gonthier.

Fescourt, Henri. *La Foi et les montagnes.* Paris: Plan de la Tour, 1979.

Flichy, Patrice. *Les Industries de l'imaginaire.* Grenoble: Presses Universitaires de Grenoble, 1980.

Francastel, Pierre. *Art et technique.* Paris: Etudes de Sociologie de l'Art, 1970.

Gauthier, Guy. *Initiation à la sémiologie de l'image.* Paris: Cahiers de l'Audiovisuel, 1979.

———. *Vingt leçons sur l'image et le sens.* Paris: Edilig "Médiatheque" Collection, 1982.

Genette, Gérard. *Figures II*. Paris: Editions du Seuil, 1969.
———. *Narrative Discourse: An Essay in Method*. Ithaca: Cornell University Press, 1980.
Gledhill, Christine. *Home Is Where the Heart Is*. London: British Film Institute, 1987.
Godard, Jean-Luc. *Godard on Godard*. Ed. Tom Milne. New York: Viking Press, 1972.
Gombrich, E. H. *Art and Illusion*. Princeton: Princeton University Press, 1972.
Greimas, A. J., and J. Courtés. *Sémiotique: Dictionnaire raisonné de la théorie du langage*. 2 vols. Paris: Hachette Universitaire, 1986.
Guback, Thomas. *The International Film Industry*. Bloomington: Indiana University Press, 1969.
Halliday, John. *Sirk on Sirk*. London: Secker and Warburg, 1971.
Hennebelle, Guy, et al. "Le Cinéma militant." Special issue of *Cinéma d'aujourd'hui* (March–April 1976).
Hjelmslev, Louis. *Prolegomena to a Theory of Language*. Madison: University of Wisconsin Press, 1961.
Jacobs, Lewis. *The Rise of the American Film*. New York: Teachers College Press, 1968.
Jost, François, and Dominique Chateau. *Nouveau cinéma, nouvelle sémiologie*. Paris: Coll. "10/18," UGE, 1979.
Jowett, Garth. *Film: The Democratic Art*. New York/Boston: Little & Brown, 1976.
Kaplan, E. Ann. *Women in Film Noir*. London: British Film Institute, 1980.
Kepley, Vance. "Lenin and the Soviet Cinema: The Nationalization Decree Reconsidered." *Journal of Film and Video* 42/2 (Summer 1990): 3–14.
Kirihara, Donald. "A Reconsideration of the Institution of the Benshi." *Film Reader* 6 (1985): 41–53.
Koszarski, Richard. *Hollywood Directors*. 2 vols. New York: Oxford University Press, 1976.
Kracauer, Siegfried. *From Caligari to Hitler*. Princeton: Princeton University Press, 1974.
———. *The Theory of Film: The Redemption of Physical Reality*. New York: Oxford University Press, 1960.
Kuleshov, Lev. *Kuleshov on Film*. Ed. Ronald Levaco. Berkeley: University of California Press, 1974.
Kuntzel, Thierry. "The Film-Work." *Enclitic* 2/1 (1973): 38–61.
———. "The Film-Work 2." *Camera Obscura* 5 (1980): 7–68.
Lebel, Jean-Patrick. *Cinéma et idéologie*. Paris: Editions Sociales, 1971.
Lemon, Lee T., and Marion J. Reis. *Russian Formalist Criticism: Four Essays*. Lincoln: University of Nebraska Press, 1965.
Leutrat, Jean-Louis. *Le Western*. Paris: Editions A. Colin, 1973.
Lévi-Strauss, Claude. *Structural Anthropology*. 2 vols. Trans. Monique Layton. Chicago: University of Chicago Press, 1976.
———. *Structural Study of Myth and Totemism*. London: Tavistock, 1967.

Leyda, Jay. *Kino: A History of the Russian and Soviet Cinema.* London: George Allen & Unwin, 1960.

L'Herbier, Marcel. *Intelligence du cinématographe.* Paris: Correa, 1946.

Lherminier, Pierre. *L'Art du cinéma.* Paris: Seghers, 1960.

Lipton, Lenny. *Independent Filmmaking.* San Francisco: Straight Arrow, 1972.

Lotman, Jurij. *Semiotics of the Cinema.* Trans. Mark E. Suino. Ann Arbor: University of Michigan Press, 1976.

Lowry, Edward. *The Filmology Movement and Film Study in France.* Ann Arbor: UMI Research Press, 1985.

Marin, Louis. *Essais sémiologiques, écritures, peintures.* Paris: Klincksieck, 1971.

Marks, Elaine, and Isabelle de Courtivron, eds. *New French Feminisms.* Amherst: University of Massachusetts Press, 1980.

Martin, Marcel. *Le Langage cinématographique.* Paris: Editeurs Français Réunis, 1977.

Mast, Gerald, and Marshall Cohen, eds. *Film Theory and Criticism.* New York: Oxford University Press, 1979.

Matejka, Ladislav, and Krystyna Pomorska, eds. *Readings in Russian Poetics: Formalist and Structuralist Views.* Ann Arbor: University of Michigan Press, 1978.

Mercillon, Henri. *Cinéma et monopoles.* Paris: Editions A. Colin, 1953.

Metz, Christian. *Essais sémiotiques.* Paris: Klincksieck, 1977.

———. *Essais sur la signification au cinéma.* 2 vols. Paris: Klincksieck, 1976.

———. *Film Language.* New York: Oxford University Press, 1974.

———. *The Imaginary Signifier.* Trans. Celia Britton, Annwyl Williams, Ben Brewster, and Alfred Guzzetti. Bloomington: Indiana University Press, 1982.

———. *Langage et cinéma.* Paris: Albatros, 1977.

———. *Language and Cinema.* The Hague: Mouton, 1974.

Mitry, Jean. *Esthétique et psychologie du cinéma.* 2 vols. Paris: Editions Universitaires, 1980.

———. *Histoires du cinéma.* 5 vols. Vols. 1–3, Paris: Editions Universitaires, 1967, 1969, 1973; vols. 4–5, Paris: Jean-Pierre Delarge, 1980.

Morin, Edgar. *Le Cinéma ou l'homme imaginaire.* Paris: Editions de Minuit, 1978.

———. *Les Stars.* Paris: Editions du Seuil, 1972.

Mulvey, Laura. "Visual Pleasure and Narrative Cinema." *Screen* 16/3 (Autumn 1975): 6–18.

Münsterberg, Hugo. *The Film: A Psychological Study.* New York: Dover, 1970.

Nattiez, Jean-Jacques. *Densité 21.5 de Varèse: Essai d'analyse sémiologique.* Montreal: Université de Montreal, 1975.

Navasky, Victor S. *Naming Names.* New York: Viking, 1980.

Nichols, Bill, ed. *Movies and Methods.* 2 vols. Berkeley: University of California Press, 1976, 1985.

Noguez, Dominique. *Eloge du cinéma expérimental.* Paris: Editions du Centre Pompidou, 1979.

———. *Trente ans de cinéma expérimental en France (1950–1980).* Paris: ARCEF, 1982.

Odin, Roger. "Dix années d'analyses textuelles de films." *Linguistique et Sémiologie* 4 (1977).

———. "Modèle grammatical, modèles linguistiques et étude du langage cinématographique." In *Cahiers du 20e siècle: Cinéma et littérature.* Paris: Klincksieck, 1978.

Oldfield, R. C. "La Perception visuelle des images du cinéma, de la télévision et du radar." *Revue Internationale de Filmologie* 3–4 (October 1948).

Oudart, Jean-Pierre. "L'Effet du réel." *Cahiers du Cinéma* 228 (March/April 1971).

Panofsky, Erwin. "Iconography and Iconology: An Introduction to the Study of Renaissance Art." In *Meaning in the Visual Arts.* Garden City, N.Y.: Doubleday Anchor, 1955.

Pasolini, Pier Paolo. *Heretical Empiricism.* Translated by Ben Lawton and Louise K. Barnett. Bloomington: Indiana University Press, 1988.

Poisson, Jacques. "Cinéma et psychanalyse." *Cahiers du Mois* 16–17: 176.

Propp, Vladimir. *Morphology of the Folktale.* Trans. Laurence Scott. Austin: University of Texas Press, 1968.

Pudovkin, V. I. *Film Technique and Film Acting.* Trans. Ivor Montagu. New York: Grove Press, 1970.

———. "From *Film Technique.*" In *Film Theory and Criticism,* ed. Gerald Mast and Marshall Cohen. New York: Oxford University Press, 1979.

Renoir, Jean. *My Life and My Films.* Trans. Norman Denny. New York: Atheneum, 1974.

Rohmer, Eric. *L'Organisation de l'espace dans "Faust" de Murnau.* Paris: UGE, 1977.

Ropars, Marie-Claire, Michèle Lagny, and Pierre Sorlin. *Octobre.* Paris: Albatros, 1976.

———. *La Révolution figurée.* Paris: Albatros, 1980.

Rosen, Philip, ed. *Narrative, Apparatus, Ideology.* New York: Columbia University Press, 1986.

Rosolato, Guy. *Essais sur le symbolique.* Paris: Gallimard, 1964.

Sadoul, Georges. *Le Cinéma français (1890–1962).* Paris: Flammarion, 1962.

———. *Dictionary of Films.* Berkeley: University of California Press, 1972.

———. *Histoire générale du cinéma.* 6 vols. Paris: Denoël, 1973.

Saussure, Ferdinand de. *Course in General Linguistics.* Trans. Wade Baskin. New York: McGraw-Hill, 1966.

Schéfer, Jean-Louis. *L'Homme ordinaire du cinéma.* Paris: Gallimard, 1980.

Silver, Alain, and Elizabeth Ward, eds. *Film Noir.* Woodstock, N.Y.: Overlook Press, 1979.

Silverman, Kaja. *The Acoustic Mirror.* Bloomington: Indiana University Press, 1988.

Simon, Jean-Paul. *Le Filmique et le comique.* Paris: Albatros, 1979.

Soriano, Marc. "Lire, assister." *Revue Internationale de Filmologie* 3–4 (October 1948): 299–304.

Sorlin, Pierre. *The Film in History.* Oxford: Basil Blackwell, 1980.

———. *Sociologie du cinéma.* Paris: Editions Aubier, 1977.

Souriau, Etienne. "Filmologie et esthétique comparées." *Revue Internationale de Filmologie* 10 (April–June 1952): 113–149.

———. *L'Univers filmique.* Paris: Flammarion, 1953.

Spottiswoode, Raymond. *A Grammar of the Film.* Berkeley: University of California Press, 1951.

Sternberg, Meir. *Expositional Modes and Temporal Ordering in Fiction.* Baltimore: Johns Hopkins University Press, 1978.

Truffaut, François. *Hitchcock.* New York: Simon & Schuster, 1967.

Vanoye, Francis. *Récit écrit—Récit filmique.* Paris: CEDIC, 1979.

Vernet, Marc. *Figures de l'absence.* Paris: Cahiers du Cinéma, 1988.

Vertov, Dziga. *Kino-Eye.* Trans. Kevin O'Brien. Ed. Annette Michelson. Berkeley: University of California Press, 1984.

Walker, Alexander. *The Shattered Silents.* New York: William Morrow, 1979.

Wollen, Peter. *Signs and Meaning in the Cinema.* Bloomington: Indiana University Press, 1976.

Zazzo, René. "Niveau mental et compréhension du cinéma." *Revue Internationale de Filmologie* 5 (n.d.): 29–36.

SUPPLEMENTARY BIBLIOGRAPHY
(from 1994 French Edition)

The first edition of *Esthétique du film* was published in France in 1983. Since then the book has been reissued in subsequent editions and translated into several languages, proving the usefulness of an introductory text on the theoretical and aesthetic dimensions of film studies. However, since 1983 many aspects of the discipline have developed and shifted a great deal, both in France and abroad. These new developments signal both the vitality and the institutional stabilization of theory and aesthetics within our universities and other research institutes.

Creating a minutely detailed international bibliography is certainly beyond the scope of an introductory text like *Aesthetics of Film*. This book, conceived and written in the early 1980s, traces the important effects of semiotics, which dominated the field from 1965 to 1975. But it also outlines other modes of inquiry, be they ideological or psychoanalytic, that shaped numerous debates as critical film journals became more sensitive to theory.

It was during the middle of the 1980s that philosopher Gilles Deleuze brought out his two volumes devoted to the moving image: *Cinema 1: The Movement-Image* and *Cinema 2: The Time-Image* (see citation in section 7.1 below). This simple fact actually offers an extraordinary acknowledgment by one of the world's most prominent philosophers: that the cinema is an art that is also an original and specific mode of thought. These two volumes by Deleuze proposed a new conceptual framework that has certainly influenced film analysis and aesthetics since 1985.

For its part, semiotics of the cinema, after 1983, developed further and perhaps more cautiously than previously in France and Italy and across Europe, following a more pragmatic slant. Semiotics then skirted alongside the cognitive sciences which have affected film theory to a remarkable extent from the American side of the Atlantic. But it also moved in relation to dominant currents in British and American philosophy, especially the work of David Bordwell, and, from a completely different perspective, Stanley Cavell, whose first book, *The World Viewed*, published in 1971, was virtually unknown in France.

More generally, theoretical research freed itself from linguistic and semiotic models to embed itself in the context of art history and philosophical reflections. To a certain degree, film aesthetics has overcome its autonomy during the last two decades, as witnessed in the new directions of research on the relations between cinema and painting (*L'Oeil interminable* by Jacques Aumont) and film analyses by Jean-Louis Leutrat (*Kaleidoscope* and *La Prisonnière du désert*) for example.

Another important trend in the second half of the 1980s was the surprising vitality of a revival of "new approaches" to film history. This delayed reaction is rather paradoxical given the wealth of historical research in France and beyond (as evident in the currency of the label "new historicism"), and new French histories have come largely in the wake of work accomplished in the USA and Italy. We need simply refer here to the exemplary work of Douglas Gomery in the United States, Gian Piero Brunetta in Italy, and the large collective text *The Classical Hollywood Cinema* by David Bordwell, Janet Staiger, and Kristin Thompson, published in 1985.

We have indicated the degree of difficulty of the books and articles listed below with the help of two symbols:

(*): An introductory work that should prove easily accessible for a student just beginning college study.

(**): More advanced work that assumes some prior knowledge of the subject matter and is written for a more experienced reader.

Titles that are not marked fall in the middle and are directed at intermediate readers.

1. Introductory Work on Film Theory and Aesthetics

Among the most introductory of works:

In French:

Aumont, Jacques. *L'Image*. Paris: Nathan "Fac-Cinéma" Collection, 1994. Principal theories of the image.

Gauthier, Guy. *Vingt leçons (plus une) sur l'image et le sens*. Paris: Edilig "Médiathèque" collection, 1989. Contains numerous examples of analyses.(*)

And two special-issue journals:

Kermabon, Jacques, ed. "Les Théories du cinéma aujourdhui." *CinémAction* 47 (1988).(*)

Magny, Joel, ed. "Histoire des théories du cinéma." *CinémAction* 60 (July 1991).(*)

While the following are not introductions to film theory in the strictest sense, they are recommended for their historic pertinence and analytical descriptions of practical techniques:

Chion, Michel. *Le Cinéma et ses métiers*. Paris: Bordas, 1990.(*)
Mitry, Jean. *Esthétique et psychologie du cinéma*. Paris: Jean-Pierre Delarge, 1990. This is a single-volume edition of Mitry's two-volume 1963 classic.

In English:

Andrew, Dudley. *Concepts in Film Theory*. New York: Oxford University Press, 1988.
———. *The Major Film Theories*. New York: Oxford University Press, 1976.(*)
Bordwell, David, and Kristin Thompson. *Film Art: An Introduction*. New York: McGraw-Hill, 1993.(*)
Carroll, Noel. *Mystifying Movies: Fads and Fallacies in Contemporary Film Theory*. New York: Columbia University Press, 1988.(**)
———. *Philosophical Problems of Classical Film Theory*. Princeton: Princeton University Press, 1988. Carroll's two books offer more difficult and fairly polemical arguments.(**)
Lapsley, Robert, and Michael Westlake. *Film Theory: An Introduction*. Manchester: Manchester University Press, 1988.

In Italian:

Casetti, Francesco. *Teorie del cinema, 1945–1990*. Milan: Bompiani, 1993. A history of theories of the cinema.(**)

2. Film as Audio-Visual Representation

2.1. Cinema Aesthetics and the Plastic Arts

Arnheim, Rudolf. *Film as Art*. Berkeley: University of California Press, 1957.
Aumont, Jacques. *Du visage au cinéma*. Paris: Cahiers du Cinéma, 1992.(**)
———. *Introduction à la couleur*. Paris: Armand Colin, 1994.(*)
———. *L'Oeil interminable: Cinéma et peinture*. Paris: Séghiers, 1989.(**)
Belloi, Livio, ed. *Revue Belge du Cinéma* 31 (1992).
Bellour, Raymond. *L'Entre-images: Photo, cinéma, vidéo*. Paris: La Différence, 1990.(**)
Bellour, Raymond, and Anne-Marie Duguet, eds. *Communications* 48 (1988).
Bonitzer, Pascal. *Décadrages*. Paris: Editions de l'Etoile / Cahiers du Cinéma, 1985.
Cavell, Stanley. *The World Viewed*. Cambridge: Harvard University Press, 1979.(*)
DuBois, Philippe. *L'Acte photographique et autres*. Paris: Nathan, 1990.(**)
———, ed. *Revue Belge du Cinéma* 10 (Winter 1984–1985).
Eisenstein, Sergei Mikhailovich. *Le Cinématisme: Peinture et cinéma*. Bruxelles: Complexe, 1980.
———. *Eisenstein et le mouvement de l'art*. Paris: Cerf, "7ième Art" Collection, 1986.
Kurtz, Rudolf. *Expressionisme et cinéma*. Grenoble: Presses Universitaires de Grenoble, 1987. Original German version, 1927. This is a classic text on film aesthetics.(*)
Moholy-Nagy, Laszlo. *Painting, Photograph, Film*. Cambridge: MIT University Press, 1969. Original German edition, 1926.
Noguez, Dominique. *Une renaissance du cinéma: Le Cinéma "underground."* Paris: Klincksieck, 1985. Offers a vast panoramic summary of experimental cinema.

Paini, Dominique, and Marc Vernet, eds. *Iris* 14–15 (1992). A conference presentation from the Musée du Louvre, April, 1991.
Revault d'Allonnes, Fabrice. *La Lumière au cinéma.* Paris: Cahiers du Cinéma, 1991.(*)
Schaeffer, Jean-Marie. *L'Image précaire: Du dispositif photographique.* Paris: Seuil, 1987.(**)
Sorlin, Pierre. *Esthétiques de l'audiovisuel.* Paris: Nathan, 1992. A stimulating essay for the experienced reader.
Villain, Dominique. *L'Oeil à la caméra: Le Cadrage au cinéma.* Paris: Editions de l'Etoile / Cahiers du Cinéma, 1984.(*)

There is also a university journal entitled *Admiranda* that devotes much of its space to issues surrounding visual aesthetics. Readers may also wish to consult the following special issues of *Cahiers d'Analyse du Film et de l'Image* (Aix-en-Provence): no. 1 (1986) "Problèmes formels"; nos. 2 and 3 (1988) "Le Cadre, la présence"; no. 4 (1990) "Le Jeu de l'acteur"; and nos. 5, 6, and 7 (1991) "Figuration, défiguration"; all edited by Nicole Brenez.(**)

2.2. Sound Representation and the Cinema

Chion, Michel. *Audio-Vision: Sound on Screen.* Translated by Claudia Gorbman. New York: Columbia University Press, 1990.(*)
Gorbman, Claudia. *Unheard Melodies: Narrative Film Music.* Bloomington: Indiana University Press, 1987.
Masson, Alain. *L'Image et la parole: L'Aveuglement du cinéma parlant.* Paris: La Différence, 1989.(*)

3. Montage

This concept currently plays a much more modest role than during "classical" film theory days. Nonetheless, we call attention to:

Albera, François. *Eisenstein et le constructivisme russe.* Lausanne: L'Age d'Homme, 1990.
Albera, François, Ekaterina Khokhlova, and Valérie Posener. *Kouleshov et les siens.* Locarno: Editions du Festival de Locarno, 1990.
Aumont, Jacques, ed. "The Kuleshov Effect." *Iris* 4, 1 (1986).
Cremonini, Giorgio. *La scena e il montaggio cinematografico.* Bologna: Il Mulino, 1983.
Crittenden, Roger. *The Thames and Hudson Manual of Film Editing.* London: Thames and Hudson, 1981.
Kuleshov, Lev. *Kuleshov on Film.* Edited by Ronald Levaco. Berkeley: University of California Press, 1974.
Le Montage dans tous les états. Conference of the Collège d'Histoire de l'Art Cinématographique 5 (Spring 1993). Paris: Cinémathèque Française / Musée du Cinéma.
Ropars-Wuilleumier, Marie-Claire. *Le Texte divisé.* Paris: PUF, 1981.(**)
Sánchez-Biosca, Vincente. *Teoría del montaje cinematográfico.* Valencia: Ediciones Filmoteca, 1991.
Villain, Dominique. *Le Montage.* Paris: Cahiers du Cinéma, 1991.(*)

4. Film Narration

Today, instead of montage stealing all the attention, the area of film theory under most active development includes diverse inquiries into narratology. Interested readers can find detailed bibliographies in André Gaudreault and François Jost's *Le Récit cinématographique* and in Edward Branigan's *Narrative Comprehension and Film*. An abbreviated bibliography on narratology follows.

Bordwell, David. *Narration in the Fiction Film*. Madison: University of Wisconsin Press, 1985.

Branigan, Edward. *Narrative Comprehension and Film*. New York: Routledge, 1992.(**)

———. *Point of View in the Cinema: A Theory of Narration and Subjectivity in Classical Film*. New York: Mouton, 1984.(**)

Gardies, André. *Approche du récit filmique*. Paris: Albatros, 1980. Devoted primarily to studying Alain Robbe-Grillet's *The Man Who Lies*.

———. *L'Espace au cinéma*. Paris: Méridiens-Klincksieck, 1993.

Gaudreault, André. *Du Littéraire au filmique: Système du récit*. Paris: Méridiens-Klincksieck, 1988.(**)

Gaudreault, André, and François Jost. *Le Récit cinématographique*. Paris: Nathan, 1994. This book refers to many examples from early cinema and the films of Orson Welles.

Jost, François. *L'Oeil caméra: Entre film et roman*. Lyon: Presses Universitaires de Lyon, 1989. Theorizes focalization and occularization, or audio and visual point of view.

Masson, Alain. *Le Récit au cinéma*. Paris: Cahiers du Cinéma, 1994. Analyses of narratives in seven films that deliberately ignore all narratological perspectives.

Neupert, Richard. *The End: Narration and Closure in the Cinema*. Detroit: Wayne State University Press, 1995.

Vanoye, Francis. *Récit écrit, récit filmique*. Paris: Nathan, 1994. This is a virtual reference manual for study of film narration.

Vernet, Marc, ed. "Cinema and Narration, 1 and 2." *Iris* 7 and 8 (1986, 1988).

An additional valuable journal is the special issue, "Le Récit saisi par le film," *Hors Cadre* 2 (1984).

5. Narrative Dimensions of the Script

5.1. Scriptwriting Manuals

Since 1983, many of the scriptwriting manuals published have been easy, mediocre menus for amateurs. We will cite here only a few texts that take into account theories of narration and narratological issues.

In French:

Chion, Michel. *Ecrire un scénario*. Paris: Editions de l'Etoile / INA, 1987. This book analyzes scripts from four films and provides a critical study of English-language manuals in its glossary.

Jenn, Pierre. *Techniques du scénario*. Paris: FEMIS, 1991. A rereading of Aristotle applied to classical Hollywood cinema, and in particular to films by Charles Brackett and Billy Wilder.(*)

Maillot, Pierre. *L'Ecriture cinématographique*. Paris: Méridiens-Klicksieck, 1989. From story to script and techniques of organization and continuity.(*)

Torok, Jean-Paul. *Le Scénario: L'Art d'écrire un scénario; Histoire, théorie, pratique*. Paris: Artifact / Henri Veyrier, 1986. For the most part, a history of scriptwriting and a defense and illustration of a certain French professionalism vs. myths of the power of improvisation.(*)

Vanoye, Francis. *Scénarios modèles, modèles de scénarios*. Paris: Nathan, 1991. This book is the more original since, in addition to a personal typology of scripts, it offers a psycho-biographical and social perspective rarely envisioned.

In English, reference manuals include:

Horton, Andrew. *Writing the Character-Centered Screenplay*. Berkeley: University of California Press, 1994.

Stempel, Tom. *Framework: A History of Screenwriting in the American Film*. New York: Continuum, 1988.

Swain, Dwight V., and Joye R. Swain. *Film Script Writing: A Practical Manual*. Boston: Focal Press, 1988.

Vale, Eugene. *The Technique of Screen and Television Writing*. New York: Simon and Schuster, 1982.

5.2. Realism (a concept addressed in Chapter 3, "Cinema and Narration")

Berdardini, Aldo, and Jean A. Gili. *Cesare Zavattini*. Paris: Editions du Centre Georges Pompidou, 1990.

Grierson, John. *Grierson on Documentary*. London: Faber and Faber, 1966. The great theoretical reference text by the famous English documentary filmmaker.

Lyant, Jean-Charles, and Roger Odin, eds. *Cinémas and réalités*. Saint-Etienne: CIEREC, 1984. Published proceedings from a February 1983 conference with a very useful and complete bibliography.

Nichols, Bill. *Ideology and the Image: Social Representation in the Cinema and Other Media*. Bloomington: Indiana University Press, 1981.

———, ed. *Newsreel: Documentary Filmmaking on the American Left (1971–1975)*. New York: Arno Press, 1980.

6. Cinema and Language: Classical Film Critics and Theorists

6.1. Classical Theories

Besides Jean Epstein, the bulk of whose philosophical and aesthetic writings were reissued by the French publisher Seghers in 1974, the collected works of Louis Delluc, today available thanks to a complete edition offered by Pierre Lherminier and the Cinémathèque Française, help shape the discipline. Delluc's writings, unlike Epstein's, which reaffirm theoretical and philosophical perspectives, reveal more about the history of criticism.

Delluc, Louis. *Ecrits cinématographiques*. Edited by Pierre Lherminier. 4 vols. Paris: Cinémathèque Française, 1985, 1986, 1990.

Epstein, Jean. *Ecrits de cinéma*. 2 vols. Paris: Seghers, 1974.

6.2. Semiotics of the Cinema, Language, Generative Theories, Cognition

Bettetini, Gianfranco. *La conversazione audiovisiva: Problemi dell'enunciazione filmica e televisiva*. Milan: Bompiani, 1984.(**)
Bordwell, David. *Making Meaning: Inference and Rhetoric in the Interpretation of Cinema*. Cambridge: Harvard University Press, 1989.(**)
Carroll, J. M. *Toward a Structural Psychology of Cinema*. La Haye: Mouton, 1980.(**)
Chateau, Dominique. *Le Cinéma comme langage*. Paris: Publications de la Sorbonne, 1986.(**)
Colin, Michel. *Cinéma, télévision, cognition*. Nancy: Presses Universitaires de Nancy, 1994.(**)
———. *Langue, film, discours: Prolégomènes à une sémiologie générative du film*. Paris: Klincksieck, 1985.(**)
Gardies, André, ed. "25 ans de sémiologie du cinéma." *CinémAction* 58 (1991).
Marie, Michel, and Marc Vernet, eds. "Christian Metz et la théorie du cinéma." *Iris* 10 (1990). Includes a detailed bibliography compiled by Metz himself.
Metz, Christian. *L'Enonciation impersonnelle ou le site du film*. Paris: Klincksieck, 1991. Metz's final book; this critical synthesis of enunciation theories is based on a great number of examples.
Mitry, Jean. *La Sémiologie en question*. Paris: Cerf, 1987. A very polemical study.
Mourgues, Nicole de. *Le Générique de film*. Paris: Méridiens-Klincksieck, 1994.
Odin, Roger. *Cinéma et production*. Paris: Armand Colin, 1990.(*) A very clear account of diverse didactic and synthetic perspectives.
Pasolini, Pier Paolo. *Heretical Empiricism*. Translated by Ben Lawton and Louise K. Barnett. Bloomington: Indiana University Press, 1988.
Ropars-Wuilleumier, Marie-Claire. *Ecraniques: Le Film de texte*. Lille: Presses Universitaires de Lille, 1990.(**) The author deepens her theorization of filmic écriture.

Two additional journals offering special issues include "Théories du cinéma et crise dans la théorie," *Hors Cadre* 7 (1989), and "The Current State of Theory," *Iris* 1 and 2 (1983).

7. Film and Its Spectator

7.1. Cinema and Psychoanalysis; Cinema and Philosophy

Casetti, Francesco. *D'un regard à l'autre: Le Film et son spectateur*. Lyon: Presses Universitaires de Lyon, 1990. Original Italian version is *Dentro lo sguardo: Il film e il suo spettatore*. Milan: Bompiani, 1986.(**)
Deleuze, Gilles. *Cinema 1: The Movement-Image*. Translated by Hugh Tomlinson and Barbara Habberjam. Minneapolis: University of Minnesota Press, 1986.
———. *Cinema 2: The Time-Image*. Translated by Hugh Tomlinson and Barbara Habberjam. Minneapolis: University of Minnesota Press, 1989. These two volumes assume a prior knowledge of film history, diverse critical discourses that have informed film studies, and the central concepts from Deleuze's philosophical writings.(**)
Dhote, Alain, ed. "Cinéma et psychanalyse." *CinémAction* 50 (1989).
Lacoste, Patrick. *L'Etrange Cas du Professeur M.: Psychanalyse à l'écran*. Paris: Gallimard, 1990.(**)

Vernet, Marc. *Figures de l'absence: De l'invisible au cinéma.* Paris: Cahiers du
Cinéma, 1988.
Zizek, Slavoj, ed. *Tout ce que vous avez toujours voulu savoir sur Lacan sans
jamais oser le demander à Hitchcock.* Paris: Navarin, 1988. A collection of
very original essays.(**)

7.2. British and American Theories (Feminist, Sociocultural, Marxist)

These theories are often based on Freudian psychoanalysis and its various exten-
sions. For an introduction to this school of thought, which is very important
within American universities, see:

Burch, Noel, ed. *Revoir Hollywood: La Nouvelle Critique anglo-américaine.* Paris:
Nathan, 1994.
Reynaud, Bérénice, and Susan Vincendeau, eds. "20 ans de théories féministes
sur le cinéma." *CinémAction* 67 (1993). An anthology whose texts are unfortunately truncated in their theoretical development.

In English:

de Lauretis, Teresa. *Alice Doesn't: Feminism, Semiotics, Cinema.* Bloomington:
Indiana University Press, 1984.
Doane, Mary Ann. *The Desire to Desire: The Woman's Film of the 1940s.*
Bloomington: Indiana University Press, 1987.
Dyer, Richard. *Now You See It: Studies on Lesbian and Gay Film.* London:
Routledge, 1990.
Flitterman-Lewis, Sandy. *To Desire Differently: Feminism and the French Cin-
ema.* Champaign: University of Illinois Press, 1990.
Gledhill, Christine, ed. *Home Is Where the Heart Is.* London: BFI, 1987.
Penley, Constance, ed. *Feminism and Film Theory.* New York: Routledge, BFI,
1988.

8. History of Cinema; History and Cinema

We provide only a very selective list here and refer the interested reader to more
complete bibliographies published in Michèle Lagny's *De l'histoire du cinéma,*
Robert Allen and Douglas Gomery's *Film History,* and François Garçon's special
edition of *CinémAction.* Our condensed list features works that address methodological issues of historiography.

Allen, Robert C., and Douglas Gomery. *Film History: Theory and Practice.* New
York: Knopf, 1985. A very clearly written text, well-supported by eight case
studies.(*)
Altman, Rick. *The American Film Musical.* Bloomington: Indiana University
Press, 1987.
Berriatua, Luciano. *Los proverbios chinos de F. W. Murnau.* Madrid: Filmoteca
Espanola, 1990. Vol. 1, *Etapa alemana;* Vol. 2, *Etapa americana et documents.*
Bertin-Maghit, Jean-Pierre. *Le Cinéma sous l'occupation.* Paris: Olivier Orban,
1989. Interesting for its bibliography of original and unpublished sources.
Burch, Noel. *Life to Those Shadows.* Translated and edited by Ben Brewster. Ber-
keley: University of California Press, 1990. An essential book on the cinema's
first fifteen years and the development of cinematic language.

Ferro, Marco, ed. *Film et histoire*. Paris: Ecole des Hautes Etudes en Sciences Sociales, 1984.(*)

Garçon, François, ed. "Cinéma et histoire: Autour de Marc Ferro." *CinémAction* 65 (1992).

Gaudreault, André, ed. *Pathé 1900: Fragments d'une filmographie analytique du cinéma des premiers temps*. Paris: Presses de la Sorbonne Nouvelle, 1993. An exhaustive analytical filmography that pushes film archaeology to its limits.

Henriet, Gérard, and Jacques Mauduy. *Géographies du western: Une nation en marche*. Paris: Nathan, 1989. Methodologically original, with numerous examples, sketches, and maps.

Lagny, Michèle. *De l'histoire du cinéma: Méthode historique et histoire du cinéma*. Paris: Armand Colin, 1992. Very clear and epistemologically pertinent study.

Lagny, Michèle, Pierre Sorlin, and Marie-Claire Ropars. *Générique des années 30*. Vincennes: Presses Universitaires de Vincennes, 1986.(**)

Leutrat, Jean-Louis. *L'Alliance brisée: Le Western des années 20*. Lyon: Institut Lumière, Presses Universitaires de Lyon, 1985. A very scholarly study.(**)

————. *Le Cinéma en perspective: Une histoire*. Paris: Nathan, 1992. An original and stimulating argument.

Leutrat, Jean-Louis, and Suzanne Liandrat. *Les Cartes de l'ouest*. Paris: Armand Colin, 1990. A didactic introduction to the western with an analysis of John Ford's *Stagecoach*.

Mannoni, Laurent. *Le Grand Art de la lumière et de l'ombre: Archéologie du cinéma*. Paris: Nathan, 1994. Exemplary for its return to original sources from the sixteenth century on.

Journals specializing in relations between history, aesthetics, and theory of the cinema include:

Archivos de la Filmoteca. From the Filmoteca Gereralitat in Valencia, Spain, which has published seventeen issues.

Cinémathèque. Five issues appeared from 1992 to 1994.

1895. Since September 1986, published by the Association Française de Recherche sur l'Histoire du Cinéma. Sixteen issues have appeared, including "L'Année 1913 en France" (October 1993), edited by Thierry Lefebvre and Laurent Mannoni.

Film History. Published since 1987.

Vertigo. A review of film aesthetics and history, with ten issues published from 1987 to present.

9. Auteur Theory, Writings by Directors, Mise-en-scène, and Film Criticism

Arnaud, Philippe, ed. *Sacha Guitry, cinéaste*. Crisnée, Belgium: Yellow Now, 1993.

Baecque, Antoine de. *Cahiers du Cinéma: Histoire d'une revue*. Vol. 1, *A l'assaut du cinéma*; Vol. 2, *Cinéma, tours détours*. Paris: Cahiers du Cinéma, 1991. Very scholarly yet very clear.

Bertetto, Paolo, and Bernard Eisenschitz, eds. *Fritz Lang: La Mise-en-scène*. Turin, Paris: Cinémathèque Française, 1991.

Biette, Jean-Claude. *Poétique des auteurs*. Paris: Cahiers du Cinéma, 1988.

Daney, Serge. *Devant la recrudescence des vols de sac à main: Cinéma, télévision, information*. Lyon: Aléas, 1991.

———. *L'Exercice a été profitable, Monsieur.* Paris: P.O.L., 1993. Very original critical ideas that strongly marked the beginning of 1990s criticism in France. Its continuation can be found in the journal *Trafic*, which has eleven issues to date.

———. *La Rampe: Cahier critique, 1970–1982.* Paris: Cahiers du Cinéma and Gallimard, 1983.

Douchet, Jean. *L'Art d'aimer.* Paris: Cahiers du Cinéma, 1987.

Godard, Jean-Luc. *Godard on Godard.* Translated by Tom Milne. New York: Viking, 1972.

Hors Cadre 8 (1990), "L'Etat d'auteur."

Leenhardt, Roger. *Chroniques de cinéma.* Paris: Cahiers du Cinéma, 1986.

Mourlet, Michel. *La Mise en scène comme langage.* Paris: Henri Veyrier, 1987.

Truffaut, François. *The Films in My Life.* Translated by Leonard Mayhew. New York: Simon and Schuster, 1978.(*)

———. *Le Plaisir des yeux.* Paris: Cahiers du Cinéma, 1987.(*)

10. Film Analyses

In terms of sheer numbers of new titles, this is the area that has developed the most in recent years. We strongly urge readers to consult the bibliography in Jacques Aumont and Michel Marie's *L'Analyse des films*, which complements *Aesthetics of Film*. See in particular:

Aumont, Jacques, and Michel Marie. *L'Analyse des films.* Paris: Nathan, 1988.

Casetti, Francesco, and Federico Di Chio. *Analisi del film.* Milan: Bompiani, 1990.

Vanoye, Francis, and Anne Goliot-Lete. *Précis d'analyse filmique.* Paris: Nathan, 1992.(*) Designed for true beginners.

Interested readers should also consult the many monographs on individual directors that have appeared in the last ten years; we have included in our list only those offering methodologically significant analyses of the films.

Arnoldy, Edouard, and Philippe Dubois. "*Un chien andalou:* Lectures et relectures." *Revue Belge du Cinéma* (1993).

Berthome, Jean-Pierre, and François Thomas. *Citizen Kane.* Paris: Flammarion, 1992. This book offers a synthetic analysis of a very heavily studied film.

Coremans, Linda. *La Transaction filmique: Du Contesto à Cadaveri eccellenti.* Berne: Peter Lang, 1990.

Dewismes, Brigitte, and Gérard Leblanc. *Le Double Scénario chez Fritz Lang.* Paris: Armand Colin. A study of *The Big Heat.* Offers an exemplary and masterful analysis of the sources of Lang's film and its various transformations at each stage of production. Includes numerous working sketches and frame enlargements.

Gaudreault, André, ed. *Ce que je vois de mon ciné: La Répresentation du regard dans le cinéma des premiers temps.* Paris: Méridiens-Klincksieck, 1988. Examines twelve early films in narratological terms.

Hayward, Susan, and Ginette Vincendeau. *French Film: Texts and Contexts.* New York: Routledge, 1990. Textual and contextual analyses of twenty French films, from Germaine Dulac to Agnès Varda.

Leutrat, Jean-Louis. *Kaléidoscope.* Lyon: Presses Universitaires de Lyon, 1989.

Sellier, Geneviève. *Jean Grémillon: Le Cinéma est à vous.* Paris: Méridiens-Klincksieck, 1989.

Taranger, Marie-Claude. *Luis Bunuel: Le Jeu et la loi.* Saint-Denis: Presses Universitaires de Paris-VIII, 1990.
Turk, Edward. *Child of Paradise: Marcel Carné and the Golden Age of French Cinema.* Cambridge: Harvard University Press, 1989. An original examination of Marcel Carné's work, particularly significant for its British-American approach to film history. Strongly marked by psychoanalytical and ideological perspectives.

There are also several series of critical monographs. Four major French series include:

Collection "Film(s)." Lyon: Interdisciplinaire. Four titles have been published since 1989: *Citizen Kane, India Song, Rules of the Game,* and *Pierrot le fou.*
Collection "Image par image." Paris: Hatier. Four titles have appeared since 1990: *Citizen Kane, M, Rules of the Game,* and *Contempt.*
Collection "Long métrage." Crisnée, Belgium: Yellow Now. Fifteen titles have appeared since 1988; monographs of particular interest include Roberto Rossellini's *Voyage to Italy,* by Alain Bergala; Fritz Lang's *Man Hunt,* by Bernard Eisenschitz; Jean-Luc Godard's *Band of Outsiders,* by Barthelémy Amengual; and Carl Dreyer's *Vampyr,* by Jacques Aumont.
Collection "Synopsis." Paris: Nathan. Eighteen volumes have appeared since 1989: *Rules of the Game, City Lights, Citizen Kane, M, Barry Lyndon, Rear Window, Contempt, The Leopard, The 400 Blows, Children of Paradise, Senso, The Seventh Seal, Battleship Potemkin, Some Like It Hot, The Passenger, Mon Oncle, Un chien andalou* and *L'Age d'or,* and *Grand Illusion.* The didactic structure of these critical analyses does not interfere with their subtlety, originality, or historical scholarship.

The two most important English-language monograph series are:

British Film Institute, collection "Film Classics," featuring in particular *Citizen Kane* by Laura Mulvey (1992), *Olympia* by Taylor Downing (1992), *Singin' in the Rain* by Peter Wollen (1992), and *L'Atalante* by Marina Warner (1993). Their iconography is remarkable.
"Wisconsin / Warner Brothers Screenplay Series." Madison: University of Wisconsin Press. Begun in 1979 by Tino Balio, the series now boasts twenty titles, beginning with *The Jazz Singer: Edited with an Introduction by Robert L. Caringer* (1979).

INDEX